LOBBYING for HIGHER EDUCATION

★ ★ ★ ★ ★ ★

VANDERBILT ISSUES IN HIGHER EDUCATION is a timely new series that focuses on the three core functions of higher education: teaching, research, and service. Interdisciplinary in nature, it concentrates not only on how these core functions are carried out in colleges and universities but also on the contributions they make to larger issues of social and economic development, as well as the various organizational, political, psychological, and social forces that influence their fulfillment and evolution.

LOBBYING for HIGHER EDUCATION

HOW COLLEGES AND UNIVERSITIES INFLUENCE FEDERAL POLICY

Constance Ewing Cook

Vanderbilt University Press
Nashville and London

This publication is made from recycled paper and meets the minimum requirements of
American National Standard for Information Sciences—Permanence of Paper for Printed
Library Materials. ∞

Support for this work was provided by the Spencer Foundation, the W.K. Kellogg
Foundation, and the Research Office of the University of Michigan. However, the data presented, statements made, and views expressed are solely the responsibility of the author.

Library of Congress Cataloging-in-Publication Data

Cook, Constance Ewing.
    Lobbying for higher education : how colleges and universities
influence federal policy / Constance Ewing Cook. -- 1st ed.
    p. cm. -- (Vanderbilt issues in higher education)
    Includes bibliographical references and index.

    ISBN 0826513166 (cloth : permanent paper)
    ISBN 0826513174 (pbk. : permanent paper)
    1. Universities and colleges--Government policy--United States.
2. Higher education and state--United States. 3. Lobbying--United
States. 4. Education--United States--Societies, etc. I. Title. II.
Series.
    LC173 .C66 1998
    379.1'18'0973--ddc21
                                                                98-8885
                                                                CIP

for Jim

CONTENTS

FIGURES AND TABLES

Tables

FOREWORD

As the initial offering in the series Vanderbilt Issues in Higher Education, Constance Ewing Cook's *Lobbying for Higher Education* provides an insightful analysis and discerning conclusions regarding the Washington arena in which some of the most fundamental issues facing higher education in this country are addressed. In many significant ways, federal policies and financial support directly affect teaching, research, and service, the three core functions of higher education on which this new series principally focuses. Federal student financial aid programs and federal funding of faculty research are only two of the essential areas affected by this complex and crucial relationship. Constance Cook's impressive empirical research and the theoretical grounding in political science and public policy that she brings to this study add an interdisciplinary perspective that will characterize future volumes in the series as well.

By providing such a full and incisive account of the ways in which American colleges and universities and their representative associations in Washington collaboratively work to influence the shaping of relevant federal policies, Professor Cook has made a signal contribution to our understanding of one of the most important issues confronting the future of American higher education.

John M. Braxton
General Editor,
Vanderbilt Issues in Higher Education

PREFACE

An illuminating story is told in certain Washington circles. Three dogs are sitting on the corner outside a restaurant when a meat truck pulls up. As the driver steps out to deliver the meat, the dogs begin strategizing about how to get some for themselves. One dog says, "I used to be a lawyer. Let me negotiate with the driver and talk him into giving us the meat." The second dog says, "I used to be an architect. I know a secret passageway to the kitchen. I can lead us to the meat." The third dog says, "I used to be a college president. I'm sure they will give us all the meat we want if we just sit here on the corner and whine and beg." This story is a favorite of public officials because it says so much about what has been wrong with higher education lobbying.

This book concerns the ways that higher education associations and the American colleges and universities they represent try to influence federal policy, especially congressional policy. The focus is primarily on lobbying changes that occurred in 1995–96 after the arrival in Washington of the first Republican congressional majority in forty years, since 1954. The book describes how the Washington higher education community organizes itself for political action, how its major interest groups are perceived by their members and public officials, and how it makes decisions about lobbying strategies and tactics. The associations and institutional representatives that comprise the community have always devoted considerable resources to federal relations because the government's impact on them is so substantial. It soon became apparent, however, that more than usual was at stake during the Republican revolution that brought in the 104th Congress.

The book is designed for a variety of readers. Students of higher education policy will be most interested in its description of Washington players and processes. It will provide insights for those directly involved in Washington higher education advocacy and policy making, especially college and university presidents and federal relations officers, higher education association leaders and staff, and public officials in Congress and the executive branch. Many of them will recognize their own voices on these pages because they responded to the initial survey on which the book is based, or participated in interviews. Finally, this book is for interest group scholars and other social scientists who study organizations trying to affect public policy decisions.

PREVIOUS LITERATURE

The inspiration for this book comes from social science, especially political science, literature on interest groups (otherwise known as *special interests, pressure groups,* or *organized interests*). The definition provided by David B. Truman in the 1950s still is applicable, "An interest group is any group that is based on one or more shared attitudes and makes certain claims upon other groups or organizations in the society . . ." (1951, 33). Thus, an interest group is defined by its involvement in public policy advocacy and its active interest in governmental decisions.

A review of the literature on interest groups shows it is grounded in seminal works with broad theories regarding representation, such as Truman's *The Governmental Process* (1951). To inform the development of those theories, or to illustrate them, scholars have done case studies of individual groups, such as Lawrence S. Rothenberg's *Linking Citizens to Government* (1992), which concerns Common Cause, and comparative studies of one type of group, such as Jeffrey M. Berry's *Lobbying for the People* (1977), which concerns public interest groups more generally. Scholars have also looked at a single bill and traced the impact of interest groups on its passage, as was done in Jane Mansbridge's *Why We Lost the ERA* (1986), and they have looked at the outcome of a broader set of policy issues and analyzed group involvement in them, as in Jo Freeman's *The Politics of Women's Liberation* (1975). Additionally, there are empirical studies of large numbers of Washington associations, such as Jack L. Walker's *Mobilizing Interest Groups in America* (1991), as well as studies of the individuals who join or contribute to groups, such as Terry M. Moe's *The Organization of Interests* (1980b). One author of a study of interest group literature has noted the "burst of new intellectual energy and research" that has characterized the field in recent years (Petracca 1992, 363). That makes sense, given that organized interests are playing an increasingly influential role in American politics.

One of the bigger bursts of intellectual energy in the interest literature, and the one to which this book contributes, is the study of policy *domains*. A policy domain consists of individuals and groups outside of government who lobby on a particular public policy topic and consider each other's activities and positions as they plan their own. While a domain's boundaries are permeable and participants sometimes pursue their interests outside the domain, a domain is characterized by its ability to meet most of the needs of its participants and serve as the gate through which most policy matters must pass (Browne 1995, 204–5). This book uses *community* synonymously with *domain* to refer to the nongovernmental players in a policy sector, in this case the higher education policy sector.

The value of domain research is that it provides a new frame, or lens, to illuminate other theoretical approaches. One of those who has called for more studies of this nature is Jack L. Walker, who wrote about the need for research on how "internal characteristics of policy networks determine public policies . . . , the consequences of conflict and consensus within such networks . . . , and [how] policy communities exert their influence on the broader political system" (1991, 199). Similarly, Mark Petracca has concluded that "it's time that the interest group subfield begin gathering systematic data about the Washington interest group community" (1992, 356). That is a big task because there are hundreds, probably thousands, of policy communities in the Washington, D.C., policy-making arena.

Several previous studies of Washington policy domains serve as early models for this one, including Edward O. Laumann and David Knoke's *The Organizational State* (1987), a sociological study that concerns the energy and health communities, with an emphasis on organizational theory and its application to the two communities under review. It identifies the core actors, examines the interrelationship of actors in each community, and analyzes the structures of conflict and consensus.

The most comprehensive work on domains is *The Hollow Core: Private Interests in National Policy Making* (1993), by John P. Heinz, Edward O. Laumann, Robert H. Salisbury, and Robert L. Nelson, which concerns the domains of energy, agriculture, labor, and health. John P. Heinz and his colleagues describe the structure of group interactions, look at levels of conflict, and try to "assess the extent to which various patterns of behavior are domain specific" (1993, 248).

In their commentary on interest group literature, Virginia Gray and David Lowery note that there are two distinct types of research: one concerns mobilization and organizational maintenance, and the other concerns lobbying and other strategies for influencing policy outcomes (1996a, 91). *The Organizational State* primarily concerns the former, while *The Hollow Core* is an example of the latter. William P. Browne's *Private Interests, Public Policy, and American Agriculture* (1988), includes both strands of the interest group literature, as they apply to agricultural groups. It maps the various players in the agricultural community, describes their constituencies, emphasizes coalition building and other lobbying strategies, and then measures policy impact. Because this book describes the higher education policy community in depth and also includes both strands of the literature, it is more similar to Browne's study than to the other two.

This book also borrows from previous research on higher education policy that appeared in the 1970s and early 1980s (e.g., Bailey 1975, Bloland 1985, Breneman and Finn 1978, Finn 1978, Gladieux and Wolanin 1976, and King 1975). That literature described the higher education players in Washington and highlighted major policy issues, such as the 1972 Higher Education Act. Two more recent books provide thorough analyses of substantive policy issues, namely, *The Bill* (1995) by Steven Waldman, which chronicles the enactment of the National and

Community Service Trust Act of 1993, and *Power and Politics: Federal Higher Education Policymaking in the 1990s* (1997) by Michael D. Parsons, which describes the reauthorization of the 1992 Higher Education Act. The focus in this book is on advocacy more than substantive policy issues, and it provides the first broad overview in more than a decade of the Washington higher education community and its major policy concerns.

QUESTIONS THIS BOOK ADDRESSES

This book addresses a number of normative questions about the nature of representation and advocacy, as well as discipline-oriented questions about interest group theory. The major theoretical topics it highlights are the following:

- How does an institutional association differ from one with individual members in regard to organizational maintenance and representation?

    This book examines the difference between groups in which the members are separate individuals who make their own decisions about affiliation and groups in which the members are institutions. The interest literature is full of information about organizational maintenance and representation in membership-based groups, and this book augments that literature by describing the same issues for institutional associations. The institutional associations under consideration here are the six major Washington higher education associations (see chapter 1), and their members are colleges and universities.

    Economist Mancur Olson (1965) contended that each interest group member undertakes a personal cost-benefit analysis before joining or renewing a membership commitment. The *exchange theory* of interest group membership, developed by Robert H. Salisbury (1969), took that idea one step further and conceptualized the relationship between leaders and members according to an economic model in which the interest group leaders sell benefits, and the prospective members buy those benefits for the price of affiliation with the group. This book addresses the question of how these theories of membership incentives apply to an institutional association. Most importantly, it explores the difference between the incentives needed to attract and retain an institutional member, in this case a college or university, and those needed to satisfy the institutional representative to the association, in this case a college or university president. It also examines the importance of federal relations as a membership incentive.

    A number of authorities (e.g., Truman 1951; Berry 1997; Hansen 1985; Walker 1991; Chong 1991) have remarked that when a policy community is embroiled in a political crisis, associations become more important to their members, and advocacy takes on new significance. This book explores that proposition by comparing the views of higher

xiv

education association members prior to the arrival of the 104th Congress with those after it had begun.

A second question concerns membership participation. A democratic model usually serves as the standard for judging membership-based interest groups (e.g., Truman 1951; Rothenberg 1992), but often that model does not operate in practice (e.g., Berry 1977). The application of the democratic model to institutional associations is one of this book's topics.

A third question concerns membership renewal. While most individuals in a membership-based group simply terminate their affiliation when they are dissatisfied, others may choose to remain. Such factors as loyalty to the organization (Hirschman 1970), reputational concerns about withdrawal (Chong 1991), or worry about neglect of civic duty (Wilson 1973) are among the major reasons why some members consider it unacceptable to be an unaffiliated free-rider who benefits from the group nonetheless (Olson 1965). This book addresses membership renewal issues in institutional associations to show how they conform to or diverge from those in other groups.

- What effect does the proliferation of Washington associations and representatives within a policy community have on its lobbying?

Students of American politics have documented an increase in Washington representatives in most policy areas over the last few decades (see, for example, Walker 1991; Salisbury 1984; Salisbury 1992; Schlozman and Tierney 1986; Pratt 1993). William P. Browne (1995) noted that there was an increase in Washington groups of as much as 700 percent during the period from 1947–1984, and Jonathan Rauch (1994) showed that the number of national associations doubled from 1956–1970 and then doubled again by 1990.

The social science literature on what constitutes success for an interest group discusses the impact of numbers. In their study of four policy domains, Heinz and his associates (1993) found that if there are a large number of representatives and organizations opposing a proposal, then it becomes necessary to have a large number supporting the proposal. In other words, "the percentage of active players supporting a proposal is significantly associated with success" (346). Nonetheless, they concluded that most often it is neither the number of representatives nor the number of associations supporting a policy proposal that seem to determine its outcome, and increased political activity may actually lead to increased uncertainty for a domain (380–81). The interest group universe has been destabilized by its sheer numbers, both collective numbers and numbers within each domain. As Browne pointed out in his study of the agricultural policy community, "the new universe of interest groups is beyond manageable proportions" (1988, 252). Petracca concluded, "more interest groups are engaging in more activity and yet are receiving less of the government's largesse than ever before" (1992, xxiv). Rauch said, "The more you try to beat the other guy, the more the game expands" (1994, 63). Salisbury (1990) called it a paradox of "more groups, less clout."

Just as in other policy communities, there has been a huge influx of new Washington representatives of higher education in recent decades, including specialized associations, campus representatives, and "hired guns" (i.e., for-profit law, consulting, and lobbying firms). This book examines its impact to ascertain whether it seems to have had a positive effect on higher education policy making.

- How does a policy community organize itself in Washington, and what role does an umbrella association play?

Recent studies of the internal dynamics of policy communities (especially Heinz et al. 1993, Browne 1988, Laumann and Knoke 1987) have concluded that they no longer have single umbrella (or peak) associations to integrate and mediate the demands of various segments and serve as intermediaries among contending interests. As the numbers of players in the communities have grown, it has become more and more difficult to avoid fragmentation and friction within· them (Heinz et al. 1993). The fragmentation of interests has contributed to the difficulty of creating coalitions and working collectively (e.g., Salisbury 1992, 145–46). Because there are so many groups, they tend to cancel each other out, leaving public officials to make their own independent choices without as much reference to group preferences as there would be if fewer groups were involved. Salisbury (1992) noted that the officials "find themselves with choice and discretion, able to select policy alternatives and take positions knowing that almost any position will have some group support and none can prevent opposition from arising" (347). They know that there are interests on all sides of an issue, both supporters and opponents, so there is no way they can please every group anyway. As a result, they can make their own decisions without regard to interest group consequences, so "the balance of power may have shifted in favor of governmental actors" (Heinz et al. 1993, 405). John Kingdon pointed out that "if a group is plagued by internal dissension, its effectiveness is seriously impaired" (1984, 55). A balkanized policy community invites policy makers to follow their own policy preferences.

An umbrella association can maximize cohesion and minimize internal rivalries. Communities with little internal conflict are more likely to be able to shape legislators' views effectively than those with much internal conflict, and group cohesion is an important resource in convincing government officials to listen as a community tries to influence policy agendas, decisions, and implementation (Kingdon 1984, 55; Laumann and Knoke 1987, 387).

A division of labor usually emerges within the policy community, especially if there is an umbrella association to facilitate it. Associations find their own policy niches by interacting with similar groups and looking for ways to coordinate their activities without overlapping (Browne 1990; Heinz et al. 1993; Gray and Lowery 1996a and 1996b). To achieve that coordination, the higher education community has what it calls an umbrella association, and this book examines the role it plays and how the community organizes itself in Washington. While personalities are clearly important in shaping group structure, this book tries to look beyond personalities and uncover some basic organizational principles for the higher education community.

• How does a change in party control of Congress with its attendant political turmoil affect the strategies and tactics of a policy community?

An extensive study of Washington interest groups (Schlozman and Tierney 1986) concluded that during periods of political turmoil, interest groups engage in more political activity. However, it also concluded that groups go on using the same approaches to advocacy that they used in the past. They continue to do what they used to do but in greater amounts (Schlozman and Tierney 1986). It is not until they suffer substantial policy defeats that they are likely to change their approach (Gais and Walker 1991). In 1995 when the 104th Congress came to town, the new Republican leaders proposed major changes in higher education funding, with sharp reductions and some restructuring. Their proposals ushered in a period of policy turmoil, with the relative consensus on higher education policy which had characterized the Democratic Congress for decades suddenly subject to debate and criticism. Therefore, part of this book's story is a description of a policy community's reaction when a change in party control upsets the status quo. It asks whether that change led the higher education community to alter its attitudes and approach to lobbying.

METHODOLOGY

Both qualitative and quantitative research methods were used to answer the questions posed above, as well as many more that are pertinent specifically to the higher education community. The first stage involved survey data collection; the second stage involved exploratory field work and interviews.

A four-page survey was sent to the presidents of 2,524 colleges and universities listed in the 1994 *Higher Education Directory* (see survey instrument in Appendix A) between May and October, 1994. It went to those in all types of institutions except specialized ones, such as music schools, medical schools, or theological seminaries. The presidents of proprietary (for-profit) institutions were not included in the survey because their institutions are sufficiently numerous and sufficiently different from other types of postsecondary institutions to merit a study of their own.

The survey had a 62 percent response rate, with 1,554 of the institutions returning the questionnaire. A majority of all types of institutions responded, from a low of 51 percent of the associate of arts colleges to a high of 89 percent of the doctoral universities (see figure P.1).[1]

Figure P.1
Survey Response Rates, by Carnegie Classification

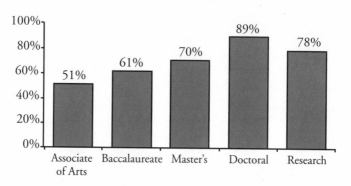

Note: Surveys were mailed to presidents of 2,524 colleges and universities, and 1,554 responded.

The questionnaire asked presidents about their institutions' federal relations, their preferences regarding lobbying strategies, and their perception of higher education's effectiveness in Washington. It also asked about their membership in the major higher education associations and their satisfaction with them, whether the benefits were worth the costs, the presidents' level of commitment to membership, and their reasons for withdrawal. The appeal and relevance of these topics was evident from the fact that almost every one of the presidents who responded returned the enclosed reply card asking for a copy of the survey results.[2] Presidents said they ordinarily have no way to evaluate the major associations to which they belong and for which their institutions pay substantial dues, so they saw this study as a useful way to learn more about the associations and, especially, their federal relations.

Since more than half of the institutions of each type were represented in the survey results, one would expect to be able to generalize from the survey respondents to the population as a whole, and tentative generalizations are made throughout this book. The tentative nature of the generalizations stems from the fact that institutions that were members of the six major associations at the time of the survey could have been more likely to respond to the questionnaire, given that its primary focus was on the associations.

The second, qualitative stage of the research involved 140 telephone or face-to-face interviews, mostly the latter. All interviews were done by the author, and almost all took place during 1995 and 1996, with the majority in the early months of the 104th Congress.

The interviewees were a sample of college and university presidents who serve on the six major Washington association boards, campus lobbyists, the presidents and government relations personnel of the six associations and other influential Washington associations, plus many of the personnel on Capitol Hill (both members of Congress and their staffs) and in the executive branch (both appointed and career officials) who were identified by association personnel as being particularly influential in shaping higher education policy outcomes. (A list of interviewees appears after the bibliography.) Many of the interviewees asked not to be identified by name, and names appear in the text and citations only for those who did not request anonymity and whose identity is important to an understanding of the significance of their remarks.

Just as those surveyed responded enthusiastically, so did potential interviewees. Almost every one of the presidents who serve on the six major association boards agreed to a telephone interview, if requested, and even during the hectic first year of the 104th Congress, it was not difficult to schedule interviews with association personnel and with congressional staff and executive branch officials. (Admittedly, however, it was more difficult to arrange interviews with members of Congress.) Although most of the interviews were scheduled for only a half hour, the face-to-face interviews frequently lasted from sixty to ninety minutes. It was clear that the interviewees had an intense interest in the topic and were eager to reflect on the higher education community and the nature of the work that they do.

The interviews covered many of the same topics as the survey, but in more detail. Association leaders were questioned about the nature of their membership incentive systems. College and university presidents answered questions about the reasons for their institutions' affiliations with the associations and the membership benefits they personally and their institutions collectively receive. The level of membership participation in the decision making of these institutional associations was examined through questions for presidents and association leaders about the ways the associations learn about presidents' views, the extent to which those views are taken into account for association policy decisions, and the role the presidents play on the association boards of directors. Institutional presidents, campus lobbyists, and the leaders of specialized associations were interviewed about the functions of the six major associations, the community's division of labor, and whether the proliferation of Washington representatives has diminished the importance of major associations. They were also asked about the extent to which the American Council on Education (ACE) serves as higher education's Washington voice, facilitates community consensus, and coordinates messages to policy makers. Public officials were asked in interviews about the value to the policy community of achieving consensus and presenting a unified position, as well as about their perception of whether the higher education community succeeds in doing so.

Fortuitously, the mail survey of college and university presidents took place just prior to the 1994 election of a Republican congressional majority, while most interviews came after that election. It is possible, therefore, to use the survey data as a backdrop showing the higher education community's traditional attitude toward lobbying and then use the interview data to document the ways that a period of political turmoil altered the community's approach to it. Association leaders and campus lobbyists were questioned, along with the presidents, about the nature of the strategies and tactics they used during the 104th Congress: what was new, and why they did what they did. Public officials were asked their views of the community's effectiveness.

Many of the survey and interview questions for this book built on the findings from a study done nearly two decades ago. In 1979 the Ford Foundation sponsored a project at the Center for the Study of Higher Education of the University of Michigan on the role of the major higher education associations (Cosand et al. 1979). Specifically, all college and university presidents were surveyed in regard to their perceptions of the major associations, both collectively and individually. Mail survey questions dealt with the relationships among the associations, their federal relations roles, and the perceptions and expectations of their member institutions. In addition, there were interviews with national observers (e.g., association leaders, members of Congress and their staffs, and members of the federal bureaucracy), along with a comparison of their views and those of the institution presidents. Although the Ford Foundation sponsors and the major associations received a summary of the research findings, the study was never published. This book is the only sequel to the original study, and it draws its structure and methodology from that early research. The 1979 study data appear throughout the book, where relevant, because they provide a useful way to describe changes in higher education representation over time.

OUTLINE OF THE BOOK

Chapter 1 discusses the federal role and structure for higher education policy making. The chapter introduces the major associations, as well as other higher education representatives in Washington, and explains the reasons for the proliferation of representatives over time.

Chapter 2 provides a brief history of the six major associations. It also has a section on early higher education lobbying, especially the associations' debacle during the enactment of the 1972 Higher Education Act, and the criticism of the associations that followed. The chapter includes a review of higher education policy issues and lobbying through the 1980s.

Chapter 3 explains the erosion of public confidence in higher education, and its implications for policy making in the early 1990s. The chapter offers detailed narratives regarding two major policy issues, earmarked funding and the State Postsecondary Review Entities (SPREs), both of which demonstrated the limitations of major association lobbying. The chapter explains the community's deteriorating relationship with the Clinton administration in its first two years in office.

Chapter 4 concerns the arrival of the 104th Congress and describes its leaders' vocal criticisms of academia. The chapter then gives an overview of higher education policy issues that came before the 104th Congress when it convened in January 1995.

Chapter 5 describes the Washington higher education community. It details the role of the American Council on Education (ACE), as well as other major associations and specialized groups. It explains their relationship to campus lobbyists and hired guns. It also shows how and to what extent ACE performs its coordinating role.

Chapter 6 concerns the relationship between the six major associations and their college and university members. Its topics are: the costs and benefits of membership, the role of federal relations as a membership incentive, the extent of members' participation in the associations, the factors influencing renewal decisions, and the nature and extent of the institutional members' commitment to the associations.

Chapter 7 characterizes differences among institutional types, especially public and private, two- and four-year, and research and other types of institutions. It contrasts their differing issues and approaches to federal relations, especially their attitudes toward consensus within the community, and the way each chooses to represent itself in Washington.

Chapter 8 analyzes the lobbying strategies and tactics of the higher education community, comparing them with those of other communities. Because higher education lobbying has changed over time, this chapter explains how the community lobbied prior to the advent of the 104th Congress and describes the new tactics it began to use in 1995–96.

Chapter 9 examines the issue of interest group effectiveness in two ways. First, it reviews higher education policy outcomes in the 104th Congress and second, it describes public officials' perceptions of effectiveness and their recommendations to the higher education community.

Chapter 10, the concluding chapter, summarizes the book's major contributions to the interest group literature and provides a set of questions that warrant further study.

Chapter 11, an epilogue of sorts, is a brief overview of the points that are of particular relevance to college and university presidents.

Appendices include the actual text of the survey sent to college and university presidents and a comparison of the survey respondents with the overall population of colleges and universities in the United States. A list of interviewees follows the bibliography.

ACKNOWLEDGMENTS

This book was four years in the making, and I received wonderful encouragement and assistance along the way. An early grant of seed money from the Office of Research at the University of Michigan funded part of the original survey, and subsequent grants from both the Spencer Foundation and the W. K. Kellogg Foundation made possible the survey and interviews, as well as graduate student research assistance. The three grants were significant not only in monetary terms but also because they bestowed legitimacy on this unusual project. I very much appreciate the funders' confidence, but I hasten to add that the statements made and views expressed here are solely the responsibility of the author.

Professor of Higher Education Marvin Peterson, my colleague at the Center for the Study of Higher and Postsecondary Education (CSHPE) at the University of Michigan, initially encouraged me to pursue this study. He was part of a team that did a similar research project in 1979 (Cosand et al.), and its findings provide a baseline for evaluating some of the data I have collected. My thanks go also to University of Michigan Professor of Political Science Richard Hall, who first proposed that my work include a map of the higher education landscape in Washington.

It has been a pleasure to work on this project with CSHPE's talented graduate students. Mark Nemec and Catherine Millett contributed research and survey assistance early on. Mark handled the questionnaire distribution and then presented a preliminary version of chapter 5 with me at the 1995 meeting of the Association for the Study of Higher Education (ASHE). Catherine contributed in multiple ways, including analysis of open-ended survey data, and she and Mark devised Figure 5.3. Two other students are responsible for the information that went into specific tables: Julia Davis for Table 5.1 and Kathleen Kelly for Table 1.2. Additionally, Gertrude Arnold and Michael McLendon worked closely with me for a six-month period in 1996. As a result of our teamwork, Michael is listed as co-author of chapter 3 and Gertrude of chapter 7 (which grew out of a paper we presented at the 1996 ASHE annual meeting). Both Michael and Gertrude made contributions to other chapters as well, especially chapters 2, 4, and 9, and Gertrude is responsible for formatting most of the figures in this volume. Additionally, I want to express appreciation to students in my graduate seminar on Public Policy in Higher Education, especially Denise Green and John Cole, for providing good advice on the manuscript.

ACKNOWLEDGMENTS

There are others at the University of Michigan to whom I owe many thanks. By far the most important is Rachel Stivenson, whose intelligence, diligence, good humor, and secretarial skill sustained me during the final two years of this project. She arranged interviews, typed transcripts, and then formatted the manuscript repeatedly as it went through various iterations. She also formatted the "maps" of the higher education community, Figures 1.1, 5.1, and 5.2. I simply could not have completed this project without her. Rachel's predecessor, Marilyn Parrent, also did a superb job of arranging interviews and typing transcripts. Another contributor was Holde Borcherts, senior librarian, whose thoughtfulness and speed make her research skills even more valuable. My colleagues at the Center for Research on Learning and Teaching (CRLT) contributed their encouragement; Lisa Mets was particularly gracious about offering administrative assistance and reassurance as I worked on the manuscript.

Several people generously read early drafts and offered insights that improved the manuscript markedly. Especially helpful were Professor Robert Berdahl of the University of Maryland, Professor Jeffrey Berry of Tufts University, Professor Harland Bloland of the University of Miami, Professor William Browne of Central Michigan University, Jon and Carol Fuller of the National Association of Independent Colleges and Universities, Professor Allan Cigler of the University of Kansas, Professor Kenneth Kollmann of the University of Michigan, and John Vaughn of the Association of American Universities. All shaped the manuscript in significant ways. Others who offered wise suggestions about portions of the manuscript were Robert Samors and Thomas Butts of the University of Michigan Government Relations Office, David Baime of the American Association of Community Colleges, Chancellor James Renick of the University of Michigan—Dearborn, and President Gunder Myran of Washtenaw Community College. Additionally, there were several anonymous reviewers whose wise advice I have taken.

I owe special thanks to Charles Backus and his capable staff at Vanderbilt University Press, who quickly appreciated the unique aspects of this manuscript and gave it more personal attention than any author has a right to expect. They demonstrated the risk-taking and creativity that should be, but are not always, the hallmarks of a good university press. I am grateful as well for the support of Professor John Braxton and the editorial advisory board of the series Issues in Higher Education.

My husband, Jim, to whom this book is dedicated, cheered me on every step of the way, even when he would have preferred to have me play golf with him. My thanks also go to my children, Jay and Amy Cook, and my parents, Margaret Ewing and the late Reid Ewing, for their consistent interest in my work.

Most importantly, I am beholden to well over a hundred college and university presidents, association leaders, and public officials who generously submitted to interviews, often lengthy ones, and offered their own candid insights on higher education organization and advocacy in Washington, D.C. I hope they will see in this volume an accurate and comprehensive summary of their views. I was often struck by the interviewees' eagerness to tell the story of higher education lobbying and their conviction that it is a story worth telling. I am honored to be the storyteller.

LOBBYING for HIGHER EDUCATION

★ ★ ★ ★ ★ ★

Chapter One

HIGHER EDUCATION POLICIES AND REPRESENTATION

"You often hear that higher education doesn't lobby. Victorian phrases crop up in the debate about government relations. There is the use of words like tainted. *"*
A lobbyist from one of the "Big Six"
higher education associations in Washington

It is not unusual to encounter a book on lobbying. What is unusual about this particular book is that the policy community that is under examination, higher education, is one that prided itself for decades on how little lobbying it did and how little it knew about the craft of advocacy. Higher education has always thought of itself as a national treasure, a public good whose value should not be questioned. Historically, its leaders believed that politics is a dirty business, one unworthy of a lofty enterprise like higher education. Observers agree that, as a result, the Washington representatives of colleges and universities remained on the sidelines during the early congressional debates on federal aid to higher education. For most of their history, the Washington higher education associations did not even want their representatives to be called "lobbyists" (Hawkins 1992, 124).

There are still vestiges of that attitude, and there are many reasons for it. Twenty years ago those who chronicled higher education's federal relations commented on the prevailing view of politics in the higher education community. One said, "Distaste for the art and practice of politics is mixed with a genuine concern that aggressive political action would somehow be inappropriate to the academic enterprise and might even be counterproductive" (Gladieux 1977, 272). Another commented that higher education associations tried to "ride above the waves" so as to avoid the "demeaning and lowly" political process. He said higher education lobbying was often "passive" because, "To enter the game of partisan politics as a traditional lobby would strip academia of its privileged status in society" (Murray 1976, 90–92).

Given the impact of federal funding and regulations, it is vital for colleges and universities to be well-represented in Washington. Simply put, higher education representatives are faced with a difficult paradox: On the one hand, higher education's image as a public good garners it the support of many public policy makers. If it lobbies just the same way other "special interests" do, it can look just like the others and risk a loss of support from those who consider it high-minded, above the fray.[1] On the other hand, if higher education does not lobby the same way as others, its gentility can lead to an absence of public attention and a low priority on the public agenda. To complicate the issue further, higher education institutions and associations have legal restrictions on their lobbying as a result of their non-profit tax status.[2]

For all these reasons and others, a Washington policy analyst noted, "Higher education lobbying is treated by higher ed folks as if it is a different kind of undertaking. . . . They think this is a genteel endeavor, not an industry." A university lobbyist agreed, saying, "Those in higher ed are gun-shy about lobbying. They don't like combative situations." As a result, the higher education community historically lobbied in a somewhat half-heart-ed manner, if at all.

In the course of the 104th Congress, during 1995–96, a paradigm shift occurred in higher education advocacy. While the quantity and quality of higher education lobbying had been growing for a long time, it was not until the so-called Republican revolution that the community decided it was more important to keep higher education issues on the public agenda than to worry about losing support from those who thought colleges and universities should avoid political involvement. As one lobbyist put it, "We decided to stop looking like a 'country bumpkin promoting the public good'." Another commented, "During the 104th Congress we tried new tactics. . . . What a novel approach! Higher ed meekly stuck their toes in the water of modern lobbying. This is a timid crowd." For the first time, the higher education community focused full attention on advocacy and, without apology, engaged in vigorous lobbying activity.

This chapter gives an overview of the federal role in higher education, which shows how much is at stake. It then describes the Washington higher education community, especially the six major associations, and explains the diverse types of colleges and universities in the United States. Finally, it discusses the proliferation of federal access points which, in turn, has encouraged the proliferation of higher education actors in Washington.

THE FEDERAL ROLE IN HIGHER EDUCATION

What makes higher education and its federal relations worthy of special study is the sheer importance of American colleges and universities. They are considered the finest in the world. Historically, national policy has con-tributed to their excellence and value, so the higher education community seeks to ensure that the government continues to be a positive force.

There is much at stake in higher education policy making, especially because higher education has such an impact on the U.S. economy. College graduates command higher salaries and provide higher tax revenues than those who do not attend or graduate from college, and the higher education

4

enterprise constitutes a $100 billion industry, accounting for 3.1 percent of the gross domestic product (Horton and Andersen 1994). As of 1996, there were 3,688 American colleges and universities, enrolling 14.3 million students either part-time or full-time (*Chronicle of Higher Education,* 2 September 1996).[3] Additionally, there are 800,000 instructional and research staff and one million administrative and support staff employed by these institutions (American Council on Education 1993). The American economy, prosperous by comparison with others, prospers in part because of the knowledge and skills taught by colleges and universities and the research done by their faculty. Both basic and applied university research contribute to American economic competitiveness in the global market.

Apart from its direct impact on the economy, higher education is important because it enriches the lives of the citizenry. Americans believe in upward mobility and typically consider education the key to mobility. In the contemporary era, it is a college degree or, increasingly, a graduate school degree that best promotes upward mobility. Furthermore, during their college years young people develop skills necessary for informed involvement in a participatory democracy, and policies promoting access serve to blur societal divisions, especially since more than half of high school graduates now attend college. Communities are enriched by the arts, sports, cultural events, and other resources of their local educational institutions, and millions of people benefit from various public service programs undertaken by colleges and universities. In short, it is difficult to imagine the quality of life experienced by Americans without the quality and quantity of higher education available to them.

In spite of the significance of the higher education enterprise, there is no comprehensive federal policy regarding colleges and universities. Federal involvement in higher education policy making has always been piecemeal, and the role of the national government is ambiguous. The U.S. Constitution is silent on the subject of all education, not just higher education, and although George Washington championed the establishment of a national university, the founding fathers ultimately decided against it. The Tenth Amendment of the Bill of Rights says that all power not specifically delegated by the Constitution to the federal government is reserved for the states, so the states have primary responsibility for higher education. As a result, it has been the state governments that have established and funded public institutions, and they continue to provide the largest share of institutional funding.

Before public institutions developed in this country, there were already private (independent) colleges and universities. Their autonomy was ensured by the Supreme Court's decision in the Dartmouth College case in 1819, which said the incorporation of an institution under government charter did not bring it under government control. Eventually an extensive system of public state-funded education began to appear side by side with private higher education, but neither the public institutions nor the privates developed under the aegis of the federal government. Nonetheless, the federal policy making role has not been insignificant.

The federal government first involved itself in higher education in 1787 when Congress passed the Northwest Ordinance requiring that each newly formed state should receive two townships dedicated toward support of a university. Although a few states appropriated the proceeds from this land to existing private institutions, most created new state universities. Nearly a century later, the Morrill Act of 1862 provided federal land in each state, from which the proceeds were to be used to support a college offering agricultural and mechanical education, and not excluding more traditional disciplines. Today, the institutions funded by the Morrill Act are those most commonly considered *land-grant* universities.

The federal government then passed the Hatch Act (1887) and the second Morrill Act (1890) to fund certain types of institutional research. Additionally, the federal government founded the service academies and has chartered institutions such as Howard University. The Reserve Officers' Training Corps, established on university campuses in 1916, was another form of federal support, and during the 1930s the federal government enacted a variety of other forms of financial aid.

It was not until after World War II that federal funding for higher education became quite substantial, based on national needs. For example, the GI Bill of 1944 (called the Servicemen's Readjustment Act) provided federal support for veterans' education, which served as a reward for their military service. In the 1950s the federal government also financed education for specific careers, and with the goal of contributions to global understanding.

Sponsorship of vital research became a major federal initiative in the postwar era. In 1945 President Truman's science advisor, Vannevar Bush, issued a report in which he argued that the federal government should develop a partnership with the nation's research universities and fund them to train young scientists and develop new scientific knowledge through basic research. His proposal was adopted, and the result was a large number of federal research initiatives, many of which were tied to strategic national defense objectives. The 1945 Fulbright Act, which financed the international exchange of scholars, was followed by the 1958 National Defense Education Act (NDEA). That Act, passed after the Russian launch of Sputnik, was one of many examples of higher education funding resulting from the Cold War mentality and competition with the Soviet Union. The NDEA encouraged students to study science and mathematics in return for federal financial aid.

Next came a series of agencies created to bolster American research capacity. The creation, in 1949, of the National Institutes of Health (NIH), which supports university-based medical research and is a division of the

Department of Health and Human Services, was followed in 1950 by the establishment of the National Science Foundation (NSF), which funds other university-based scientific research. Then came the National Endowment for the Arts (NEA) and the National Endowment for the Humanities (NEH), both of which were created in 1965 to extend federal funding to non-scientific research and programs. (While the NEA has a very small budget, with little linkage to higher education institutions, faculty artists, poets, and creative writers occasionally receive NEA grants. The NEA is included in this list not because of its budget but because those faculty members in the arts and humanities so value its work.) Additional federal departments have provided large amounts of research funding to higher education, especially the Departments of Defense, Agriculture, Energy, and Health and Human Services, and the amounts grew especially when the Cold War was at its height. (By far the largest share of federal dollars fund scientific and medical research, as opposed to other types of university-based research. Although science policy issues are addressed only peripherally in this book, since they affect a relatively small number of colleges and universities, the observations and conclusions made here are broadly applicable to lobbying for the scientific realm as well.)

The federal government has been especially instrumental in regard to affirmative action in higher education. Affirmative action involves measures to correct or compensate for past discrimination or to prevent discrimination from recurring in the future, and it especially affects higher education employment, admissions, retention, and student financial aid. The principal piece of affirmative action legislation is the Civil Rights Act of 1964 (amended in 1972, 1978, and 1991), which was the cornerstone of President Lyndon Johnson's Great Society programs. The Act prohibits all forms of discrimination on the basis of race, color, gender, religion, or national origin. Title VII of the Act specifically applies to public and private employers with fifteen or more employees and, therefore, includes colleges and universities. Other employment-related federal statutes concern discrimination on the basis of age, physical or mental disability, veteran status, citizenship status, and disabilities.

Policies concerning student admission and retention in selective higher education programs have also been shaped by federal affirmative action goals. While landmark judicial decisions like the 1978 *Bakke* case have altered the way that institutions implement affirmative action legislation, the federal government has in fact acted for decades as a force for nondiscrimination in higher education.

Affirmative action legislation has also shaped institutional policies toward student aid, especially because the Civil Rights Act of 1964 was interpreted to allow institutions to take race into account in financial awards. The Higher Education Act (HEA) of 1965, developed during the early civil rights movement, differed not only in the magnitude of federal

7

assistance, which was substantial, but also in its objective. It sought to remove barriers to educational opportunity by initiating a variety of types of federal grants, loans, and fellowships to both undergraduate and graduate students. In addition, the Act provided institutional funding for certain purposes. The 1965 Act thus constituted a far-reaching federal effort on behalf of higher education, and it has been amended and reauthorized five times since 1965—in 1972, 1976, 1980, 1986, and 1992 (and is scheduled for renewal in fiscal year 1998). (The federal *fiscal year* means the period from October 1 of each calendar year through September 30 of the following year.[4]) Along with the carrot has come the stick: Washington has used its financial aid, as provided in the Higher Education Act and its amendments, to enforce affirmative action objectives by threatening to cut off student financial aid at institutions that do not comply with federal mandates. One such mandate is Title IX of the 1972 HEA which prohibits discrimination on the basis of sex and is best known for its provision of better athletic opportunities for women students.

The magnitude of the federal role in higher education funding has grown substantially over the years. While states continue to supply about twice as much money, the federal share now constitutes nearly 15 percent of all college and university revenues. Unlike state aid, most federal funding goes directly to individuals (typically to students or professors), rather than to the institutions themselves. By 1996, federal student financial aid, both grants and loans, reached a high of $35.1 billion, and about a third of the students in postsecondary education were receiving some form of federal aid. As for federal grants and contracts for university-based research, they totaled $11.8 billion in 1996 (*Chronicle of Higher Education*, 2 September 1996) and were the major source of faculty members' research dollars. In addition to student aid and research money, there are other forms of federal funding (e.g., funding for critical foreign languages, or library support, or teaching improvement projects) that provide some of the *extras* that the higher education community counts on to fill in the gaps. However, federal funds remain largely uncoordinated and come from a wide variety of agencies and programs to serve a wide variety of purposes.

Along with the massive federal funding for higher education has come a proliferation of regulations. For example, the federal tax code has a substantial impact on higher education funding and institutional policies. While American institutions have an unusual amount of independence and autonomy by comparison with institutions in most other countries, it is increasingly difficult to find a single aspect of college or university activity that remains unaffected by the federal government in one way or another. Besides student aid, research, and affirmative action, Washington affects higher education policies on such diverse topics as, for example, campus safety, accreditation, faculty retirement age, graduation rates, substance abuse, telecommunications, and assessment of student learning. The variety of topics means that advocacy on behalf of higher education is a complex task.

THE HIGHER EDUCATION COMMUNITY

The task of advocacy for the American higher education community is further complicated by its diversity. There are more than 3,600 colleges and universities, and they are located in every part of the country, including every state and city, and many towns. They vary from two-year community colleges granting associate degrees to research universities granting doctoral degrees. Of these institutions, 55 percent are private (i.e., independent) institutions whose budgets come largely from student tuition and private donations. Some state dollars go to private institutions, especially in the form of student aid, but the amount of state funding for private institutions is minuscule by comparison with the amount for public ones. About 22 percent of the 14.3 million students in American higher education are enrolled in private institutions (*Chronicle of Higher Education*, 2 September 1996).

The remaining 78 percent of American students, both undergraduate and graduate students, are enrolled in public institutions. Public colleges and universities, which are funded largely by state governments, are also dependent on student tuitions and private donations, but to a lesser extent than private institutions. State governments typically pay for most of the operating expenses and new buildings at public institutions. The fifty state governments have fifty different systems for interacting with their own higher education institutions, and there is tremendous variation in the degree and types of controls they exercise. To monitor and influence policy making, colleges and universities send staff members both to their state capitals and also to Washington.

There is as much variation in institutional representation in Washington as there is in every other aspect of higher education. Large numbers of institutions have staff whose job descriptions include federal relations in whole or in part, and many of them commute regularly to the nation's capital. Beginning in the early 1970s, a few individual institutions began establishing their own Washington offices, and now there are more than a dozen of them. In addition, most of the large state systems of higher education have offices in the capital to represent the interests of all their member institutions.

Also in Washington are hundreds of associations representing higher education. For example, there are regional and state coalitions of colleges and universities and consortia of institutions of the same general type (e.g., church-related institutions, or historically black institutions). There are associations of people in the same roles in their institutions (e.g., chief financial officers, or members of governing boards, or professors within each discipline), associations of people with the same general concerns (e.g., about the quality of graduate education, or the nature of international education), and associations of personnel with the same type of tasks to perform for the higher education community (e.g., accreditation). In fact, *The Encyclopedia of Associations* now lists several hundred groups whose customary work concerns various aspects of higher education, more than two hundred of which are located in the Washington area. Many of these groups do no federal relations at all, but some are engaged in educational or lobbying activities of one sort or another. Additionally, law, lobbying, and consulting firms are sometimes retained by individual institutions to advance their interests with the federal government, and ad hoc groups often spring up to work on a specific policy issue and then disband when the issue has been resolved.

To create order in the jumbled Washington landscape, a set of major associations serve as the principal voices of higher education. Like the organizations representing many other policy domains (see, for example, Heinz et al. 1993, 57), the major higher education associations have been the important players in the domain for several decades and are viewed as permanent fixtures. These six major associations differ from most other Washington higher education associations in that they are presidentially based. In other words, the presidents of colleges and universities are designated as the principal institutional representatives. It is customarily the presidents who make the final decisions about whether to join or renew membership, and it is the presidents who most often attend the association meetings. Nonetheless, the real members of these six associations, known as the *Big Six*, are the institutions themselves.[5]

The heads of the Big Six associations spend much of their time on federal relations and consider that activity to be their personal priority. As one of the major association presidents noted, "Federal relations is the reason we are in Washington instead of Jackson, Wyoming, where I would rather be." While all have some staff assigned to governmental affairs, with the number growing in recent years, the staff size and the proportion of the association budgets devoted to federal relations are usually quite modest, though they vary by association. Nonetheless, these groups stay in regular contact with members of Congress and the executive branch.

One of the Big Six associations, the American Council on Education (ACE), is the national coordinating body for American higher education. ACE represents all accredited colleges and universities, both public and private. ACE's membership is composed of individual institutions as well as national and regional higher education associations, including the other five major associations. Thus, ACE is, in part, an association of associations.

While the other five major associations have some association members as well, their main function is representation of a specific type of institution. Most American colleges and universities have memberships in one or more associations. Nonetheless, most institutions think of one of the five specialized associations as their *primary* association because it is the only one to which they belong, or the one they consider primary for federal relations. Because the jurisdictions of the five associations overlap to some extent, some institutions choose to belong to two of the five. These overlapping memberships will be explained further in chapter 5.[6] However, the majority of institutions are members of the single association that best represents their own type of institution, and then they usually join ACE as well (see figure 1.1).

Figure 1.1
**Relationship of the
Big Six Associations**

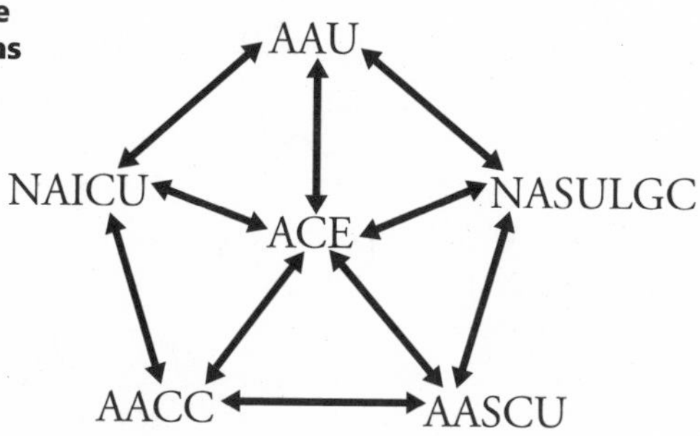

The five major associations are the American Association of Community Colleges (AACC), the Association of American Universities (AAU), the American Association of State Colleges and Universities (AASCU), the National Association of Independent Colleges and Universities (NAICU), and the National Association of State Universities and Land-Grant Colleges (NASULGC). The overlap among them occurs because AACC represents two-year institutions, both public and private; AASCU represents public master's (comprehensive) universities, most of which are four or more years, but a few of which have two-year degree programs as well; NASULGC represents mostly public universities that range from research and doctoral to master's; AAU represents the elite research universities, both public and private; and NAICU represents private institutions, ranging from research universities to two-year colleges. ACE represents all these major presidentially based associations, as well as other more specialized higher education associations, and also every type of college and university. (See chapter 5 for more discussion of this organizational structure.)

With the exception of AAU, which has the same dues for all its member institutions, the Big Six associations' annual charges are based either on size of enrollment or on a combination of enrollment and general expenditure data. The 1995 dues of the Big Six ranged from a low of $600 for the smallest NAICU college to a high of $38,200 for the largest NASULGC university.[7] The University of Michigan, for example, which has both a large enrollment and a large budget, paid about $90,000 in 1995 for its memberships in three Big Six associations (i.e., AAU, NASULGC, and ACE).

The memberships of the Big Six range from 60 to 1,800 institutions and associations. After ACE, AACC is the largest. Its members are public and private two-year degree-granting colleges. AAU has the smallest membership because it is the voice of the elite research institutions and is the only one of the Big Six whose membership is by invitation only. AASCU's members are master's institutions and state systems of public higher education, and the degree programs of its institutions range from the associate degree to the doctorate. NAICU's members are independent (or private) institutions, plus organizations that coordinate private higher education within the states and some other smaller associations of private institutions. NASULGC's members are almost entirely public colleges and universities, especially land-grant institutions and the state flagship universities, as well as public higher education systems. It is smaller than all of the Big Six except AAU. (See chapter 5 for more detailed information about the membership of the Big Six.)

The principal differences among higher education institutions are those of control (i.e., public and private), length of program (two-year and four-year), and research institutions as compared to others. By virtue of its control, program, and emphasis or lack of emphasis on research, each higher education institution develops some basic attitudes on federal relations that are shared with others of the same type. Additional factors such as size and location also play a role in institutional attitudes. Through analysis of survey results, this book shows which of the differences seem especially important in setting an institutional approach to federal relations. (See chapter 7 for an analysis of the different attitudes of different types of institutions.)

The Carnegie classification system is often used to differentiate among various types of colleges and universities, so its terminology appears throughout this book and bears explanation. First developed in 1970, the classifications have been modified and updated periodically, including as recently as 1994. The current system uses the following descriptions:[8]

Research Universities. These institutions give high priority to research, have a minimum of $15.5 million in annual federal support for research, and award fifty or more doctoral degrees each year, as well as having a full range of baccalaureate programs. In 1994 there were 125 institutions classified as Research Universities by the Carnegie system. Those with the most federal funding and the largest numbers of doctoral degrees are members of AAU, and some of these elites are also members of NASULGC. The other Research Universities are often members of NASULGC or, less frequently, AASCU. Examples of Research Universities are the University of California at Berkeley and Yale University.

Doctoral Universities. These institutions are committed to graduate education through the doctorate, and they also offer a full range of baccalaureate programs. The Doctoral Universities award a minimum of ten doctoral degrees in three or more disciplines or twenty or more doctoral degrees in one or more disciplines. In 1994, 111 institutions qualified as Doctoral Universities. These institutions are primarily members of NAICU if they are private institutions, and either NASULGC or AASCU, or both, if public. Boston College and Western Michigan University are both examples of Doctoral Universities.

Master's (or Comprehensive) Colleges and Universities. These institutions also offer a full range of baccalaureate programs, plus graduate education through the master's degree. They award a minimum of twenty or more master's degrees annually in one or more disciplines. There were 529 Master's Colleges and Universities in 1994, about half of which are public and are likely to be members of AASCU; the other half, the privates, are likely to be members of NAICU. Examples of Master's Colleges and Universities are Mankato State University in Minnesota and Elon College in North Carolina.

Baccalaureate (Liberal Arts) Colleges. These institutions are primarily undergraduate colleges and emphasize their baccalaureate degree programs. Many of them award large percentages of their baccalaureate degrees in liberal arts fields. There were 637 Baccalaureate Colleges in 1994, and since most of them are private institutions, most are members of NAICU. The few public baccalaureate institutions are most likely to be members of AASCU. Williams College in Massachusetts and York College of the City University of New York are both examples of Baccalaureate Colleges.

Associate of Arts Colleges. These institutions offer associate of arts certificate or degree programs and usually do not offer baccalaureate degrees. There were 1,471 of these colleges in 1994. About one-third are private institutions which may be members of NAICU, and all of them, both public and private, may be members of AACC. Miami Dade Community College in Florida and Schoolcraft College in Michigan are both Associate of Arts Colleges.

Specialized Institutions.[9] These institutions offer degrees ranging from the bachelor's to the doctorate, and at least half of the degrees are in a specialized field, such as medicine, and the allied health fields, including pharmacy and chiropractic medicine; religion or theology; art, music, and design; business and management; engineering and technology; teachers colleges; and law. Other types of specialized institutions are military institutes, graduate centers, maritime academies, and tribal colleges. These specialized institutions may be members of ACE but are not ordinarily members of the other five major associations, except for some in NAICU.

The Carnegie classification system does not include proprietary (for-profit) schools. The 6,500 proprietary schools in the U.S. are mostly two-year or less-than-two-year technical and vocational schools, and they often differ from community colleges in the duration and breadth of their degree and certificate programs. However, the most important difference between the proprietaries and the community colleges is the locus of control. While community colleges are publicly funded and chartered, proprietary schools usually have a single owner or a board without external community accountability. The difference in profit motive and control mechanisms translate into differences of policy and operation, and most proprietary schools have the characteristics of small businesses. The 1,200 largest proprietary schools are members of the Career College Association (CCA), their umbrella organization. Although CCA is a member of ACE, most of its member institutions are not in ACE because most are not accredited.

For the purposes of this book, discussion of the higher education community is limited to the nonprofit institutions and does not include the vocational, proprietary schools because they differ so substantially from other types of postsecondary institutions. However, even with the exclusion of the proprietaries, higher education remains a diverse sector because of the substantial differences among nonprofit colleges and universities.

The higher education community overcomes some of the communication problems inherent in its diversity by having a common vehicle for information sharing, i.e., the *Chronicle of Higher Education*. The *Chronicle* is a weekly news magazine with subscribers in government, in associations, and, of course, in colleges and universities. Its news stories deal with legislative, judicial, and executive branch issues in the federal and state governments, as well as association news and issues of interest and concern on the campuses. While there are many other journals and magazines in higher education, the popularity of the *Chronicle* means that it provides a common base of knowledge for the higher education community and, therefore, contributes in Washington and elsewhere to cooperation and collaboration among its many players.

In spite of this common base of information, however, the higher education community's diversity makes consensus building difficult. Nonetheless, consensus is highly prized by academia since a collegial consensus building process defines college and university decision making and operates in faculty meetings on most campuses. Many of the community's Washington representatives, especially the major associations, operate through a similarly slow and deliberate consensus building process.

PROLIFERATION OF WASHINGTON LOBBYISTS

Jonathan Rauch called the American interest group sector "a classic growth industry" (1994, 58), and that characterization applies to higher education as much as to other communities. As early as 1960 an ACE publication worried publicly about the Washington "babble of many voices speaking for higher education" (Gladieux and Wolanin 1976, 44), and the growth had only begun at that point. Of the new players in the Washington higher education community, some are newly hired federal relations personnel commuting to Washington from their college or university offices elsewhere. Still others are new staff in already well-established Washington associations who have been hired to accommodate the increased level of federal relations activity. The majority, however, are the staff of associations that have newly established Washington offices. In fact, the volumes of the *Encyclopedia of Associations* show an increase of about 400 percent from 1956 to 1996 in the number of associations in the Washington, D.C., area that include higher education as a significant component of their activities (see table 1.1).

Table 1.1
Higher Education Associations in the Washington, D.C., Area

Year	Number of Associations
1956	44
1968	86
1976	102
1986	180
1996	221

Source: *Encyclopedia of Associations* (1956, 1968, 1976, 1986, & 1996).
Note: Data were derived from the *Encyclopedia of Associations* because that publication includes all types of associations, including those that do not feature higher education as their primary focus but do include it as a major concern. Given the difficulties of counting across categories in the *Encyclopedia of Associations* and determining association focus from textual description, the figures reported here may be slightly higher or lower than the actual number of associations. (The *Higher Education Directory* is also a good source of information about associations, but it includes only those that feature higher education as the primary focus, so the numbers in the *Directory* are lower than those in the *Encyclopedia*.)

The explosion in the number of higher education lobbyists has resulted from a variety of factors, many of which pertain to other communities as well. The increasing numbers of governmental actors is a major reason for the increasing numbers of groups (Gray and Lowery 1996b) because more federal access points have led to more people seeking access.

All three branches of the federal government make higher education policy,[10] and the relevant executive branch departments and agencies are numerous. College and university representatives maintain regular contact with them concerning budget requests, implementation of higher education legislation, and promulgation and implementation of regulations. For most of the higher education community, the most important executive branch agency is the Department of Education. It was established in 1979 as the successor, along with the Department of Health and Human Services, to the Department of Health, Education, and Welfare. The Department of Education houses a large number of higher education programs, including student financial aid (e.g., student loans, Pell grants, and a variety of graduate student fellowships), TRIO programs for at-risk students (Talent Search, Upward Bound, and Student Special Services, as well as the newer Equal Opportunity Centers and McNair Incentive Scholars Program), programs for developing institutions, international programs, and grants competitions of various kinds, especially the well-regarded Fund for the Improvement of Postsecondary Education (FIPSE). They are all administered by the assistant secretary for postsecondary education. Other executive branch departments and independent agencies are also critical to the higher education community, especially the Departments of Defense, Agriculture, Energy, the National Aeronautics and Space Administration (NASA), NSF, NEH, and NEA, and the Department of Health and Human Services, especially NIH.

The representatives of policy communities typically prefer interactions with one branch of government or another (Salisbury 1992, 97), and higher education representatives are like many others in devoting the largest share of their efforts to the legislative branch (Heinz et al. 1993, 215; Browne 1988, 209) because it is the part of government that the higher education community has historically influenced most successfully. Almost every congressional committee and subcommittee deals with topic(s) of

Table 1.2
Congressional Committees with Which Colleges and Universities Deal Most Often

Senate	House
Labor and Human Resources Committee and its Subcommittee on Education, Arts and Humanities	Economic and Educational Opportunities Committee[a] and its Subcommittee on Postsecondary Education, Training and Lifelong Learning
Appropriations Subcommittee for VA-HUD-Independent Agencies (NSF and National Service)	Science Committee[b]
Senate Appropriations Committee Subcommittee on Labor, Health and Human Services, and Education	Appropriations Subcommittee on Labor, Health and Human Services, and Education (Education Department and NIH)

[a] Prior to the 104th Congress, this was called the Education and Labor Committee, with its Subcommittee on Postsecondary Education.
[b] Prior to the 104th Congress, this was called the Space, Science & Technology Committee.

interest to colleges and universities from time to time. However, there are certain committees (see table 1.2) that handle higher education issues most frequently, and the list is long enough to show why higher education lobbyists have their hands full.

It once was the case that lobbyists could carry the day if they could convince two or three Senate and House leaders to support their positions. That era is over. Although the congressional leadership has regained authority it lost in the 1970s and 1980s, the weakening of the congressional seniority system has allowed every member of Congress, not just the committee chairs, to introduce and affect legislation, including killing it. Each member of Congress has more staff than previously, and the staff have substantial influence. In addition, congressional reorganization has led to more committees and subcommittees, each of which has a burgeoning portfolio. Thus, it is necessary for lobbyists to stay in contact with large numbers of members of Congress, as well as with their staff members.

Another factor affecting the number of lobbyists is the increase in congressional activity, both appropriations and regulations. The federal government is simply doing more than it used to, so policy communities think they need more representation simply to deal with the increase in activity. Additionally, the policy issues themselves are technical and complex, which in turn calls for more people to develop the necessary expertise to address them. As a result, the division of labor among lobbyists has grown, with more expert consultants and more for-profit, specialized firms. The costs of organizing have declined in this high-tech era, so organizing and mobilizing political activists gets easier all the time, which means that it is done more frequently. Finally, because there are so many more interests competing in Washington, each group thinks it has to mount more and more political activity to keep up with the interest group equivalent of the Joneses. Each group competes with others to get its concerns on the Washington radar screen or to protect what they have already achieved. The bottom line is that Washington representatives are much busier than they used to be.

Other factors leading to the proliferation of Washington representatives are more particular to higher education itself. For example, the increasing availability in the 1980s and early 1990s of *earmarked funds* (i.e., those funds that members of Congress designate for a specific use without an open competition or traditional review process) often have given the institutions that hired more lobbyists a good return on their investment in terms of new buildings or funded projects. Therefore, many institutions increased their Washington presence to respond to the opportunity. Additionally, the institutional missions of colleges and, especially, universities have expanded as they have engaged in more and more activities—from business development to nuclear waste disposal. Thus, institutions themselves have created more potential points of intersection with the federal government as their own portfolios have expanded.

CONCLUSIONS

The higher education community is an especially interesting subject for study, in part because of the significance of the higher education enterprise to the future of the country. Additionally, it is interesting because there are so many federal higher education policy issues. A third aspect of the community is the variation in needs and preferences of the many different types of colleges and universities. The fact that the community has always had a very stable and structured set of associations and now finds itself with a multitude of new Washington higher education representatives adds to its challenges as well as its opportunities.

All of the factors cited above would make higher education lobbying an intriguing subject even without the arrival of the 104th (Gingrich) Congress. Yet that arrival tested the durability of the community's structures and the collegiality of its representatives as never before. The new Congress provided an unwelcome opportunity for the higher education community to examine the effectiveness of its lobbying skills. Those skills had been developing slowly, over a number of decades, as the following chapter will show.

Chapter Two

A HISTORY OF ASSOCIATION LOBBYING UP TO 1990

"Daniel Moynihan characterized higher education as the worst lobby in Washington. . . ."
Comment about Daniel Patrick Moynihan,
then counselor to President Richard Nixon
(Gladieux 1978, 266)

The Big Six associations are located in Washington, D.C., expressly for the purpose of representing higher education to the federal government. Since the establishment of the first of the comprehensive associations in 1887, that has been one of their principal functions (Hawkins 1992, 124), but they have not always performed it well.

This chapter concerns the history of higher education lobbying, beginning with the development of the six major associations. It describes the debacle suffered by the associations during the enactment of the 1972 Higher Education Act, an episode which shaped the lobbying that followed. Even now there are periodic references in the Washington higher education community to lessons learned in 1972, so it is useful to understand that defining event. It points out how inept higher education lobbying was in its early years and how much colleges and universities had to learn about Washington. The community rallied after 1972 and fared remarkably well in the late 1970s and 1980s. This chapter includes a review of higher education lobbying and policy issues during that period in order to set the stage for a description of the turbulent 1990s.

What follows is a brief history of the formation of the Big Six associations and then an enumeration of the lobbying lessons the associations tried to learn in the 1970s, lessons that were still applicable during the 104th Congress in 1995–96. This chapter also describes the associations' major successes and failures during the decades prior to the 1990s.

THE BIG SIX ASSOCIATIONS[1]

College and university leaders have always entrusted the major Washington higher education associations with primary responsibility for federal contacts on their behalf. The Washington association structure has been remarkably stable, and all of the major associations have a long history. Their history is described here in the order in which they were formed, including information about why they were founded and to what extent they originally focused on federal relations. While some associations focused on federal relations right from the beginning, each eventually established a Washington office and all became engaged in federal lobbying sooner or later. What is clear from the descriptions below is that there were only a handful of federal issues of interest to the associations in their early years, so it is not surprising that lobbying did not seem to be their top priority.

National Association of State Universities and Land-Grant Colleges (NASULGC, 1963; formerly, AAACES, 1887; NASU, 1895; SUA, 1930)

The oldest association of American colleges and universities was not formally organized until 1887, but as early as 1871 "friends of agricultural education" met in Chicago to discuss ways of extracting more support from Congress. Some of them later lobbied for the Hatch Act, passed in 1887, which provided ongoing financial support for agricultural research in each state (Stewart 1975, 17–18). Stimulated by their success, the presidents of land-grant universities also formed the Association of American Agricultural Colleges and Experiment Stations (AAACES) in 1887. Its earliest task was to lobby Congress for the funds that had been authorized but not appropriated by the Hatch Act, and then to lobby for the Second Morrill Act, passed in 1890. In 1919, AAACES changed its name to the Association of Land-Grant Colleges (ALGC). Another name change followed in 1926, to the Association of Land-Grant Colleges and Universities (ALGCU), and an office was established in Washington in 1939. By 1945 ALGCU had a full-time executive secretary who could participate in the discussion about veterans benefits that followed World War II.

While some state universities were beneficiaries of the Morrill Acts, most were not. In 1895 a group of state university presidents formed the National Association of State Universities (NASU), an association with institutional members. As its first federal relations activity, NASU petitioned Congress for land-grants for each state university, but the bill that was introduced was never passed. Although it was considered more of a president's club than an association involved in federal relations, NASU initially established degree standards and collected educational statistics. The Association of American Universities (AAU) then took over the standardization and accreditation mission and the United States Bureau of Education began to collect institutional data. Although NASU established a Washington office in 1955, the association's federal relations were generally weak.

Because the memberships of NASU and ALGCU overlapped substantially, it was the latter, the land-grant association, that spoke for most members on federal issues. State universities without land-grant status were left unrepresented, so twenty of them formed a third association in the 1920s, the Association of Separated State Universities. It was renamed the State Universities Association in 1930. NASU members did not leave that association to join SUA, but continued in both. Described as a "something of a menace" to ALGCU, the new association was particularly concerned that the land-grant institutions not be allowed to dominate or receive disproportionate federal funding, particularly for social science, engineering, and business (Hawkins 1992, 127). SUA established a Washington presence in 1950.

As early as 1901, there were proposals to unite the land-grant association with the state universities, but decades of competition between institutions in a given state and among the associations nationally made joining together difficult. Finally, in 1963, both NASU and SUA merged with the land-grant association. It was renamed the National Association of State Universities and Land-Grant Colleges (NASULGC).

Association of American Universities (AAU, 1900)

Sometimes described as a "boutique organization," the Association of American Universities (AAU) was founded in 1900 with fourteen charter members. It was exclusive from the beginning, and dedicated to issues of quality, particularly in graduate education and research. AAU members were concerned about the use of the word *university* by unworthy institutions, and even by NASU. The association hoped that by calling attention to the prestige of its member institutions, the lower quality of others would be recognized.

Some criticized AAU for not revealing the standards that defined eligibility for its membership. Therefore, AAU adopted from the United States Bureau of Education the role of setting accreditation standards and published an annual "approved list" of colleges and universities that suitably prepared their students for graduate study. Leaders of nonmember institutions then asked AAU to assess their graduate programs as well. Because it was unwilling to take on this role, the association discontinued accreditation altogether in 1945.

AAU still continues its tradition of selectivity. Memberships are by invitation, with a new offer extended every few years, and an approximate balance of public and private institutions is maintained. Until relatively recently AAU was minimally involved in federal relations; it did not establish a Washington office until 1962.

National Association of Independent Colleges and Universities (NAICU, 1976; developed from AAC, 1915)

The newest member of the Big Six, the National Association of Independent Colleges and Universities (NAICU) speaks as the voice of private higher education in the United States. Its roots date back to the Association of American Colleges (AAC). AAC was established in 1915 by more than 150 institutional presidents, in part to counter the AAU *approved list* and the growth in political influence of NASU. AAC provided a voice for small liberal arts colleges, many of which were affiliated with Christian denominations, though it also had a few members that were public institutions.

From the beginning AAC had more members by far than any of the existing associations and was the first of the associations to establish a paid position as executive secretary. The first one temporarily moved the office to Washington in 1918 and provided administrative support to ACE in its infancy. The association first established quarters in Chicago, then relocated to New York, and finally settled permanently in Washington in 1947.

By 1976 AAC membership exceeded 850 institutions, both public and private, but the organization was not a cohesive body. The mostly small, private institutions wanted a single, identifiable voice to speak on their behalf. Member discontent grew as they worried about church-state separation and, therefore, opposed direct institutional aid from the federal government (Gladieux and Wolanin 1976, 45).

In 1976 NAICU was created specifically to address the needs of *independent* higher education. At great cost in membership and resources, AAC (which later became the Association of American Colleges and Universities, AAC&U) returned to its original cause, that of liberal education, leaving NAICU as the Washington voice of private higher education for the Big Six. After debate about whether NAICU should be a direct institutional membership organization or a confederation of state independent college associations, the former view prevailed. The state associations are also NAICU members. In some respects, NAICU is like ACE in being an association of associations, as well as serving individual institutional members.

American Council on Education (ACE, 1918)

At a National Education Association (NEA) meeting in 1898, Burke A. Hinsdale, a University of Michigan professor, proposed a new organization, a federation of colleges and universities "that would tend to raise standards and prevent duplication" (Hawkins 1992, 9). Although a committee was appointed to explore such a development, it never completed the task, and the idea was put to rest for a time. World War I provided just the occasion for reconsideration. Colleges and universities across the nation were dramatically affected by the war, and while wanting to appear patriotic by supporting the military effort, presidents were gravely concerned about protecting their institutions as enrollments dropped. It was difficult to learn what support the War Department needed and expected of the colleges.

In January 1918, the president of AAU began arranging meetings with other association leaders. The eight associations that eventually came together formed the Emergency Council on Education in March 1918, which began to lobby Congress in the interests of what now might be called enrollment management. Expressing concern that educated military officers would be needed on an ongoing basis, they hoped to keep students in college as long as possible, slowing the mass exit of men on campus. Relationships were established with representatives of the War Department and with the United States Bureau of Education, and communication was improved (Stewart 1975, 15–16).

When the war ended a few months later, the presidents chose to continue their association, changing its name to the American Council on Education (ACE). The head of the Bureau of Education became the first director in 1918. Although founded as a federation of associations, ACE immediately solicited contributions from institutional members in order to compensate its director at the same level as he had been receiving in government service (King 1975, 20; Stewart 1975, 65).

Perhaps because of its establishment during the war, ACE assumed the role of liaison between the federal government and higher education. ACE kept abreast of issues of local and regional importance as well as federal issues, since its membership comprised both associations and institutions. In 1927 teachers colleges and junior colleges became eligible for membership, adding to the diversity of interests represented by the association. A few years later, state school systems and some private secondary schools joined the Council, as well as business and trade associations. After devoting considerable attention to lower schools in the 1930s and 1940s, the association again focused on higher education by the late 1950s.

As membership grew, so did the variety of Council activities. Revenues were generated through business enterprises—for example, intelligence tests, military officer exams, and contract research. According to Donald M. Stewart, "Ambiguity of role and vagueness of purpose came to plague ACE early in its history as its leaders continued doing whatever was necessary to help keep the organization alive" (1975, 27).

During World War II, ACE began distribution of a weekly newsletter, eventually entitled *Higher Education and National Affairs,* as a means of keeping the membership informed about federal issues. In the 1950s a group of Washington association leaders began regular luncheon meetings to consider issues of common concern. Since then, layers of additional meetings have developed under the ACE umbrella.

In 1950 ACE moved into new quarters in Washington, D.C., large enough to allow the higher education associations to be grouped together. In addition to ACE, fifteen other associations occupied the new center. In 1968, the National Center for Higher Education relocated to One Dupont Circle, a building funded by the Kellogg Foundation in order to house all of the major higher education association leadership under one roof and promote communication and collaboration among them. More than forty higher education associations eventually shared this well-known Washington address. Except for NAICU, all of the Big Six were located at

One Dupont Circle until 1997.[2] (See chapter 5 for a description of the interrelationships of the Big Six associations.)

American Association of Community Colleges
(AACC, 1992; formerly AAJC, 1920; AACJC, 1972)

In 1920 leaders of the nation's junior colleges (i.e., two-year institutions) were invited by the U. S. Commissioner of Education to meet in St. Louis, Missouri, for a two-day conference, the first event dedicated to junior colleges. The American Association of Junior Colleges (AAJC) was founded at this time. Junior colleges had been established by some local school boards as the thirteenth and fourteenth grades of the high school curriculum and by some religious denominations as teaching colleges (Pedersen 1995, 26). The junior colleges provided preparation for transfer to a four-year university and/or educational opportunities to residents of the local community.

By 1939, a new constitution had defined public relations as the major AAJC role, and a Washington office was established. The timing of the move was fortuitous since the association became actively involved in lobbying during World War II to promote inclusion of junior college students in draft deferments, the GI Bill, vocational education, and the Reserve Officers Training Corps (Brick 1963, 126–29).

AAJC grew quickly, particularly in the 1960s, when a new two-year college was created every ten days (Hamilton 1977, 41). The staff was second in size among the Big Six only to ACE. Eventually, the association's name changed, first to the American Association of Community and Junior Colleges (AACJC) in 1972 and, finally, to the American Association of Community Colleges (AACC) in 1992. The association is the primary advocacy organization for two-year degree-granting colleges.

American Association of State Colleges and Universities (AASCU, 1961)

The last of the major associations formed to represent public institutions, the American Association of State Colleges and Universities (AASCU), was established in Washington in 1961. AASCU was created because NASULGC and AACC left unrepresented a host of public institutions, including comprehensive state universities, technological institutes, four-year colleges begun as junior colleges, and former teachers colleges. These colleges and universities experienced tremendous growth, especially in the late 1960s and early 1970s. According to AASCU's own literature, member institutions graduate "one-third of our nation's bachelor's degree recipients; one-quarter of its master's degree recipients; six percent of all doctorates; and one-half of America's teachers" (AASCU 1995).

AASCU has an unusual structure. An institutional president, elected from each state to the Council of State Representatives, facilitates communication between member institutions and the national staff. The state representatives collaborate to develop the policy agenda of the association (AASCU 1994). This structure provides a liaison between member institutions and the national organization and promotes the interaction of AASCU institutions at the state level. Interestingly, within their own states, AASCU institutions compete with the land-grant institutions and junior colleges for resources, but at the federal level they tend to be allied with NASULGC.

EARLY HIGHER EDUCATION LOBBYING
AND THE 1972 DEBACLE

The higher education community participated only sporadically in the political process as early federal policy was being crafted. Initially it was unsure that it wanted federal aid, so the Washington associations' job, when they did lobby, was often to block government involvement with colleges and universities, not to ask for assistance (Hawkins 1992, 131). For example, higher education representatives initially opposed the GI Bill, fearing that it would flood colleges and universities with unqualified students (Berdahl interview, 1996).

Individual associations dipped into and out of the policy making process according to their own interests at a given time. As a result of the associations' passivity and reluctance, the community's congressional allies often found it frustrating to support federal aid to colleges and universities, and to their students. For example, when Congress was considering and then enacting federal aid in the early 1960s, especially the Higher Education Act of 1965, Senator Joseph S. Clark (D-Pennsylvania), a proponent, was angry about the associations' refusal to organize and lobby for federal aid without a lengthy process in which they would ask their entire membership to endorse a position before taking a stand. He said, "Let us remember that educators are not monks who take a vow of poverty, both for themselves and for the institutions they serve. They, too, are American citizens with the right, indeed the duty, to petition for redress of grievances and to indicate to their elected representatives how they would like those grievances redressed" (King 1975, 75).

Higher education lobbying had not improved when, in 1971, Representative Edith Green (D-Oregon), who supported aid to higher education institutions, compared the attitude of academia to college students writing their parents: "Don't worry. Everything's fine here. Send money" (Gladieux and Wolanin 1976, 118). And in 1972, Senator Wayne Morse (R-Oregon) urged the higher education community to do a better job of organizing and "get it all together," speaking as one voice (Bailey 1975, 73). Senator Claiborne Pell (D-Rhode Island) in the previous year had characterized the higher education community as uncooperative and status quo oriented (King 1975, 116). As noted in the chapter epigraph, Daniel

Patrick Moynihan, then counselor to President Nixon, expressed similar frustration with the Washington higher education lobby during this period (Gladieux 1977, 266).[3]

In the decades after World War II, especially the 1950s and 1960s, it was possible for higher education to be the "worst lobby in Washington" and still fare very well. That was the Cold War era, and the threat from the Soviet Union led lawmakers to funnel vast sums into support of American higher education. Academe's relations with policy makers were so friendly that there was even a regular poker game between congressional staffers and higher education lobbyists. The "iron triangle" of support for higher education policy was in operation among the various members of the higher education issue network.[4] Colleges and universities enjoyed high public esteem, and that esteem was reflected in federal funding decisions.

The post-war years marked the advent of vast quantities of student financial aid (e.g., the GI Bill and the Higher Education Act of 1965), as well as the birth of major federal agencies whose principal assignment was to fund university-based research. (See the brief history of federal higher education policy in chapter 1.) Student populations were growing, new campuses were springing up, and faculty were being hired and tenured in large numbers. It was a period of prosperity and expansion for the higher education community, and the role of its umbrella association, ACE, was simply to "urge that, whatever else was done, more money should be spent" (Wilson 1973, 268). The Washington lobbying requirements were minimal. The higher education community could sit back and let the money roll in.

Although the 1960s were generally prosperous for higher education, as the decade drew to a close, higher education faced increased scrutiny. Congress and the public were concerned about campus unrest, and possible reductions in federal research funding combined with inflation to create an unstable financial picture for many institutions. The higher education community turned to Congress for help.

When the Higher Education Act of 1965 (HEA) faced renewal in 1972, most of the associations saw value in unity and converged under ACE leadership with a common interest: direct federal support for colleges and universities. The associations argued that lower tuition, and therefore access and affordability, would result from general institutional funding. Working together to try to devise a funding formula acceptable to all types of institutions, association leaders appeared oblivious to the forces working against them. In fact, Congress and the White House preferred to provide funding directly to students, who would then use it at the institution they chose. The associations acted as if the educational issue of 1972 was *how* to award institutional funding, while policy makers were questioning *whether* funding should go *directly* to institutions, or *indirectly,* through students.

Higher education found an important ally in Representative Edith Green, head of the House Special Subcommittee on Education. With her support, the associations were confident that the legislation authorizing institutional support would pass.

Meanwhile, Senator Claiborne Pell proposed an alternative bill establishing grants to be awarded directly to students. Other members of Congress who were traditionally supportive of higher education, such as Representatives John Brademas (D-Indiana) and Albert Quie (R-Minnesota), worked alongside Pell. Community colleges and proprietary schools strongly supported Pell's bill as well because they saw that it would benefit many of the neediest students, and those were the ones who often attended their institutions.

The 1972 HEA eventually incorporated the Pell bill, so the major associations found themselves on the losing side. Congress had ignored their efforts to augment institutional funding, and direct student aid passed with tremendous support. This was not just a loss of face but a major political debacle for the Washington higher education associations. One result of the 1972 Amendments was that its financial aid programs, known as *Pell Grants*, "let the students make their own choices in the marketplace of postsecondary education" (Gladieux and Wolanin 1976, 225). A second result was that eligibility to participate in financial aid programs was granted to students not only at community colleges but also at vocational and technical schools, including proprietary (for-profit) institutions. In fact, the language in the 1972 HEA was changed from "higher education" to "postsecondary" in order to include every type of institution.

CRITICISM OF THE ASSOCIATIONS

The associations' position against student aid and in favor of institutional aid made them appear greedy and paternalistic as well as politically inept during the debate over the 1972 legislation. They were attacked for their focus on only one issue, their lack of good policy analysis, and their inability to collaborate effectively. Critics contrasted the naiveté of the higher education lobby with the increasing professionalism of other Washington lobbies. The associations were perceived as out of touch with both Congress and the nation (C. Brown 1985; Gladieux and Wolanin 1976).

ACE received the most criticism because it had led the higher education associations in their unsuccessful lobbying. It was especially awkward for ACE to have the junior colleges and proprietary institutions on the side of the victors. Even before the 1972 debacle, there was a Washington joke told at an AAC annual meeting that "ACE had died long ago as an organization but no one had been kind enough to tell its officers or to give it a decent burial" (Stewart 1975, 5).

Honey-Crowley Report

Because ACE was fast losing support from its association and institutional members, an evaluation of ACE government relations efforts was solicited by ACE's new president, Roger Heyns. The report, delivered in September 1972 by John Honey and John Crowley of Syracuse University, was harshly critical of ACE. According to Stewart, "There seemed to be almost universal agreement that the Council had lost its edge with Congress and the Executive, that it was out of touch with its own long established constituencies, and that it did not comprehend the new forces shaping public policy and the future of higher education" (1975, 391). The report criticized ACE for its inertia and its tendency to work only for adjustments and expansions of existing programs, rather than for departures to current practice (King 1975, 107; Bloland 1985, 51). ACE was also criticized for its inflexibility, its reactive decision-making as opposed to anticipatory strategizing, its lack of data-based policy analysis, and its confused, overlapping federal relations structure (King 1975, 97).

The Honey-Crowley Report proposed the elimination of several ACE offices and programs and the reorganization of others, as well as the addition of a new policy analysis service. Arguing that ACE return to its original role as an umbrella association, the report supported the elimination of institutional memberships in favor of association representatives, and urged inclusion of associations representing black colleges, proprietary schools, and students themselves.

Although the Honey-Crowley Report was helpful in building an understanding that changes were necessary, only some of its proposals were adopted. Others were set aside. Invitations to participate were extended to the associations of black colleges, proprietary schools, and students (Stewart 1975, 397–405). Government relations was given a more prominent role, and a Policy Analysis Service was established to support that role, with a widely respected political scientist, Stephen K. Bailey, directing that effort as vice president (Bloland 1985, 57–60; Stewart 1975, 404). Heyns described the Service as "a direct response to the criticism that higher education is unable to reply to public policy issues with adequate data and analysis. . . . The service will be . . . concerned with systematically analyzing plans and proposals to support the legislative stance of the American Council on Education and its affiliated associations" (Stewart 1975, 404).

Roger Heyns resigned as ACE president in 1977, and was replaced by Jack Peltason. Peltason established three priorities for ACE: first, to strengthen federal relations and move into state government relations as well; second, to expand policy research and analysis; and third, to provide more programs for higher education administrators, particularly women and minorities (Bloland 1985, 68–69). The other associations became concerned that Peltason was changing ACE's role, especially after he created

28

committees on intercollegiate athletics and academic affairs. Specifically, they worried that ACE's role as a coordinating agency was being downgraded in favor of providing services to the institutions that might compete with services already provided by other associations. As one association leader commented, "In developing more membership services, the council seems to be responding more as a membership association than as a coordinating body." Many of the member presidents seemed to share the associations' concerns about ACE's new direction. One president stated, "Excessive duplication in a time of belt-tightening doesn't make sense" (*Chronicle of Higher Education*, 25 August 1980).

Cosand Report

In the late 1970s two additional studies evaluated the effectiveness of the higher education associations and considered options for the future. In addition to the Big Six, both studies included the Association of American Colleges and the Council for the Advancement of Small Colleges. The first study was funded by the Ford Foundation and administered by the Center for the Study of Higher Education at the University of Michigan, with the concurrence of the major associations. It was led by Joseph Cosand, a former junior college president who had chaired the boards of both ACE and AACC, as well as serving in the U.S. Office of Education, and was then serving as professor of higher education at the University of Michigan. Professor Cosand and his colleagues surveyed nearly 3,000 college and university presidents across the nation, including members and nonmembers of the Big Six. The findings indicated that presidents generally supported the major associations and intended to continue institutional membership. However, the presidents indicated a need for increased coordination and cooperation among the associations, and expressed concern that ACE was providing services in competition with the other associations, inhibiting the Council's traditional role as "coordinator, convener, and catalyst" (Bloland 1985, 60, 76–78; Cosand et al. 1979).

The survey respondents (i.e., institutional presidents) were offered a choice of five different models for ACE and the major associations. The first choice was continuation of the existing associations and the relationships among them; another choice was greater involvement and leadership from ACE; the third provided for increasing leadership from the other five major associations while diminishing ACE's role; the fourth proposed creation of a "major national organization with institutional memberships only, with special divisions for various institutional types which would replace the national presidential associations"; the final option advocated an "umbrella organization with association memberships only, which would deal only with federal relations" (Cosand et al. 1979, 9).

Although none of the proposed models received support from a majority of the presidents, the "current system" was found to be most popular, as two-thirds of the respondents rated it their first or second choice (Cosand et al. 1979, 10). The authors described as "striking" the finding that the type or size of the respondents' institutions appeared to be only minimally associated with the model supported. They concluded that "any contemplated change toward one of the models will satisfy some presidents and dissatisfy others, but the satisfaction and dissatisfaction will not be concentrated in institutions of a particular control, size or type" (10).

Cosand and his University of Michigan colleagues also interviewed national observers of the higher education community. Selected from current and former elected officials and leaders of higher education associations, agencies, and foundations, these observers also evaluated the associations positively, although they urged cooperation "to avoid duplication and to become more cost effective." They too expressed concern that ACE's expanding array of programs "seemed to reduce their potential role for providing coordination or guidance in this arena" (Cosand et al. 1979, 18).

Regarding federal relations, the Cosand Report urged the associations to cooperate in their efforts to monitor and respond to emerging issues, and suggested that new ad hoc coalitions be developed with groups within and apart from higher education when they had political interests in common (Cosand et al. 1979, 20).

Report from the "Gang of Six"

The second report was the product of a committee appointed by ACE President Peltason after member presidents protested the growing cost of multiple association memberships. The presidents were questioning the value of their institutions' investments, particularly when associations were duplicating efforts. A group described by Bloland as "dissident" institutional and association leaders in higher education (1985, 77), the "Gang of Six" became legitimate when Peltason appointed them to a committee. Their goals were three: to study association relations within the present structure and make recommendations to improve the representation of institutions; to investigate the proliferation of specialized associations in higher education; and to explore other means by which a coordinated, effective system of representation for higher education could be established (Fretwell 1981, 78).

The committee, led by E. K. Fretwell, Jr., chancellor of the University of North Carolina at Charlotte, expanded to include additional institutional presidents, as well as the heads of AAU, NASULGC, and the Council for the Advancement of Small Colleges. In 1980 they gave ACE's coordinating committee a document entitled *A Report to the Coordinating Committee from the Subcommittee on Association Relations*. A summary of its recommendations appeared in ACE's quarterly *Educational Record* early in 1981, several months after the Cosand Report had been completed.

Although the group did not recommend any significant structural changes, they urged ACE to clarify and strengthen its coordinating role, particularly in the areas of federal relations and policy analysis. The report proposed that a vice president be "responsible for improved communication between ACE and other associations, eliminating surprises as well as any excessive duplication of programming, designating lead agents, improving representation from the totality of higher education, possible merging of associations when appropriate, and avoiding proliferation of new associations" (Fretwell 1981, 79).

The report directed the other seven associations to be responsive to their members, to avoid activities conflicting with other associations, and to fulfill their responsibilities as ACE members by "responding to the lead agency concept" (Fretwell 1981, 79–80). Unlike the Cosand Report, which was directed mainly to the leadership of ACE and the other major associations, the second report also outlined expectations for institutional presidents, encouraging them to be active participants and advocates for the associations.

IMPROVEMENTS AND OUTCOMES IN THE 1970s AND 1980s

Having studied their options in the 1970s, the leaders of the higher education community decided to continue supporting the presidentially based associations (i.e., the Big Six) and to keep ACE in its role as the coordinating body. Nevertheless, in response to the criticisms of their lobbying, especially in the Gang of Six report, they began to change the way they conducted federal relations.

One way that the community tried to improve was through better coordination among the associations. In 1975 ACE was described as a "mythical monolith . . . capable of presenting views which represent only the lowest common denominator of consensus among its members and supporters" (Stewart 1975, 7–8). Yet ten years later the associations seemed to have improved their coordination, as evidenced by Bloland's 1985 observation, "The associations are much more open in their exchange of information than they were in the 1960s, and the community is much the richer for it" (85). While none of the associations' federal relations offices was large in size or resources, each could request assistance from the others in their joint enterprise.

The associations also initiated better policy analysis to support their lobbying efforts and to bolster the members of Congress who were their champions. Observers commented on the importance of providing better information and analysis to federal policy makers and noted the improvements in the research capability of the higher education associations in the 1970s (Bailey 1975; Gladieux and Wolanin 1976).

A third issue concerned visibility. The resources devoted to government relations had been inadequate (Stewart 1975, 414), so the associations augmented their staffs after the 1972 debacle. The numbers of federal relations personnel began to grow dramatically, not only in the major and many specialized associations, but also with the establishment of new campus offices and with the greater presence of campus federal relations personnel, who began commuting regularly to Washington. Along with the larger numbers came an increase in the higher education community's visibility in the nation's capital. One scholar described the improvement in higher education lobbying in the 1970s by saying, "The wallflower began to dance. . ." (Bloland 1985, 67).

It was fortunate that the associations had made improvements in their lobbying acumen because they faced major challenges during the administration of President Ronald Reagan, from 1981 to 1988. President Reagan regularly expressed his doubts about federal support for higher education, and his reluctance was evident in the budget requests he submitted to Congress. For the 1983 fiscal year, for example, the administration proposed a 50 percent cut in need-based student aid programs. In each of the years of his administration except the last, the 1989 fiscal year, the president proposed other cuts amounting to hundreds of millions of dollars. The budget requests during the presidency of George Bush, from 1989 to 1992, were not much better for the higher education community. These funding threats took on special urgency because there was also, during the 1980s and early 1990s, less state government funding for higher education. Observers of higher education appropriation trends noted that state funding was reallocated to other budget priorities, like building and operating new prisons and providing health care and other social services for the poor.

For the Washington higher education associations, a major objective throughout the 1980s and early 1990s was increased funding for student assistance programs. The associations fought for increases in the maximum Pell Grant award and for a full payment schedule for it. Although total funding for Pell Grants increased significantly throughout the 1980s, the size of each maximum grant declined in constant dollars. As a result, by the end of the 1980s, the maximum Pell award covered only 28 percent of average total college costs, down from 40 percent at the beginning of the decade. During this same time period, all other federal grant programs for college students (the Supplemental Educational Opportunity Grants, the College Work-Study program, Perkins Loans, and State Student Incentive Grants) also declined in constant dollars.

Another of higher education's concerns was the growing imbalance between federal student grants and loans. Over the decade of the 1980s, at the same time that grant aid was not keeping pace with inflation, loans became the largest federal budget item for student aid. This trend was particularly disturbing for the associations because the neediest students were forced to rely increasingly on the loan programs, which were originally intended to assist middle-income students.

An additional concern for the higher education community was a weakening of the federal government's commitment to academic research. Federal spending on academic research and development stagnated between 1980 and 1984, but after that it began to grow steadily. Between 1985 and 1990, its funding grew from a little under $9 billion to approximately $11 billion (Honan, *New York Times*, 19 June 1996), with the National Science Foundation receiving substantial increases throughout this period. In spite of the decline in the overall value of student assistance programs and the initial stagnation in research funding that occurred in the early years of the Reagan administration, overall higher education held its own in federal funding during the 1980s and early 1990s. That was true in spite of the Reagan and, later, the Bush administrations' lack of support for increases. Congress always appropriated more funding than the administrations requested, thanks in part to the advocacy of the higher education associations.

The associations considered themselves reasonably successful during the Reagan era, and scholars tend to agree. For example, Bloland (1985) concluded his review of higher education lobbying during this period by proclaiming that the associations had been "solid successes." He praised the associations, saying they "were influential in helping to shape and preserve federal funding for higher education (particularly student aid), and in the process they transformed themselves from a passive, partially informed, often divided, nonpolitical community into a keenly attentive, highly informed, and skillfully assertive body of associations participating daily in Washington higher education policy and events" (1985, 90). That may be an overstatement, given that the associations used a limited number of lobbying tactics (see chapter 8). Nonetheless, it is true that higher education lobbying in the period between the 1972 debacle and the early 1990s was more adept and spirited than it had ever been before. Still to come, however, was a whole new series of lobbying challenges for the higher education community, which will be the subject of the next two chapters.

Chapter Three

CHALLENGES IN THE EARLY 1990S

co-authored with Michael K. McLendon

"Never in my memory has higher education been so much under siege."

Robert Atwell, president of the American Council on Education, at its 1992 annual meeting

This chapter sets the stage for the arrival of the 104th Congress by describing the major higher education policy issues in the early 1990s. It details first the growing erosion of public confidence in higher education and then explains two issues that demonstrate the problems the higher education community was having even before the congressional Republicans came to power. The two issues provide a window into higher education association lobbying.

The first issue is academic earmarking, which many members of Congress consider an example of lack of integrity in higher education lobbying. Other than issuing declarations about the inappropriateness of institutional requests for earmarks, the associations remained uninvolved in the academic earmarking controversy, ignored both by Congress and by their institutional members. The second issue is student loan defaults, which led Congress to create state oversight bodies, the State Postsecondary Review Entities (SPREs), in order to have more accountability in higher education. In regard to the SPREs, the associations realized belatedly that they had been asleep at the switch when the legislation was passed, and they hurried to make amends by lobbying intensively for its elimination.

Together, these two issues show that the higher education community faced serious challenges in Washington even before the 104th Congress convened. To emphasize that point, the chapter concludes by detailing the community's uneasy relationship with the Clinton administration in its first two years.

EROSION OF PUBLIC CONFIDENCE

Members of Congress are especially sensitive to public opinion, as they should be in a representative democracy. Because the president and his party need electoral support as well, appointed officials in the executive branch also keep an eye on public opinion. Therefore, when a community is highly regarded by the public at large, officials are more likely to be sensitive to its needs than when the public has lost confidence in it. The gradual erosion in public confidence in higher education during the 1980s and 1990s has made it more difficult for the representatives of colleges and universities to lobby effectively.

The fact that the public has seemed to lose faith in all its established institutions in recent years, not just higher education, has not made the erosion any less worrisome for the higher education community. Derek Bok, the former president of Harvard University, aptly observed that while there were internal problems on the campuses in the 1960s and 1970s, now higher education's problems are primarily external, with much public criticism (*Change*, 1992). In the decade leading up to the 104th Congress, colleges and universities found themselves subjected to wide-ranging charges, including high college tuitions, unfocused curriculum content, political correctness, the imbalance of teaching and research, athletic scandals, scientific fraud, low graduation rates, and student loan defaults.

In 1985 William Bennett, the new Secretary of Education, began using his bully pulpit to focus attention on these problems and others. Bennett unleashed a barrage of criticism of higher education. He characterized academe as a bastion of privilege that expected to be treated differently from other sectors of American society, an ivory tower divorced from the realities of societal needs. He alleged, "There has developed a sense of separateness and detachment from the affairs of other people. This in its worst manifestation comes across as insufferable moral superiority . . ." (Vobejda, *Washington Post National Weekly Edition*, 9 March 1987).

Perhaps the single most damaging criticism of academia was Secretary Bennett's contention that rapidly escalating tuition charges at both public and private colleges and universities reflected higher education's greed. It was true that tuition cost hikes had begun to outpace the growth in incomes in the 1980s. Between 1980 and 1981 and between 1994 and 1995, for example, tuition increased 234 percent, according to a General Accounting Office report, by comparison with an 82 percent increase in income level and a 74 percent increase in the cost of consumer goods. Consequently, the proportion of household income needed to pay for college nearly doubled during that period (*Chronicle of Higher Education*, 6 September 1996). Public opinion surveys showed an increasing skepticism about college affordability. A 1990 report by the Council for the Advancement and Support of Education (CASE), based largely on the results of a survey conducted by the Gallup Organization, found that the percentage of Americans who believed college costs were rising at a rate that would put college out of reach for most people was 87 percent, compared with 77 percent of those surveyed in 1985. Moreover, the percentage of people who agreed that most people could afford a college education declined fourteen points over the same six-year period, from 39 percent in 1985 to just 25 percent in 1990 (CASE 1990).

In addition to concern about the high cost of a college education, there were growing doubts about its value. The doubts had originally gained attention with the publication of a series of critical reports in the 1980s. The reports noted that most institutions had responded to the student activism of the 1960s by relaxing their curricular requirements and providing more electives and fewer obligatory courses. They said the result was a lack of substance and direction in the typical college curriculum, as well as excessive vocational specialization. Since undergraduates were no longer required to have a common general education experience, the reports charged that a college degree had lost its coherence and even its value. Among those reports were *To Reclaim a Legacy: A Report on the Humanities in Higher Education* (Bennett, 1984), *Involvement in Learning: Realizing the Potential of American Higher Education* (National Institute of Education, 1984), and *Integrity in the College Curriculum: A Report to the Academic Community* (Association of American Colleges, 1985). Many other critical reports and proposals followed these three.

Secretary Bennett especially criticized the public's return on investment in higher education. Specifically, Bennett contended that many of the most elite, prestigious colleges and universities had capitulated to left-wing ideologues and, as a result, higher education had become intellectually and morally bankrupt. That charge helped launch the anti-political correctness movement of the late 1980s and early 1990s. As a major salvo in his campaign, Secretary Bennett publicly lambasted Stanford University's 1988 decision to broaden its curriculum and require all first-year students to study gender, race, and class issues.

In addition to Secretary Bennett's attacks, a series of exposés written by university insiders made their unlikely appearance on *The New York Times'* Bestseller List in 1987. *The Closing of the American Mind: How Higher Education Has Failed Democracy and Impoverished the Souls of Today's Students,* by University of Chicago Philosophy Professor Allan Bloom, and *Cultural Literacy,* by University of Virginia English Professor E. D. Hirsch, Jr., were immensely popular books, both of which accused American higher education of having surrendered to "cultural relativism" (i.e., a value-free education) and blasted universities for their supposed capitulation to superficial academic trends. Both books urged a return to the classical liberal arts tradition with the Great Books of the Western canon at the center of the curriculum. Other popular accounts of higher education's moral and intellectual decline followed. Particularly well-publicized was Dinesh D'Souza's *Illiberal Education* (1991), which catalogued and ridiculed cases of political correctness at some of the nation's most prestigious universities, such as Duke, Harvard, Stanford, the University of California at Berkeley, and the University of Michigan.

Besides charging that higher education did not value liberal learning, the critics said that higher education no longer cared about the students it was supposed to be serving, especially the undergraduates. For example, Martin Anderson's *Impostors in the Temple* (1992) lamented the betrayal of the academic profession by "corrupt priests" who disdained teaching, and Charles Sykes' *Profscam* (1988) claimed that faculty workloads were ridiculously light. An increasingly frequent criticism of higher education concerned the imbalance of teaching and research, which resulted in too few classes taught by faculty members and too many taught by graduate student teaching assistants. Critics typically commented that the result was excessively large class sizes, over-enrolled required courses, incompetent academic advising, unavailable professors, disinterested part-time instructors, and unintelligible teaching assistants.

These criticisms came not just from higher education's enemies but from some of its long-time friends and supporters as well. Harvard President Derek Bok observed, "Although there are smaller colleges where teaching remains the overriding priority, in the modern university the incentives are not weighted in favor of teaching and education—indeed, quite the contrary is true" (*Change*, 1992). Similarly, Ernest Boyer, the president of the Carnegie Foundation for the Advancement of Teaching, stated that "Institutions ooze affection when they want you to enroll, but the fact is that freshmen and sophomores are not a priority." And *Policy Perspectives*, a publication of the Pew Higher Education Research Program, similarly concluded, "Too many [faculty] academic calendars begin after ten a.m. and end just before three p.m. with time out for weekends, fall breaks, Thanksgiving and Christmas holidays, spring vacations and summer recesses" (Grossman, Jouzaitis, and Leroux, *Chicago Tribune*, 21 June 1992).

Not surprisingly, the national debate captured the attention of many members of Congress, some of whom, such as Representative Patricia Schroeder (D-Colorado) convened hearings to address the criticisms. Summarizing the results of a report commissioned by her committee, Representative Schroeder said, "Among the one hundred public colleges where tuition went up the most, the amount of teaching time went down and the class size went up. The costs are hidden behind the 'magical' field of research where professors are freed up from their classes and given more money for travel, research assistants, and laboratories" (*Washington Post*, 15 September 1992).

Notwithstanding the torrent of other criticisms of academe, it was probably the allegations of misuse of federal research money that became the single most damaging and far-reaching public embarrassment for higher education. The popular television program *60 Minutes* aired a damaging exposé alleging university misuse of federal research funds in 1991, and a frenzy of other publicity soon followed.

Indirect costs are those expenses, such as utilities and capital depreciation, that universities incur as an indirect yet attributable result of conducting research in their facilities. Indirect cost recovery rates are set at a percentage of the total cost of the research grant. They are negotiated between the individual institution and the federal agency which sponsors the research. In 1990 and 1991 many of the nation's leading research universities were charged with misuse of millions of dollars of federal indirect cost reimbursements and excessive charges to the federal government for the research they were doing.

Although many of the nation's most prestigious universities were implicated, Stanford University was made the center of the controversy. Among other charges, the *60 Minutes* exposé claimed that Stanford had used some indirect cost money to renovate the president's home and the university's yacht. Representative John Dingell (D-Michigan), Chair of the House Energy and Commerce Committee, called special congressional hearings on the matter and made the indirect cost investigations the primary object of the committee's attention throughout 1991. Dingell summoned university presidents and administrators to testify before the committee, while teams of Internal Revenue Service investigators, and investigators from a variety of other government agencies as well, descended on some campuses for extended stays in order to conduct audits of institutional research budgets. Ultimately, the cloud of accusations and the pervasive media attention forced the resignation of Stanford University President Donald Kennedy in August 1991, even though Stanford was eventually cleared of the charges.[1] The indirect cost scandal attracted national media attention and became a symbol of the self-serving over-indulgence of higher education, especially its over-emphasis on university research.

By 1992, higher education had suffered a decade-long string of embarrassing criticisms and disclosures. These had had an undeniable effect upon the morale of those in the higher education community. For example, George Mason University President George W. Johnson, reflecting on the impact of years of public scrutiny, said, "I'm kind of overwhelmed. I've never been so attacked from so many different points of the compass. I feel a little ineffectual and futile" (McMillen, *Chronicle of Higher Education*, 24 July 1991).

Thus, going into the 104th Congress it was clear that public confidence in the integrity and performance of higher education had been seriously eroded. A campus lobbyist asserted, "Higher ed is no longer the fair-haired child." An association president characterized the situation as follows: "Higher education's values don't speak for themselves anymore. It has fallen from grace; it has fallen off the pedestal. The public no longer trusts any powerful institutions, and higher ed is seen as a monolith—arrogant, with deep pockets, and removed from social problems." Martin Anderson captured the cumulative effect of the various criticisms of academe when he wrote, "It has been quite a while since anyone spoke of the world of American higher education as a place of integrity" (Anderson 1992, 9).

GROWTH AND PRACTICE OF ACADEMIC EARMARKING

One cannot fully understand the erosion of confidence in higher education without understanding earmarked funding. Members of Congress regularly received requests from higher education institutions for academic earmarks, or "pork" as opponents of the practice called them, and those requests made academe look just like other special interest lobbies.

Academic earmarks are special appropriations made to specific colleges and universities or to groups of institutions, that have not been authorized by the relevant congressional committee. Though special appropriations are occasionally included in statutory language, they more typically result from influential members of Congress adding "report language," usually a brief sentence or two, to spending bills. The language directs agencies of the federal government to fund specific research-related endeavors. Unlike competitively funded scientific research, academic earmarks bypass the formal peer review process and are made without a review of their merit. Often the lawmakers who vote for earmarks are not even aware of how much money was appropriated or exactly how the money will be spent. Nonetheless, they vote for the earmarks because they think their chances for re-election improve when they can bring new funding to institutions in their districts or states. The justification that members of Congress often give for the earmarks is that they spread money beyond the one hundred top research universities to which the peer review process allocates more than 80 percent of federal research and development funding. Thus, the earmarks give more institutions the opportunity to engage in research and other educational endeavors. However, some of the top research universities also receive earmarked funds. Earmarked funds for special facilities and equipment are especially prized because there are no other federal funds available to support and upgrade institutions' research infrastructures. Since the 1960s, with the exception of federal earmarking, institutions have relied on state governments to fund facilities and equipment, but the states have not always been able to pay the bills.

During the decade from 1982 to 1992 earmarks for colleges and universities increased dramatically. They grew from $11 million to $700 million annually, with approximately $2.5 billion expended on academic earmarks during that ten-year period (Pianin, *Washington Post*, 23 September 1992). According to a 1993 report by the House Committee on Space, Science, and Technology, in the 1992 fiscal year, 170, or roughly 5 percent, of the nation's colleges and universities were recipients of earmarked funds (Brown 1993).

The practice of congressional earmarking for higher education often pits the larger national scientific research agenda against the particular interests of individual institutions and members of Congress. Leaders of the national scientific research community clearly oppose the practice of earmarked funding. Albert Teich, Director of Science and Policy at the American Association for the Advancement of Science, has asked, "Should the criteria be, 'Who has the most political clout and can hire the best lobbyists?' or, 'Who can do the best science as judged by scientists?'" (Jordan, *Washington Post*, 3 November 1993). In a similar vein, Eric Bloch, former director of the National Science Foundation (NSF), has criticized earmarked funding for its circumvention of the quality control process that is ensured by competitively funded science. Asked Bloch, "Where's the quality control? With peer review, there's quality control on the research" (Davis, *Wall Street Journal*, 2 May 1990).

Academic earmarks also pit colleges and universities against the higher education associations that represent them in Washington. AAU, along with other higher education associations, has over the years issued several moratoriums against accepting earmarked gifts, and has urged members to refrain from the practice. Testifying before the House Committee on Space, Science and Technology in the fall of 1992, retired AAU president Robert Rosenzweig characterized earmarked gifts in the following way, "They are destructive of high-quality science, wasteful of the public's money, and erosive of public confidence in the integrity of universities and of the political process" (Greve, *Detroit News and Free Press*, 7 August 1994). Joe B. Wyatt, chancellor of Vanderbilt University and then-chair of the board of AAU, was an outspoken critic of academic earmarks, referring to them as robbery. Said Wyatt, "I don't know what else to call it. There is a new recognition among scientists that this is not free money going to these midnight, earmarked projects. . . . It's money coming right out of competitive science funding" (Jordan, *Washington Post*, 10 October 1993).

Yet even as the associations routinely issued proclamations against the practice of earmarked funding, individual institutions lined up every year to solicit these gifts from congressional patrons. As one senior administrative officer at the University of Pittsburgh put it, "I abhor the system, but I sure don't want to be the last in line" (Cordes and Ornstein, *Chronicle of Higher Education*, 3 August 1994). Institutions' pursuit of earmarks is a classic example of Olson's "tragedy of the commons" in which individual self-interest takes precedence over what is generally regarded as the common good (1965). The fact that some higher education institutions regularly sought earmarks made the entire community look just as greedy as other special interests.

As the number of congressional earmarks for colleges and universities grew during the latter half of the 1980s and into the 1990s, so too did the number of national press accounts detailing egregious examples of academic pork. An example of the kind of story that routinely found its way into newspapers around the country was an $8 million earmark to Delta College in Michigan, a two-year community college without a single major field of study in the sciences, for the purpose of building a planetarium (Gerdes, *Detroit Free Press*, 15 February 1993).

Reports of academic earmarks often focused not only on the college or university recipient but also on those members of Congress who had been particularly effective in securing earmarked funds for favored institutions. The *Washington Post*, for example, described how Senator Daniel Inouye (D-Hawaii), an alumnus of George Washington University, had conducted a three-year personal lobbying campaign to provide $50 million in funds to his alma mater for construction of a hospital (Jordan, *Washington Post*, 10 October 1993). Senator Robert Byrd (D-West Virginia) became renowned for his ability to steer enormous sums of money to colleges and universities in his home state, such as the $21 million research grant to tiny Wheeling Jesuit College—a gift almost twice the College's annual budget (Anderson and Binstein, *Washington Post*, 30 August 1993). Similarly, between 1990 and 1994 Representative John Murtha (R-Pennsylvania), chair of the House Appropriations Subcommittee on Defense Appropriations and sometimes described as the "King of Earmarks," supported Defense Department earmarks worth at least $333 million for projects related to various colleges and universities in his state. Approximately $202 million of it went to projects in his own district (Cordes, *Chronicle of Higher Education*, 2 November 1994).

Not all members of Congress support academic earmarking. In fact, many members strongly oppose the practice, believing that it undermines the nation's larger scientific research agenda and compromises the integrity of higher education. Representative Vernon Ehlers (R-Michigan) referred to earmarked funding as a "purely selfish" form of higher education lobbying (Ehlers interview, 1996), while Senator Nancy Kassebaum (R-Kansas) stated, "Earmarks have been a mistake. They detract from higher education. Higher ed should be above the fray and not grubbing at the federal trough" (Kassebaum interview, 1996). Similarly, a Senate staffer commented, "The efforts of special interests to get set-asides and earmarks have decreased the impact of higher education overall. . . . They've hurt the long-term improvement of higher education."

One source of anger and frustration for many members of Congress relates to the practice among some colleges and universities of using high-priced lobbyists to solicit earmarked funds. In a 1993 *New York Times* editorial, Vanderbilt Chancellor Joe B. Wyatt noted that some institutions paid Washington lobbying firms between $10,000 and $50,000 a month to help seek out congressional sponsors for earmarks (*New York Times*, 12 October 1993). Far and away the leader among these lobbyists is the Cassidy (formerly Cassidy and Associates) firm, whose former-congressional-committee-staff-turned-lobbyists ensure it privileged access to some of Congress' most influential members. Cassidy tells institutions that, in exchange for annual fees in the three figure range, it may gain for an institution much more in federal appropriations than the cost of its services. Cassidy's influence on Capitol Hill, particularly during the mid-to-late 1980s, earned it enormous sums of money from some of the nation's most prominent universities. In congressional committee testimony in September 1993, for example, Tufts University revealed that it had paid Cassidy in excess of $3 million over the past decade. The growing influence of lobbyists like the Cassidy firm has led even some proponents to criticize the role of lobbyists in the academic earmarking process. In 1990, Senate Appropriations Committee Chair Robert Byrd (D-West Virginia) publicly attacked Cassidy for its arrogance, while also criticizing colleges and universities for their excessive reliance upon lobbyists.

Congressional staff also regularly express their disdain for the use of lobbyists by colleges and universities. One senior congressional staffer said, "Bozo lobbyists shouldn't charge for the help that congressional staff provide for free," and then characterized universities that use lobbyists as "tacky." Other congressional staff have conveyed their amazement at higher education's use of lobbyists to the neglect of other sources of influence. For example, a Senate staffer remarked, "I tell the colleges it's a negative to use Cassidy and Associates. I try to be less responsive to them and not reward that activity. I don't understand why the schools don't call me before paying a bundle for a lobbyist to call me. The college presidents have underestimated their own influence and their own power of persuasion."

In the midst of the rapidly escalating practice of academic earmarking and growing public criticism both of Congress and of institutions that solicit earmarked funding, California Representative George Brown (D-California), Chair of the House Committee on Space, Science and Technology, launched an effort in 1993 to curb the practice. Although other powerful members of Congress, including Senators Sam Nunn (D-Georgia) and John Danforth (R-Missouri), had previously tried and failed to combat academic earmarking, Brown took on the "politically dangerous role of pork-buster" (Cordes, *Chronicle of Higher Education*, 29 June 1994) by convening committee hearings and commissioning a report on academic earmarks that received national attention during the summer and fall of 1993. Brown called Tufts University and Columbia University before his committee in September 1993 to explain their use of congressionally earmarked funds. Brown's committee also sent out fifty letters to colleges and universities that received earmarks in fiscal year 1993 appropriation bills asking for detailed information about the funds they had received and about the rationale these institutions advanced for receiving the gifts. Although these schools ranged widely in size, type, control, and location, their common thread, according to the committee report, was that they all "have friends in high places." Perhaps most damaging, the report revealed the reliance of many of them on high-priced Washington lobbying firms, concluding that of the fifty schools surveyed, twenty-one employed registered lobbyists.

Brown's report recounted the numerous and varied arguments used to defend academic earmarks: "It is claimed that they allow small, less populous states some share of federal R&D dollars; that they break the stranglehold of the 'elite' research institutions; that they stem from inadequate funding or facilities in existing programs; that they meet real national needs in targeted ways" (Brown 1993). The report conceded there is "undoubtedly" some truth in these arguments, "But all of them fail to communicate the disturbing nature of academic earmarks: it is a process that is built on closed door consultations (often facilitated by high priced lobbyists); it is a process that grows through logrolling among Appropriations Committee Members attempting to do favors for constituents; it is a process that destroys rational efforts to set priorities tied to national needs; it is a process that circumvents the right of the great majority of the House and Senate to have a voice in determining the expenditure of public funds; most fundamentally, it is process that fails to protect the taxpayers' investment."

Representative Brown's report concluded by arguing that earmarks were "beginning to eat into the base programs of the federal agencies we rely on to fund our scientific enterprise," noting that while the House Appropriations Committee had earmarked hundreds of millions of dollars for construction at individual colleges and universities in 1993, the committee had found only $93.5 million in all of the previous five years to fund the NSF's Facilities and Infrastructure Program. Clearly, the report's overarching theme was, "The fairest way to distribute our research dollars is through competitive, peer reviewed awards programs" (Brown 1993).

Brown's fight to reduce earmarks was successful briefly, though not long-term. For fiscal year 1994, congressional earmarks for colleges and universities dropped 50 percent in those spending bills (agriculture, housing and veterans programs, energy and water, and the Departments of Commerce, Justice, and State) which represent the majority of the money that is earmarked annually by Congress for academic research projects (Cordes, *Chronicle of Higher Education*, 3 November 1993).

The warfare that was waged over academic earmarks in 1993–94 left higher education with a tarnished reputation as it prepared to greet the new 104th Congress. Amidst intense public and congressional scrutiny, the Washington higher education associations alternately appeared ineffective and disinterested. A former chair of two association boards complained, "AASCU and ACE's boards say nothing about earmarking. Associations deplore earmarking but they don't do anything about it." Another university president said that he and many of his fellow presidents would have "preferred to have AAU define 'earmark' better and enforce compliance more strictly." A third president characterized academic pork as a "major policy problem for higher education," and captured the tension between the associations and individual institutions in his observation that, "While AAU and NASULGC take public positions opposed to pork barrel projects, their member institutions move aggressively ahead: an interesting paradox." Thus, the earmark debate had not only tarnished the reputation of individual institutions, it had also tarnished the reputation of the higher education associations by demonstrating their impotence in the face of a major controversy.

THE STORY OF THE STATE POSTSECONDARY
REVIEW ENTITIES

A second issue that presented a major challenge for the higher education community in the early 1990s and initially demonstrated the ineptitude of the associations concerned the State Postsecondary Review Entities (SPREs). The SPREs resulted from congressional concern about the integrity of federal student assistance programs, as well as about accountability in higher education more generally. The 1972 Higher Education Act (HEA), as described in chapter 2, had provided assistance directly to students, rather than to institutions, and had also made eligible for receipt of federal aid those students who attended proprietary (for-profit) institutions. The system of federal postsecondary assistance was vulnerable to a variety of abuses, and by the late 1980s skyrocketing student loan default rates and fraudulent institutional practices were costing the federal government $3–4 billion annually. This sum was nearly one-third of the total annual expenditures of the federal student assistance programs.

There were several reasons for the high default rates and institutional abuses. Perhaps the most significant reason was the enormous increase in the number of proprietary schools in the years since 1972, for these schools, as a group, had higher default rates than other types of institutions. Some of the proprietary schools were no more than fly-by-night schools whose practices were deceptive and often illegal. Some of them recruited students for the purpose of securing Pell Grant funding but then made little or no effort to educate or retain those students. A second reason for the high default rate and abuses was the laxity of the nation's system for monitoring institutional accountability and ensuring the appropriate use of federal student assistance funds. The system used to determine institutional eligibility to participate in federal student assistance programs involved three loosely related components: institutional accreditation by any accrediting association recognized by the U. S. Department of Education;[2] determination of eligibility by the Department of Education; and recognition of the right to operate by the state in which the school is located.

There were a number of real and potential problems endemic in this process. First, the regional accrediting associations were responsible primarily for reviewing institutions' academic programs, not their financial integrity. Second, these accrediting groups monitored mostly nonprofit colleges and universities, not trade schools or proprietary institutions. Third, the state coordinating and governing boards (i.e., those state-level statutory or constitutional boards of control which exercise varying amounts of authority over public institutions' academic and fiscal affairs) differ widely in their oversight of state institutions. In fact, many state boards exercise little or no oversight of proprietary schools. Finally, the Department of Education, which recognizes accrediting bodies, did not take a stringent approach to determining which schools could participate in the federal programs.

Intense congressional concern over federal student loan program integrity led to numerous congressional hearings in the late 1980s and early 1990s. These hearings dealt with issues of institutional accountability and forewarned of impending congressional action to remedy the perceived problems.

Congressional concerns were evident as the reauthorization process for the 1992 HEA began in earnest in 1990, but the Washington higher education associations appeared to be largely inattentive to the problem. Rather, the associations concentrated primarily on their traditional goals of increased student aid and higher loan limits for students. An association head who deals primarily with private institutions observed, "There are two reasons for the federal government to involve itself in higher education. One is access; and the other is excellence. In the reauthorization, the higher education associations concerned themselves exclusively with access, not excellence." Similarly, the director of a specialized association stated, "The associations are so dominated by the 'access' agenda that they are not really dealing with 'program integrity' and 'quality' issues that are currently engaging members of Congress." He added that the associations "deal only with self-serving issues" and that they had "underestimated the mood of Congress." Another observer, a chief congressional staffer, said, "During the reauthorization, higher ed just tried to rubber stamp traditional programs." She said the associations focused too narrowly on unimportant issues. Similarly, an association head remarked that higher education, in general, was in "denial about the importance of accountability." Accountability issues, according to this president, were "the crack in the dam."

Pell Grants are the nation's largest college student grant program, and they serve students with financial need. Because their value had declined substantially, in 1992 Representative William Ford (D-Michigan), chair of the House Education and Labor Committee, moved to make the Grants an entitlement, i.e., an automatic benefit for all who qualified based on their financial status, according to the congressional definition of eligibility. He wanted to ensure access to the program for growing numbers of low-income students. Ford's proposal led many in Congress to push for some assurance in the reauthorization that current and future federal student aid funds would be well spent. Little consideration was given to the possibility of different standards for federal funding of proprietary schools because powerful members of Congress such as Representative Ford, who was himself a proprietary school graduate, opposed that idea. Instead, Congress sought to address the loan default problem and other accountability issues across the entire spectrum of postsecondary education.

Congress decided to use the 1992 HEA to improve accountability by strengthening the nation's accrediting system through a new system of state-level review boards. The boards were to be called State Postsecondary Review Entities, or SPREs. The intent of the SPRE legislation was to step up the federal government's oversight of institutions that receive federal student aid by establishing new and stricter guidelines for state governments and accrediting bodies. Under this reconstituted "Program Integrity Triad," as it was called, in Part H of the 1992 HEA, accrediting agencies would review the quality of education offered at an institution and monitor HEA Title IV compliance with federal regulations, the federal government would monitor the financial and administrative soundness of institutions in federal student aid programs, and the newly created SPREs would review colleges that triggered certain warning signs.

Despite congressional attention to all three parts of the Triad, it was the creation of the SPREs that most concerned the higher education community. Part H of the Act specified that there should be "one State Postsecondary Review Entity in each state to be responsible for the conduct or coordination" of institutional reviews for the purpose of determining whether institutions should be allowed to continue to participate in Title IV financial aid programs. The legislation provided that plans for each SPRE be written by individual states and that the SPREs be housed in state-level boards of control, such as departments of education, or state coordinating or governing boards. The legislation set forth eleven criteria or triggers, which could call for an institution's SPRE review. Among the triggers were high student default rates, failure to submit audits in a timely manner, and excessive fluctuation in the amounts of aid received by students that were not due to changes in the federal programs themselves.

Most Washington players and knowledgeable college and university leaders believe that the passage of the SPRE legislation was a blow to the associations. They think its provisions were the result of a nighttime conference committee decision dominated by key congressional staff to which there was little or no higher education association input. A Big Six official commented that "the law about the SPREs was written at night by a conference committee and no text of it was made available to the associations for weeks. The associations were taken by surprise and were very defensive about it." Another Washington higher education leader said, "The associations had nothing at all to do with the SPREs. . . . The associations didn't anticipate them and didn't intervene." A typical college president's comment that "The SPRE legislation is a good example of involvement too late" illustrates the prevailing view that the associations were not players at a key time. Another president shared that dismay by asking, "How did subpart H slip past the major associations?"

There is another version of the same story, however, that is probably more accurate. It says that some key association officials did know about the impending SPRE legislation and agreed to it in return for potential congressional enactment of legislation making Pell Grants into entitlements. When campus lobbyists heard about the legislation and realized that non-governmental accreditation was being replaced by a federal-state agency evaluation of institutions, including assessments of academic quality never before carried out by government, they "went apoplectic," as one observer put it. The purpose of the SPREs was to reduce abuse in student aid programs, but the result was going to be evaluation of all institutions, regardless of their records on student aid management, which was a significant infringement of institutional autonomy. Campus lobbyists convinced the association lobbyists that they had misjudged the impact of SPREs. They had made a "bargain with the devil," trading new government oversight for extra federal dollars, and the campus representatives said they could not endorse this bargain.

The fallout from the incorporation of the SPRE legislation into the 1992 HEA was very detrimental to the major higher education associations. It caused infighting among association personnel because of differing views of the "bargain" that had been made, as well as antagonism between association lobbyists and campus lobbyists. The latter charged that the former lacked a campus perspective (in fact, most association lobbyists have never spent time on a campus since their own college years), and the subsequent uproar about the SPREs by college and university presidents proved them right.

Most observers and players agreed early on that the associations had mishandled the SPRE legislation. For example, a congressional staffer commented on the associations' performance by saying, "Higher education grasped a few twigs as it worked on that Act, but it missed the forest." Typical comments written in response to the 1994 survey by college and university presidents two years after the 1992 legislation showed that its impact was still being felt. One said, "The associations were not effective in stopping the HEA of 1992, which is a bureaucratic, wasteful, and often counterproductive piece of legislation." Another president commented, "They [the associations] dropped the ball on reauthorization of the Higher Education Act." A third declared, "The '92 reauthorization was a total disaster. My remarks [about the associations] would have been more positive before '92." Another agreed, "The 1992 Higher Education Act . . . reflected clear [association] failure." Similarly, then-President James J. Duderstadt of the University of Michigan remarked in an address to the Senate Assembly (the faculty governing body) on November 18, 1991, during the 1992 HEA deliberations, "The associations are completely ineffective and have been discredited." Association staff well understood the extent of the problem they had created for themselves. For example, one said, "We did not come out as we would have liked, were late to realize its [the SPREs'] potential impact, and were in fact defensive about it." In an understatement about the extent of the SPRE debacle, he called it "a bumbling start."

Because of the associations' mistakes with the enactment of SPRE legislation, the real fight occurred over the next two years, as the associations grappled with the Department of Education's rule-making process and its initial implementation. In the summer of 1993 department officials and various members of the higher education community met to discuss the Part H legislation. The department's initial draft regulations for the SPRE program were published in the *Federal Register* in January 1994 in order to have a 90-day public "notice and comment" period prior to implementing proposed regulations.

The draft regulations immediately met a firestorm of criticism from the higher education community. A NAICU official said, "The regulations were much worse than anyone had expected because they hurt institutional autonomy." David Ruffer, president of the University of Tampa, characterized the proposed set of regulations in almost catastrophic terms for the U. S. higher education system. He said that through the "federalization of the accreditation process, creation of a 50-state postsecondary review entity bureaucracy, and ill-conceived and duplicative reporting requirements, enormous financial and creative costs would be imposed on the system, leading to the demise of its role as a global leader. . . . Nothing short of rewriting the regulations is required" (Zook, *Chronicle of Higher Education*, 6 April 1994). In March 1994 the associations moved to stop implementation of the regulations by protesting to the Office of Management and Budget that the Department of Education's proposed rules would create excessive paperwork and record-keeping burdens for institutions, thereby violating President Clinton's Executive Order 12866 and the federal Paperwork Reduction Act (Zook, *Chronicle of Higher Education*, 25 May 1994).

It was clear that the private institutions, particularly the small liberal arts colleges, believed that the SPREs presented a serious threat to their independence. Therefore, throughout the debate, NAICU and many of its member institutions took an active and visible stance against the SPREs. Religiously affiliated colleges, including the Association of Catholic Colleges and Universities and the Association of Advanced Rabbinical and Talmudic Colleges, joined forces under NAICU's leadership in lobbying against the SPREs. As one private college president stated, "There have been strange bedfellows because the Talmudic and Rabbinical Colleges have been allied with the very most conservative Protestant colleges, such as Baptist institutions, since they all worry that their faith statements will be questioned and that there will be regulation of their faculty hiring policies, so there has been an unusual coalition of schools and associations."

In addition to NAICU, other Washington higher education associations joined in mobilizing college and university presidents' opposition to the regulations. Within weeks of the initial release of the draft regulations,

ACE, in coalition with the other major associations and several other regional higher education accrediting groups, released an analysis of the department's proposed SPRE regulations, characterizing them as a "threat to the academic freedom heretofore enjoyed by colleges and universities." It urged institutions throughout the country to use the required notice and comment period to register their opposition to the "potential intrusiveness, cost and burden" of the proposed regulations (*Higher Education and National Affairs*, 7 March 1994).

The ACE report, which was sent to all accredited, degree-granting institutions, claimed that the draft regulations suffered from several "fundamental flaws." The ACE document said first that the regulations exceeded the authority of the law, increasing federal and state oversight in ways unintended by Congress. Second, the regulations placed upon institutions extraordinary data collection and reporting burdens. Third, the regulations required "excessive duplication" of efforts between state governments, accrediting agencies, and the federal government. Finally, according to the report, the regulations lacked basic due process protections which would assure that institutions were treated fairly. The document also suggested that the department wanted to use the SPREs as a "massive dragnet to review a large number of colleges and universities" (Washington D.C. Higher Education Associations 1994).

The report had its intended effect. Over the next months, an "unprecedented avalanche" of more than 1700 letters, most of them negative in tone, were sent to the Department of Education by college and university presidents throughout the country in response to the associations' call for action (Zook, *Chronicle of Higher Education*, 6 April 1994). Despite repeated assurances by Assistant Secretary for Postsecondary Education David Longanecker that the proposed regulations did not and would not exceed congressional intent, the associations continued to complain. Longanecker attended the February 1994 NAICU annual meeting and received blistering criticism for the regulations. In fact, he was quoted as saying, "I almost needed an armed guard to protect me" (*Chronicle of Higher Education*, 1 November 1996). One of the NAICU college presidents declared, "Longanecker has outlived his usefulness. He issues regulations and doesn't care what you think of them. He chooses to interpret congressional language badly. . . . The SPRE triggers could still trigger Harvard and Yale if the wrong snapshot of their budgets were taken."

As a result of all this pressure, the Department of Education released a revised set of regulations in May 1994. Although the associations had made progress in curtailing the authority of the SPREs, some association leaders and institutional presidents felt that the revised regulations still went too far. For example, NAICU president David Warren stated, "I see some progress, but still some central and fundamental problems" (Jaschik, *Chronicle of Higher Education*, 4 May, 1994). He added that NAICU was considering legal challenges and he had secured pledges of support from members of Congress, presumably to restrict further the authority of the SPREs.

Additional ammunition for the higher education community's fight against the SPRE legislation resulted from the Department of Education's bungling of initial implementation in August 1994. The department sent a vaguely worded letter to over 2,000 institutions—approximately one-half of which were nonprofit colleges and universities—informing them that they were being referred to their SPREs because they had set off one or more of five review triggers, though the particular violations were not specified. The institutions later learned that, in most cases, the problem was a missing audit. In addition to the lack of specificity of the letters and the triviality of the offenses, there were problems with timing because many of the SPREs that were supposed to review the targeted institutions were not yet in place.

Association leaders, particularly NAICU and its president, David Warren, responded angrily. Although the SPRE legislation was originally intended to help reduce fraud and abuse, they said the current round of letters had little to do with the intent of the law and simply proved accurate their warnings that the SPRE system would create a new regulatory nightmare. For example, Warren stated, "We have already received about 100 calls from our members. The presidents are just furious. What does this have to do with fraud and abuse?" ACE's vice president for government relations stated, "We think they ought to be focusing on schools that have serious problems. And they ought to get it right the first time. We are telling every school that gets a letter to appeal." He added, "They [the Department of Education] sent out 2,000 letters to individual institutions and showed that they were going to make it a regulatory nightmare. They showed that they were not in control of the process" (Manegold, *New York Times*, 10 August 1994). One college president noted that the department's letter to his institution was addressed to a predecessor of his who had been gone for fifteen years, which he took to be a sign of the sloppiness and inaccuracy of the Department of Education's records. Association leaders and institutional presidents were not the only ones who criticized the ill-handled mailing from the Department of Education; anonymous sources within the department were quoted in national press accounts as questioning it. One such official said, "Why did we do this if we can't even do a serious follow-up? It is a government bust" (Manegold 1994).

As it turned out, the enactment of the SPRE legislation and the excessive and clumsy implementation that followed served to stir the entire higher education community and help prepare it for the battle over legislation proposed in the 104th Congress. The higher education community realized that it had mishandled the 1992 reauthorization of the HEA. As a congressional staffer lamented, "Part H is a monument to the ineffectiveness of the higher education lobby." Thus, the SPRE legislation produced an important legacy that affected higher education's federal relations. The leaders of the higher education community, embarrassed about past mistakes, marshaled their resources to undo what they had let slide by. The SPREs activated them to do intensive lobbying, and they resolved to be more attentive and involved in future congressional policy decisions.

RELATIONS WITH THE CLINTON ADMINISTRATION

The battle over the SPREs had another consequence. It was an important factor, though certainly not the only one, in souring relations between the higher education community and the Clinton administration. Initially, most higher education leaders had been delighted about Clinton's election because his support for education while serving as governor of Arkansas was well-known. Just prior to the 1992 presidential election, a large number of academic leaders diverged from their tradition of electoral nonpartisanship and advertised their personal (as opposed to institutional) endorsement of Bill Clinton's candidacy in the *Chronicle of Higher Education* (28 October 1992). Although higher education was not at the center of the candidate's platform, the higher education community expected to be able to advance agendas that had suffered during the Reagan and Bush presidencies. When Clinton won the 1992 election, it was the first time since the Carter administration that there was a Democratic president and Democratic Party control of both houses of Congress

Soon after the election, however, hopes that the new president would serve as a major supporter of higher education gradually began to dissipate. To begin with, Clinton ignored the nominees for executive branch positions sent to him by the major higher education associations during the transition, and he chose instead to appoint people whose education policy expertise was gained at the state level, not the federal level. As the director of an association of state representatives observed in 1994, "Clinton is moving toward more state oversight and involvement regarding higher education."

Differences between the administration and the associations became particularly obvious in regard to student financial aid. Constrained by the 1993 budget resolution that froze domestic discretionary spending at 1993 fiscal year levels for five years, discussions over federal student aid reflected the zero-sum approach that characterized budget negotiations for all federal spending. The Clinton administration's fiscal year 1994 budget called for reductions in the College Work-Study program, the Supplemental Educational Opportunity Grants program, and the Perkins Loans program, as well as termination of the State Student Incentive Grant program. Funding for the Pell Grant program fared slightly better, receiving a recommendation for a small increase for fiscal year 1994. The higher education community's concerns with President Clinton's 1994 budget grew more serious the following year, however, as the president's 1995 fiscal year budget proposal provided for the elimination of thirty-three education programs, including a number of significant and long-standing student aid programs. The administration also proposed a "pause" in indirect cost reimbursements for institutions receiving more than $10 million in federal research funds.

In response to the actions of the Clinton administration, Terry Hartle, ACE's Vice President for Government Relations, wrote, "While the Clinton budget lacks the smoke and mirrors that characterized the Reagan-Bush budgets, the result is the same; higher education does not fare well" (*Higher Education and National Affairs*, 19 April 1993a). Later, ACE then-President Robert Atwell, along with the leaders of thirteen other higher education associations, voiced their opposition, first to the stagnation, and then to the reduction, in federal student aid. In a letter to congressional budget negotiators in August 1994, Atwell wrote, "The long-term effects of inadequate grant funding will contribute to increased indebtedness and longer periods of repayment, and inhibit borrowers from saving for the education of their children" (*Higher Education and National Affairs*, 15 August 1994).

The higher education community also complained of new regulations even beyond the problem with the SPREs. One college president commented, "The Clinton administration tries to over-regulate everything. . . . Overall there has been less money and more regulation under Clinton, as well as a demeaning treatment of higher education."

Criticisms of Clinton were echoed by Democratic congressional staff. For example, while acknowledging the president's legislative successes during the 103rd Congress, one staffer commented on the manner in which the president treated higher education. He said, "Clinton's speeches debase higher education. He talks only about economics. He never mentions intellectual curiosity, or the liberal humanistic tradition, or fulfilling human potential."

By the time the 1994 election took place, the higher education community's disappointment with President Clinton was palpable. Clinton had addressed the 1994 ACE annual meeting, the first president to address that meeting since the Eisenhower era, and academe generally applauded the president for overturning the Bush administration ban on minority scholarships. Nonetheless, the conventional wisdom was that Clinton, along with his Department of Education, paid little attention to priorities of the higher education community. An association head characterized the first two years of the Clinton administration by saying, "The Clinton administration has activist people who don't listen to the associations." The higher education community's poor relations with the Clinton administration at the time of the midterm elections are illustrated by one college president's comment, "We would never have believed that Clinton would do so little for us after he was elected." Another said simply, "The Clinton Administration has become public enemy #1 of higher education." Little did they know that the November 1994 election would bring them even bigger challenges.

Chapter Four

THE ARRIVAL OF THE 104TH CONGRESS

*"This is a 'Forrest Gump' Congress. They don't know any-
thing about our issues and they don't care to learn. It is a
daunting task to educate members about programs before
they make decisions about cutting them."*
A Big Six association lobbyist early in 1995

Despite the higher education community's disappointment with the
Clinton administration, which was described in chapter 3, the November
1994 congressional elections left it with nowhere else to turn. This
Congress had the first Republican majority in both Houses in four decades,
and the change in party control presented a number of challenges for colleges and universities. The new members came into office in January 1995,
and the 104th Congress adjourned two years later, at the end of 1996. That
two-year period was a time of turmoil for the academic community because
of Republican proposals to restructure and cut the federal budget for higher
education.

REPUBLICAN "CONTRACT WITH AMERICA"

In September 1994, just weeks before the congressional elections, a
group of House Republicans led by Minority Leader Newt Gingrich of
Georgia unveiled a self-proclaimed "detailed agenda for national renewal"
entitled the "Contract With America." In the Contract, the Republicans
promised to "transform the way Congress works" and put an end to government that has become "too big, too intrusive, and too easy with the public's
money." To this end, the Contract set forth a blueprint for legislative action
during the first hundred days of a Republican-led House of Representatives.
Included among the promised bills were a balanced budget amendment and
spending cuts for various domestic programs. Although the Contract with
America made no explicit reference to higher education, it promised to
enact additional budget savings beyond those specifically stipulated in order
to reduce the federal deficit. That did not bode well for the higher education community, whose principal objectives were increases in federal funding for research and student financial aid.

Once the Republican majority was elected to Congress, their budget
reduction plans heightened the potential conflict with higher education
representatives. Early in the 104th Congress, a Democratic House staff

member correctly remarked, "The cutbacks that the Republicans are trying to make in the budget . . . make higher education's relationship with them adversarial in nature." Of course, the impending budgetary retrenchment was threatening to all domestic programs, and a Republican House staff member noted, "Everyone has adversaries in the appropriations process because everyone is fighting for the same dollars." Similarly, an ACE lobbyist stated, "The whole cadre of domestic advocacy groups are having a problem with Congress now, not just higher education." The fact that higher education had common concerns with other policy sectors did not make the situation any easier. As a Big Six official observed, "These times are not good for us, not just because the Republicans don't want to spend more money, but also because other priorities are taking precedence on the public policy agenda. It's not our fault, but the boom era is over and we're in a period of steady retrenchment."

For higher education, the reality of a Republican majority on Capitol Hill also had worrisome implications for partisan reasons. As Robert H. Salisbury has observed, most of the policy communities in Washington "find one party more responsive to their policy desires than the other" (1992, 98). In recent history members of the higher education community have usually considered the Democratic Party more responsive, principally because Democrats have been more sympathetic to its funding requests. (On a few issues, such as basic research funding, Republicans have been more responsive than Democrats; on the majority of issues, however, Democrats have more frequently supported the community's requests.) Furthermore, higher education policy making is usually done by the legislative branch to a greater extent than the executive branch, and the Democrats controlled Congress for most of the latter half of the twentieth century. For four decades, the higher education associations had forged more extensive ties with the Democratic congressional majority than with most of the Republican side of the aisle. There were exceptions, such as Republican Senators Nancy Kassebaum of Kansas and James Jeffords of Vermont with whom academia worked closely, but on the whole the community was more involved with Democratic policy makers.

Many observers commented that the vast majority of the Washington association staff, and almost all of One Dupont Circle, are Democrats. One association official estimated that in the past higher education had sided with congressional Democrats about 75 percent of the time, especially since the Democratic Party is more likely to favor funding for federal domestic programs.[1] Soon after the election, a Democratic congressional staff member said, "Higher education has always been against the Republicans and now they're out to get them. Nobody wants to be considered an adversary but some, especially the Republicans, are willing to give higher ed a very low priority." Similarly, an executive branch official remarked, "Higher ed has been part of the liberal policies of the Democrats in the past. Its friends are gone now."

When association personnel were interviewed after the 1994 election, they contended that the higher education community had always made an effort to maintain relations with Republican congressional staff when they were in the minority. Association staff regularly contrasted the bipartisanship of the higher education community with the Democratic sympathies of the elementary/secondary education lobby. AASCU's vice president for government relations, who himself is a Republican and served in the Reagan administration, was one of many who expressed a preference for bipartisanship. "AASCU is proud of being bipartisan" (Elmendorf interview, 1994). However, Republican staffers themselves were typically less impressed with the attention they had received from higher education. One of them said, "Higher ed should have started building bridges to Republicans years ago. They have worked heavily with Democrats in the past and did not focus a lot of energy or attention on Republicans. They help Democrats do fundraising." While higher education provides little campaign funding, it is indeed true that college campuses have often showcased sympathetic candidates and officeholders, and many institutions have done so for Democrats more often than for Republicans in the past.

Given the budgetary pressures facing the new Republican congressional majority, as well as their perception that higher education had a history of Democratic Party ties, it is not surprising that Republicans were unsympathetic to the policy requests of colleges and universities. However, the Republican leadership went beyond a lack of sympathy by engaging in intense criticism of higher education from an ideological perspective. As a Republican House staff member said, in a bit of an understatement, "there is a conservative distrust of academia."

At the time, House Speaker Newt Gingrich of Georgia was the chief spokesperson for the congressional majority and the Republican Party more generally, and his forceful personality had a substantial impact on policy outcomes. Gingrich expressed strong anti-higher education sentiments in his various public statements throughout 1995. His comments were particularly unsettling for the academic community because he is, in fact, one of their own. Gingrich holds a Ph.D. in history and for eight years was a professor of history and geography at West Georgia College. As Speaker, he continued to teach a course through distance education, first at Kennesaw State College, an AASCU institution, and later at Reinhardt College, a NAICU institution.[2] Some of the other Republican leadership also came from academe: for example, House majority leader Richard Armey of Texas taught economics for fifteen years at West Texas State University and elsewhere, and Senator Phil Gramm of Texas once was an economics professor at Texas A&M University.

All these former academics, as well as some other Republican leaders, unleashed a barrage of criticism of higher education at the beginning of the 104th Congress. The content and tone of the ideological siege harkened back to the earlier rhetoric of Bennett, Bloom, and D'Souza, among others (see chapter 3). This time, however, higher education's critics had even more political clout, and the criticisms took on new weight. Their comments about higher education went well beyond the need to cut the federal deficit through reductions in higher education appropriations. They emphasized religious and moral values which, they said, conflicted with the outspokenly secular values of most colleges and universities. They also opposed affirmative action and the multiculturalism practiced on most campuses.

In speaking to a business group in April, 1995, Gingrich characterized the academic world as the "nutty left" that was out of touch with the American public. Gingrich stated, "In the elite media, and in the academic world, in particular, you have two relatively tenured groups who are both obsolete" (*Ann Arbor News*, 27 April 1995). Gingrich used especially harsh language for higher education in his 1995 book, *To Renew America*. It contained a chapter devoted exclusively to what the author believed to be an impending collision between the interests of colleges and universities and those of the general public. He said this crisis resulted primarily from the fact that faculty members were "miseducating" America's children. The Speaker charged that faculty members were bent on "rejecting the culture of the people who pay their salaries" (219), and he suggested that donors inspect the curricular catalogues of colleges before giving their next donation so that their money would not be used "to subsidize bizarre and destructive visions of reality" (220). He said that colleges' annual fund-raising letters to alumni/ae said in effect, "Please give us money so we can hire someone who despises your occupation and will teach your children to have contempt for you" (221). Gingrich accused faculty of having "brain-washed" a generation of American students into denigrating Western culture. As evidence for this claim, Gingrich recounted the story of Yale University's return of a $20 million donation because, in the author's words, "the University could not get the faculty to agree to teach Western Civilization" (220).

Gingrich claimed that faculty ran college campuses for their own benefit, rather than for students or for society at large. He said the consequence was a higher education industry that was inefficient, sorely mismanaged, exceedingly costly, and unresponsive. He proposed a "thorough review of higher education by outsiders" in order to remedy the sad state of American higher education (221). He also suggested that because faculty are "simply employees," they should be subject to the same economic pressures faced by employees in other sectors of society. Finally, Gingrich urged the public to demand to be treated as consumers. In his view, "When the public begins to assert its rights as consumers of education, rather than as supplicants to an academic elite, we will begin to see rapid changes" (221).

Following the election, the Republicans showed their attitutde toward higher education in their selection of committee members. Unlike the Democrats, they chose higher education committee members who were not necessarily sympathetic to academia. A Democratic House staffer reflected on the composition of the committees and said, "After the November election, the Republican leaders assigned to this committee members who are fundamentally conservative in regard to both education and health and human services. Historically, the Democrats did just the opposite. Members self-selected themselves onto the committee and were always advocates."

Once on a higher education committee, many Republican members worked single-mindedly on budget reduction and, according to some association representatives, cared little about the substantive dimensions of the issues before them. A Big Six lobbyist said, "The members do not seem receptive to facts, much less to persuasion. Facts used to carry the day, but no longer. Current members of Congress, the Republicans that is, have preconceived notions and biases and believe that if the program is big or federal, there is a strike against it." Most higher education representatives agreed that their influence on Capitol Hill had diminished, and they understood all too well that they needed to do a better job of cultivating relations with the new Republicans. As one higher education advocate noted, "We are lucky that there isn't a Higher Ed Act reauthorization this year."

ISSUES FOR THE 104TH CONGRESS

As the 104th Congress convened, the Republican majority began consideration of a number of higher education policy issues. In addition to budget-cutting and the controversy over SPRE implementation (discussed in chapter 3), the following items affecting higher education were on the congressional agenda for 1995–96.

National service program

During the 1992 presidential campaign, Governor Bill Clinton spoke repeatedly of the need to increase access to higher education by providing loans to prospective college students. He particularly championed the development of a program to repay college costs through participation in a national service program. Clinton's proposal would allow prospective students to pay for four years of college in exchange for two years of community service and, he hoped, instill a service ethic in America's young people. This was one of the candidate's most popular campaign promises.

In the spring of 1993, soon after President Clinton took office, the associations sent a letter to the new administration outlining, among other things, the critical elements they thought should be included in a national service proposal. Most importantly, the association letter urged that such a proposal not come at the expense of the federal student loan programs or federal spending on research (*Higher Education and National Affairs*, 19 April 1993b).

With the exception of NASULGC, which lobbied on behalf of national service, the major higher education associations equivocated on the subject. At a critical juncture in July 1993, ACE, with the support of almost every major higher education association, sent a letter to Congress saying, "We are concerned in this budgetary environment that national service not be funded at the expense of already constrained support for education and research programs carried out by the nation's colleges and universities" (Waldman 1995, 197). Representative Bill Ford, a key committee chair who had come to favor national service strongly, demanded that ACE retract its letter. The result was a second ACE letter, this time clarifying the fact that the higher education community, on balance, supported national service legislation (Waldman 1995, 197). Student groups supported it especially enthusiastically.

In September 1993, President Clinton achieved a major victory with congressional passage of the National and Community Service Trust Act of 1993. Although a filibuster by Senate Republicans succeeded in reducing its duration and budget, the essence of it was that individuals who made a significant contribution to community service would receive education awards for up to two years to help them pay for postsecondary education. Participation could be either full-time or part-time, and consistent with the wish of the associations, the education awards could be used by students either before, during, or after college. The legislation provided that a newly established government agency called the Corporation for National and Community Service would either distribute the money directly to postsecondary institutions or, when participants wished to use their awards to pay off loans, directly to lenders.

The election of a Republican congressional majority in 1994 soon put President Clinton's early victory in serious jeopardy.[3] Immediately upon taking office, the Republicans began to work toward the enactment of a fiscal year 1995 rescission package. In December 1994, House Speaker Newt Gingrich announced that the GOP would seek more than $1 billion in spending cuts from the current fiscal year, and this figure, he said, could rise. In January 1995, Representative William Goodling (R-Pennsylvania) indicated that the House Economic and Educational Opportunities Committee he chaired would review all education programs and would move toward the reduction, consolidation, or elimination of some of them (*Higher Education and National Affairs*, 23 January 1995). In May, House and Senate conferees reported a sweeping $16 billion rescission package for fiscal year 1995 that targeted many of the president's favorite initiatives, including deep cuts in the national service program, then called

AmeriCorps. The rescission bill would cut nearly half of the funds already appropriated for it.

Congressional Democrats charged that the assault on the national service program was an effort to reverse President Clinton's accomplishment so that he could not benefit from it during the 1996 presidential campaign. The rescission bill quickly led to the first veto of the Clinton administration, with the president citing the threat to the national service program and deep cuts in other postsecondary education areas as the primary reasons for his veto. The Republican Congress, however, continued to threaten AmeriCorps' existence throughout 1995 including, for example, the passage of a 1996 fiscal year House appropriations package that provided for the total elimination of the program.

Direct lending

Leading up to the 104th Congress, one issue dominating discussions about the future of federal student aid programs concerned the means by which the federal student loan programs would be administered. In February 1993, President Clinton announced his intention to overhaul the federal loan system, the long-standing Federal Family Education Loan program (FFELP), under which federally guaranteed loans to college students were made by banks and private lenders, such as guarantee agencies. He planned to replace this program, which had existed since 1965, with a new initiative called the Federal Direct Student Loan program (FDSLP). Under the president's plan, called "direct lending," banks and other private sector lenders would be bypassed, and colleges and universities would make loans directly to their own students with money made available from the Department of Education. The administration promised that the proposal would simplify the process by which students receive loans, reduce the cost of student loans to borrowers, and provide borrowers with increased flexibility in repayment (Hartle, *Higher Education and National Affairs*, 17 May 1993).

Interest in direct lending was stimulated by the high costs of administering FFELP. In an analysis of the president's direct lending plan, ACE cited two reasons for the possibility of reduced costs under the proposed system. First, because the government could borrow money at a lower interest rate than private financial institutions, the cost of capital to make the direct loans would be much lower than under the existing system. Second, the federal government was also paying large subsidies to encourage private lenders to make loans to students. Elimination of these costs as part of a move toward direct lending, according to the Congressional Budget Office estimates, would save $4.3 billion over five years. The Clinton administration characterized these savings as the elimination of "excess profits to lenders" (*Higher Education and National Affairs*, 3 May 1993). The potential savings that could be made possible by direct lending seemed especially attractive because of the increasing preoccupation with federal deficit reduction.

President Clinton sent his direct lending proposal, called the "Student Loan Reform Act," to Congress in May 1993. It was opposed by the banks, the guarantee agencies, and the Student Loan Marketing Association (called "Sallie Mae"), all of which profited from the existing system. Though the higher education community was divided on its support for the proposal, the legislation contained many of the suggestions offered by the major associations. It proposed a gradual conversion to direct lending, so that all federal loans would be made directly, without the participation of banks or guarantee agencies. The proposal had support from many Democratic lawmakers, but substantial opposition emerged from Republicans. In August 1993, Congress passed the president's direct lending proposal into law, albeit with changes made in the loan conversion schedule. The legislation approved by Congress contained a compromise whereby 60 percent of new student loan volume would be made through the direct lending process by the end of the 1998–99 academic year.

The Republican control of Capitol Hill after November 1994 made the president's direct lending program one of the most hard-fought battles of the 104th Congress. Numerous Republican leaders vowed to curtail the program altogether. In January 1995, the Economic and Educational Opportunities Committee introduced legislation to cap the lending program at the 1995–96 level and limit participation in the program to those colleges and universities that had already been approved. A subsequent House bill provided for the program's complete elimination. Meanwhile, the Senate Labor and Human Resources Committee, chaired by Nancy Kassebaum (R-Kansas), proposed a more moderate plan to cap the program. Ultimately, in November 1995, House and Senate conferees agreed to a 10 percent cap on new loan volume for direct loan participation in 1996–97, but that cap was not acceptable to the Clinton administration.

Student financial aid

Another issue that dominated student financial aid discussions during the 104th Congress was the Contract with America's proposal to cut billions from the federal loan programs over a five-year period. The Clinton administration, which had disappointed higher education groups with its no-growth budgets of the 103rd Congress, emerged as a crucial advocate for student aid. An intense partisan battle ensued.

The Republican assault on federal student aid consumed all of 1995 as the House and Senate worked on their respective fiscal year 1996 budgets. In May, both the House and, to a lesser extent the Senate, passed resolutions with substantial cuts in student loans. ACE President Robert Atwell characterized the May 1995 budget resolutions as "a frontal assault on the foundations of federal student aid program that have served the nation well for 30 years" (*Higher Education and National Affairs*, 22 May 1995).

On June 13, 1995, President Clinton submitted his revised fiscal year 1996 ten-year budget which, in stark contrast to Republican budget plans, sought to balance the budget through reducing the size of federal government and cutting Medicare and Medicaid, while maintaining a strong commitment to postsecondary education spending. Specifically, the plan called for a steady and large increase in the Pell Grant program, including an increase in the maximum award. Additionally, the president sought to preserve the in-school interest exemption on student loans that House Republicans had sought to eliminate.

The Republican leadership ignored the president's plan and on June 23, 1995, a conference committee agreed to split the difference between the earlier House and Senate budget resolutions, calling for a $10.1 billion cut in federal student loan funding over seven years. This measure assumed an end to the in-school interest exemption for graduate and professional students who had taken out loans, elimination of the grace period after graduation for all student loans, and an increase in the origination fee paid by borrowers. Furthermore, the House and Senate fiscal year 1996 education appropriations bills contained significant cuts for the campus-based programs and State Student Incentive Grants.

Republican lawmakers also proposed three restrictions on student aid eligibility for legal immigrants: deportation for those who participated in student aid programs for more than twelve months, a co-signature requirement if they wanted to borrow money from student loan programs, and an eligibility or "deeming" provision which would make most of them lose eligibility for Pell Grants, campus-based programs, and Stafford Loans. Students, community and association leaders, and Democratic members of Congress all rallied on behalf of reversing the various cuts in student aid and opposing restrictions on legal immigrants' aid eligibility.

Affirmative action

Higher education had grown accustomed to decades of encouragement from the federal government to pursue affirmative action through employment, admissions and retention, and student financial aid. Various judicial rulings had modified some legislative mandates on affirmative action, and the Reagan administration had questioned them as well, but there was consistent congressional support for them. Though the 1990 Bush administration guidelines from the Department of Education had put minority-targeted scholarships in jeopardy, when President Clinton was elected his administration reversed those guidelines and again encouraged the use of such scholarships.

As the new Republican majority took their places in the 104th Congress, their leaders repeatedly questioned the legality of affirmative action measures. Accordingly, Senate Majority Leader Bob Dole (R-Kansas) introduced the Equal Opportunity Act of 1995 to curtail federal affirmative action programs, and similar legislation was proposed by Representative

Charles Canady (R-Florida) in the House. The bill eliminated consideration of gender, race, or ethnicity in federal employment, contracts, and other programs and prohibited numerical quotas and timetables. It specifically prohibited the use of affirmative action to remedy past or present discrimination.

In response, President Clinton conducted a review of federal affirmative action programs. In a speech on July 19, 1995, he gave a strong endorsement to such programs, saying that many of them had been effective and were still needed. His approach was summarized by his plan to "mend it, but don't end it." He proposed new approaches in some areas, but not in ones that would specifically affect higher education, such as employment, admissions, and student financial aid. However, congressional leaders disagreed with his approach.

Research and agency budgets

In regard to university-based research, congressional Republicans and the Clinton administration differed less on the size of appropriations than on the type. Congressional Republicans generally supported basic research, and President Clinton particularly favored applied research and industrial partnerships.

The president's 1996 fiscal year budget proposed a small increase for the National Institutes of Health (NIH), and the NIH received strong support from a number of Republican lawmakers throughout the budget process. Representative John Porter (R-Illinois), chair of the House Subcommittee on Labor, Health and Education, reportedly had an easy time securing his colleagues' support for NIH, saying, "All the costs of NIH over its 50-year history were paid for by the health-cost savings of just one of its projects, the development of the Salk vaccine" (Honan, *New York Times*, 19 June 1996). Even during the protracted negotiations over the 1996 fiscal year budget, Congress spared the NIH and in fact provided a sizable increase.

The National Science Foundation (NSF) did not fare quite as well, although it too enjoyed support from some Republican lawmakers. The president submitted a budget increase for NSF, but various appropriations proposals throughout 1995 contained substantial cuts in funding for the agency. The House Appropriations Committee in July 1995, for example, passed a spending bill with a reduction for NSF. The Republicans also advocated elimination of NSF's social and behavioral science division.

Because the Contract with America had proposed elimination of the National Endowment for the Arts (NEA) and the National Endowment for the Humanities (NEH), the congressional debate centered on how quickly the Endowments would be zero-budgeted. Many congressional Republicans held strong ideological convictions about abolishing these two federal agencies. The NEA was used as an example of the federal government's role in undermining family and religious values in American society, and the NEH became the Republicans' example of federal intrusion in curricular decisions and promotion of liberal bias among college students. The Republicans' hostility toward the two agencies was reflected in various spending bills introduced during the spring and summer of 1995. In July, the House approved a 39 percent funding cut for the NEA for fiscal year 1996 as part of a two-year phase-out of the agency, as well as a similar cut and a three-year phase-out for the NEH. Although the fiscal year 1996 spending measures introduced in the House were considerably more austere than those introduced in the Senate, committees in the latter chamber also proposed substantial spending cuts ranging from single digits to nearly 40 percent for both agencies.

The Contract with America originally championed complete elimination of the U. S. Department of Education as well. During the First Session of the 104th Congress, the Republicans discussed a variety of options, including folding Department of Education programs into the Department of Labor. The Clinton administration fought to preserve the Department of Education intact.

CONCLUSIONS

The 1994 election overturned four decades of Democratic control of Capitol Hill, bringing in a Republican Congress determined to balance the federal budget by making drastic reductions in domestic spending. President Clinton, who in 1994 had seemed to be such a disappointment to the higher education community, suddenly became its champion. By contrast, Republican leaders were vocal in their criticism of academe. On the stump and in publications, they sought to distance themselves from the academic community and contributed to the erosion in public confidence in it.

That set the stage for a bruising battle on the policy issues at the heart of federal support for colleges and universities. On all the major issues, there were sharp disagreements between the Republican majority and the Democratic administration, with the latter almost always favoring policies more attractive to colleges and universities. As the 104th Congress went to work, the skirmishes on higher education issues were fought in the public eye, with strong Republican pronouncements about restructuring higher education policy. Colleges and universities had been able to assume a low-key role in Washington for most of their history, and their lobbying had never been very aggressive. As the new Republican leadership drew its line in the sand, the community realized that its approach would have to change. Fortunately, as the next chapter demonstrates, the community has a well-organized structure, which gave it the capacity to collaborate on a new approach to lobbying.

Chapter Five

COORDINATION OF THE HIGHER EDUCATION COMMUNITY

"We try to keep the various parts of higher ed from killing each other in public."

An American Council on Educaton (ACE) lobbyist
commenting on its role

This chapter maps and describes the structure of the higher education community in Washington, especially the relationship between the American Council on Education (ACE) and the community's other Washington representatives.[1] Though ACE says it is higher education's umbrella association, recent studies of the internal dynamics of policy communities or domains (especially Heinz et al. 1993, Browne 1988, Laumann and Knoke 1987) have concluded that they no longer have single associations that coordinate their federal relations. For example, the most comprehensive book about policy domains is called *The Hollow Core,* specifically because the four communities it examines no longer have umbrella associations (which it calls "peak associations") to integrate and mediate the demands of various segments and serve as intermediaries among contending interests.[2] Is ACE actually serving as an umbrella or peak association for higher education at a time when other policy communities lack integrating associations of that nature? The question is one of importance because the structure of a policy community contributes substantially to the extent of the influence it wields (Kingdon 1984, 125; Heinz et al. 1993, 5, 22). In recent years, as the number of players in Washington policy communities has mushroomed, it has become more and more difficult to avoid fragmentation and friction within them (Heinz et al. 1993, 36–58, 254–61). The need for integrating associations has become greater at the same time that they have faded from the Washington scene.

Figure 5.1, a map of the higher education community, follows the example of Berry (1997), who mapped the telecommunications network. Berry noted that it evolved from one based on a service identity, with distinctive industry niche groups, to one characterized by alliances that cross different markets. This chapter explains that the higher education community has industry niche groups (such as private and public institutions, 2-year and 4-year, etc.), though the niche groups are not mutually exclusive and distinctive. The community also has a myriad of crosscutting alliances. The map shows that all players in the higher education community may

Figure 5.1
Map of the Washington Higher Education Community

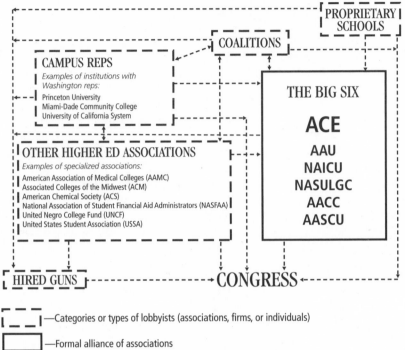

--- Categories or types of lobbyists (associations, firms, or individuals)

☐ — Formal alliance of associations

Big Six: The other five associations are all members of ACE.
Other Higher Ed Associations: Some are ACE members and some are not, and they devote varying amounts of attention to federal relations.
Campus Reps: A few institutions have Washington offices; the majority have a part-time, commuting representative, if any at all.
Coalitions: Coalitions can be of two types: standing, such as the Committee for Education Funding (CEF); or ad hoc, such as the Alliance to Save Student Aid.
Proprietary Schools: The majority of these for-profit schools have little interaction with the higher education community.
Hired Guns: These are either for-profit law, consulting, and lobbying firms or individuals who are hired for specific tasks by institutions and associations.

interact with all others, with the Big Six, especially ACE, playing a major role in facilitating interactions among the various members. While all players may contact all branches of government, Congress appears in this map because congressional lobbying is the subject of this book.

What follows is an examination of the structure and interactions of the higher education community's efforts toward federal advocacy. Included are ACE, the rest of the Big Six, other influential associations, campus representatives, "hired guns," and the proprietary schools. The community's structure is important, especially for the story of the 104th

Congress, because it facilitated coordination of higher education's decisions about policy positions and advocacy approaches.

THE AMERICAN COUNCIL ON EDUCATION (ACE)

ACE describes its principal public policy role as that of an "umbrella association." It is a massive enterprise—an independent, nonprofit association that now has 175 employees and a budget over $30 million. ACE's members include not only individual institutions of all types but also dozens of national and regional higher education associations. Like the individual institutions, the associations pay membership dues to join ACE.[3] ACE serves all accredited, degree-granting postsecondary institutions, and it tries to represent the entire higher education community. As one ACE official put it, "Everyone's got the benefit of ACE's services whether they are members or not." Many of its member institutions consider their membership in ACE "the price of good citizenship," a remark attributed by an ACE spokesperson to former Harvard President Derek Bok.

ACE's literature says that it brings together major constituent groups under a single umbrella and coordinates the interests of all segments of the higher education community into a single voice. The nonprofit nature of higher education institutions and most of their associations means that they have 501(c)(3) tax status and cannot devote full attention or substantial resources to federal relations activities, especially lobbying.[4] Nonetheless, they can determine their positions on policy and educate policy makers on their issues. Once they have reached a consensus view on a given policy issue, it is most often ACE's responsibility to publicize that view. The survey data show that the majority of college and university presidents agree that they "consider ACE to be the major voice for higher education in Washington." A review of the 1994 newspaper coverage of higher education issues indicates that the media publicize the voice of ACE more than those of the other associations (see table 5.1).

Table 5.1 **1994 Newspaper References to the Big Six Associations**

Association	Newspaper References
ACE	32
AASCU	21
NAICU	17
AAU	10
AACC	7
NASULGC	6

Note: Newspapers included are the *New York Times, Washington Post, Chicago Tribune,* and *USA Today.* This table reflects only one mention of an association per article, and since indexing is inexact, these numbers serve as approximations. The numbers may underestimate the amount of coverage the newspapers actually gave each association, but the relative amounts are probably accurate.

In order to coordinate higher education's positions, ACE organizes and hosts meetings that serve as a forum for discussion of policy issues. The president of the National Association of Independent Colleges and Universities (NAICU) described ACE's role by saying, "ACE does the call to order; it crafts the agenda; it sets the tone" (Warren interview, 1995). Whenever possible, ACE staff try to serve as brokers, framing the issues and then guiding discussion until an agreement can be reached. The meetings provide information sharing so that various constituencies can acquaint each other with their differing perspectives and try to find common ground.

The relative stature of the various associations is evident in the concentric circles of attendees at ACE's standing committee meetings (see figure 5.2). In the inner circle are the Big Six association presidents who meet

Figure 5.2
Attendees at ACE's Regular Meetings

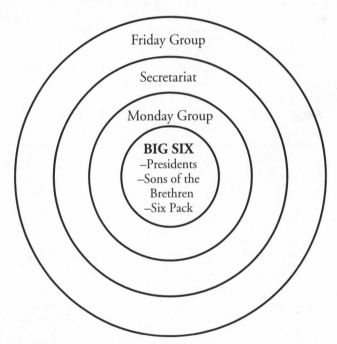

Friday Group

Secretariat

Monday Group

BIG SIX
–Presidents
–Sons of the Brethren
–Six Pack

Big Six Presidents: Leaders of the six major associations—*meets biweekly*
Sons of the Brethren: Government relations officers of the Big Six—*meets biweekly*
Six Pack: Public affairs officers of the Big Six—*meets biweekly*
Monday Group: Heads of 15 associations with greatest interest in federal lobbying—*meets every other Monday when Congress is in session*
Secretariat: Heads of Washington associations (about 40)—*meets first Tuesday of each month*
Friday Group: For information sharing; open to anyone in higher education—*meets every Friday afternoon*

biweekly, as do their federal relations officers (known as "Sons of the Brethren" or "SOBs"), and their public affairs officers ("the Six Pack"). Their staff also meet according to other areas of interest; for example, those who deal with the National Science Foundation (NSF) interact regularly.

In the next circle are the Big Six plus representatives of ten additional associations with broad policy interests, known collectively as the Monday Group.[5] It too has biweekly meetings when Congress is in session. The next concentric circle, the Higher Education Secretariat, is a little broader, and its monthly meetings include the heads of all those in the Monday Group, plus an additional two dozen associations, for a total membership of about forty. Additionally, there are regularly scheduled meetings for some specialized association personnel, such as tax experts.

In order to maximize information sharing in the Washington higher education policy community, ACE hosts weekly meetings at which everyone is welcome, including campus lobbyists and consultants. Representatives of industries dealing with higher education, such as the guarantee agencies, may also attend. The thirty-five or forty attendees at a typical Friday meeting go around the room reporting their latest news about policy issues. As an ACE official pointed out, "It serves our agenda to have as many people on board as possible."

While it may serve ACE's agenda to have many on board, it is clear that it also serves its agenda to maintain the dominance of the Big Six over higher education's policy decisions. In spite of the inclusive nature of the Friday meetings, the concentric circles imply that there are large numbers excluded from the inner circles, and some groups feel that ACE is indeed a gatekeeper: ACE decides who attends which meetings and who can help make key decisions. As one higher education representative said, "At the meetings, Terry Hartle [ACE's Vice President for Government Relations] reports to us. He does not ask us what we think. The Brethren have defined ACE's policy positions, and other ancillary groups do not have any say."

When there is uncertainty about policy preferences, it is ACE's inner circle that seeks closure on a position for the higher education community. Former President Atwell's "rules" for these meetings are illustrative of the nature of interaction in the Washington academic community: "No surprises; talk first and shoot second; higher education is best served in unity; avoid mutual vetoes" (Atwell interview, 1995). A Big Six official characterized ACE as the "U.N. blue helmets trying to keep the warring tribes away from each other." That is an important function. As the president of the American Association of State Colleges and Universities (AASCU) commented, "If ACE didn't exist, we would reinvent it." (Appleberry interview, 1995).

ACE attempts to find enough common ground on each issue so that a substantial portion of the higher education community can sign the same letter to policy makers. ACE typically drafts a letter and sends it to other associations, which can either sign it or try to persuade colleagues to make changes. When the letter is in final form, the ACE president's signature will be followed by "on behalf of," with a list of around forty other like-minded associations. Usually the co-signatories are members of the Secretariat, but sometimes there are additional signees, such as an individual university, or an association with broader interests like USPIRG (U. S. Public Interest Research Group, one of the offshoots of the Ralph Nader network).

While ACE considers itself a facilitator, it cannot deliver other groups' support or prevent others from breaking ranks. Each of its association members is sovereign, and ACE has no real power over them other than the power of persuasion. In other words, the higher education community is a loose confederation, as opposed to a federation, and ACE plays the role of convener and facilitator. The fact that ACE has been the landlord for so many of its member associations has been helpful in enhancing its role. ACE owns and controls the National Center for Higher Education at One Dupont Circle and consults its tenants about building management to ensure that they are "happy (or at least not terribly unhappy)" (American Council on Education 1996, 4). It is easier to communicate with a common location, and as an association leader said, "Having one building with all of us in it contributes substantially to the extent of consensus we develop." (All of the Big Six except the National Association of Independent Colleges and Universities [NAICU] were housed at One Dupont Circle through the end of 1996. The following year the Association of American Universities [AAU], the American Association of State Colleges and Universities [AASCU], and the National Association of State Universities and Land-Grant Colleges [NASULGC] decided to move out, leaving only the American Association of Community Colleges [AACC] under the ACE roof. The implications of their move are addressed in chapter 10.)

Those associations that disagree with ACE's positions and with the majority view on an issue are free to express their own opinions individually. The ACE-sponsored position, by definition, is the lowest common denominator. When in some instances it becomes clear that ACE's consensus position is basically "pablum" (i.e., so bland that there is nothing gained by expressing it), then groups that have stronger views are likely to express them individually. There are no sanctions for those who defy the consensus position, even when it is a member of the Big Six that does so. The president of NASULGC explained that ACE serves as a coordinator, but said, "I don't take my cues from ACE" (Magrath interview, 1995.) Similarly, the former president of AAU said, "ACE and AAU are parallel, and AAU is free standing. ACE is not its umbrella" (Pings interview, 1995). Other Big Six colleagues would agree because, as one commented, "We have a healthy respect for the differences among us." A university president who chaired ACE's board summed up ACE's role by saying, "ACE has no authority over the other associations. . . . It does not give permission."

The other purpose of the ACE meetings, especially those of the federal relations officers, besides information sharing and development of a consensual position, is coordination of advocacy. Since the period when Roger Heyns was ACE's president, there has been a "chosen instrument policy," meaning that "Whenever appropriate, one association will be responsible for discharging a particular function. . . . No one else will duplicate that function, and all will help the chosen instrument" (Heyns 1973, 94). It is usually the association with the most at stake that takes the lead on lobbying. For example, NAICU might be the chosen instrument on tax issues related to charitable contributions, since private giving was historically of greatest relative importance to the private institutions. There is also a division of labor for phone calls and other assignments. Usually, the larger associations deal with broader issues, and ACE itself usually focuses on financial aid, affirmative action, and other regulatory and legal matters.[6] ACE also finds itself dealing with some of the very specific micro-level issues that other groups cannot handle because, as an ACE staff member said, "No one has compunction about calling ACE for help."

Throughout its history ACE has been both a facilitator and an autonomous player; its dilemma is which role to play when. An inherent conflict exists between, on the one hand, representing its 1,400 individual college and university members and, on the other hand, serving as the coordinator for other higher education associations. The first role suggests that ACE be an advocate for member institutions; the second role dictates that ACE not take a position except when most of its member associations agree. According to some observers, ACE is more often an autonomous player now than it used to be;[7] for example, ACE now takes a stand occasionally without the support of AASCU or NAICU, which rarely used to be the case. Additionally, ACE has recently exercised independent leadership on accreditation, taking positions that were not endorsed by a significant segment of its membership. The dangers of autonomous positions are clear. One association leader said, "ACE gets shot at if it takes a stand when there is no consensus." More often than not, ACE still serves as a facilitator and coordinator, rather than as an autonomous player because, "When we do something autonomously, we have to be very careful because we can get into trouble."

In recent years, with the shrinking of resources, there has been more fragmentation of interests within the higher education community, so it has become more difficult to maintain a united front. AASCU and NAICU have been particularly prone to challenge ACE and go their own way from time to time. While it is to the advantage of all the associations to reach consensus as often as possible, the responsibility for bridging the policy and style differences of the five associations falls most often on ACE.

THE BIG SIX

Every higher education institution is encouraged to join ACE. Because of the associations' overlapping jurisdictions, colleges and universities may also join two of the other five major associations, each of which includes a niche group of institutions. The niche groups are not distinctive, however, because the membership of each of the five associations overlaps at least a little with two of the other four, plus ACE (see figure 5.3). For example, a private research university belonging to AAU is also likely to be a member of NAICU, while a public research university in AAU will also join NASULGC. NASULGC's membership overlaps substantially with that of AASCU. A public two-year college, when it is a component of a comprehensive university, might join both AACC and AASCU, and a private two-year college would be invited to join both AACC and NAICU. Finally, the members of all five of these associations, in order to foster the community's collaboration on federal relations, often join ACE as well. The association memberships of the 1,554 respondents to the 1994 survey demonstrate the overlapping institutional affiliations (see figure 5.4).

The Big Six encourage colleges and universities to join and pay dues to multiple groups. The 1994 survey and subsequent interview data show that some college and university presidents find this arrangement problematic and would like to see a reduction in the number of major associations. However, the majority of presidents commented that the overlapping associations serve them well. When the 1979 Cosand survey of college and university presidents asked whether a different national association structure

Figure 5.3
Overlap of Big Six Association Memberships

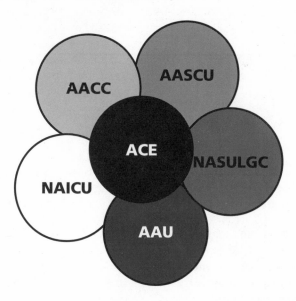

Note: The special characteristics of each college and university (i.e., public or private control, two- or four-year programs, research or land-grant mission) make it eligible to join at least two of the major associations, as well as ACE. Therefore, each Big Six association's membership overlaps to some extent with the membership of two other associations, plus ACE.

Figure 5.4
Association Memberships of Survey Respondents
(**N = 1554**)

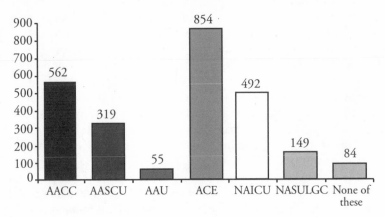

Note: Because many institutions hold multiple memberships, the total of all association memberships exceeds the survey population of 1554.

might be better, presidents said they did not want a change. Though no other organizational models were tested for the present study, the presidents' comments made clear that they have no strong interest in restructuring. As for the Big Six association staff, they often commented that the system is working because the multiple interests and identities of the associations reflect those of the member institutions. For example, one Big Six association leader said, "We have redundancy where we need it and complementarity when we need it." He went on to say that when he first arrived in Washington, he had wished for a clear organizational structure for the associations, but over time he had come to understand that the "messiness" of the division of labor was helpful in accomplishing the broad policy objectives of the higher education community.

While a handful of institutions choose to belong to more than two of the Big Six and a large minority of institutions belong to only one, the largest number of institutions are members of just two associations—ACE and one of the other five. Because of its efforts to serve the whole higher education community, and to represent every type of college and university, one would expect that ACE would not serve as the *primary association* on which institutions rely for the federal relations concerns of greatest importance to them. Surprisingly, more than one hundred survey respondents did identify ACE as their primary association. Nonetheless, the vast majority of institutions consider one of the other five associations to be their primary association (see figure 5.5). From the institutional responses, it is clear that they rely on their primary associations to handle their specialized policy concerns.

72

The largest of the Big Six associations, after ACE, is AACC, which has a membership of about 1,100. It includes more than 90 percent of all public community, technical, and junior colleges, as well as over one-third of the private two-year colleges. Its members come from every state (and most congressional districts), as well as affiliate members from several countries. AACC has traditionally been concerned with access and affordability for students, as well as vocational education and job training, school-to-work incentives, and articulation. It effectively collaborates with the American Association of Community College Trustees (AACCT) and has regularly scheduled joint meetings of their government relations personnel and an overlap of the two associations' boards, especially their legislative committees. The involvement of the trustees' association gives added weight to AACC, but both organizations regularly find they are considered a junior partner to the associations that represent the four-year institutions. (That is even true within the Department of Education, where very few staff have attended community colleges themselves and, therefore, may be more likely to call on ACE than on AACC for data and representation of the two-year institutions.) Furthermore, since the community colleges are so heavily dependent on state and local support, it is sometimes more difficult for AACC to mobilize its presidents for federal lobbying than it is for the other associations to mobilize their members.

The next largest of the Big Six is NAICU, with about nine hundred members, most of which are liberal arts colleges and comprehensive universities, but some of which are research universities and private two-year colleges. NAICU's membership also includes associations that coordinate and

Figure 5.5
Survey Respondents, by Primary Association
(N = 1430)

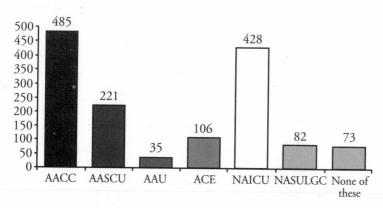

Source: 1994 Presidential Survey. The survey asked, "Which of the six major associations is most often your primary association for the federal relations of greatest importance to your institution?"

represent each state's private institutions at the state government level, as well as associations of private colleges based on religion and other common interests (such as the Women's College Coalition, for example). For these associations, NAICU serves as a confederation much the same way that ACE does for the five others in the Big Six.

NAICU's lobbying focuses especially on tax issues, on student aid for those in private institutions, and on regulatory issues, including accreditation. All these issues have a substantial effect on the budgets of independent colleges and universities. While NAICU serves as the voice of all private institutions, the research universities, most of which are NAICU members, tend to identify more closely with AAU. NAICU's liberal arts colleges are the ones most likely to consider the association's work critical to their federal relations, and the most selective of these have often taken leadership roles within NAICU in recent years.

AASCU represents more than four hundred master's (or comprehensive) state colleges and universities, with degree programs ranging from an associates degree to a doctorate; in addition, AASCU represents thirty state multi-campus systems of public higher education, such as the California State University system. It devotes much of its attention to student financial aid issues, and to other issues involving access to higher education; it also deals with state policy issues and the states' interface with federal policies.

NASULGC works closely with AASCU. The major interests of NASULGC's members (nearly two hundred in number) are agriculture, economic development, and technology transfer. NASULGC represents mostly public colleges and universities, especially land-grant institutions and the state flagship universities, as well as public higher education multi-campus systems, such as the University of Wisconsin system. Most of its members overlap with either AAU or AASCU. Since both AASCU and NASULGC were replacing their presidents at the same time early in the 1990s, there was some talk among their members about the possibility of combining the two associations into one. Instead, the two associations have chosen to work closely together and coordinate their activities. The extent of NASULGC collaboration with AASCU is apparent in the fact that the two sometimes communicate jointly with member institutions on letterhead that includes both of their names. In recent years, as agricultural issues have become less central to the roles of the member institutions, it has been more difficult for NASULGC to carve out its own special role in Washington.

The fifth and smallest of the Big Six is AAU, the group of about sixty major research universities, two of which are Canadian. Its membership was originally weighted toward private universities since research universities historically were more often independent institutions, but now there is an even split in AAU membership between publics and privates, with the board presidency alternating annually between the two. It used to be that private universities devoted more attention to Washington than publics did because the latter had to spend more time focusing on their state governments. Now, however, both publics and privates are fully engaged in federal relations. Universities have to be invited to join AAU, which makes it the only elite association of the Six. When asked why the AAU has no literature for prospective members, its president replied, "We have no literature because we have no prospective members" (Pings interview, 1995).[8]

While AAU members' principal issues are clearly research funding, science policy, health policy, and graduate education, their expectations for the association's federal relations role is more ambiguous. Unlike the other five associations, AAU assumes the role of convener more often than it serves as the voice of its member universities. All of the AAU institutions are members of other Big Six associations as well, and in any case, most of the research university presidents come to Washington quite frequently themselves. These presidents typically act as their own spokespersons, rather than expecting the president of AAU to represent their needs. The AAU institutions have their own federal relations personnel, and in many cases, their own Washington offices, so they do not have to rely on the major associations. In fact, one of the Washington lobbyists of an AAU institution expressed frustration that his staff did the major share of policy analysis for AAU and supplied it with data, rather than vice versa. Other types of institutions are more dependent on their associations for basic policy analysis.

Among the Big Six there is a lot of consultation and cooperation, as is apparent in the lengthy list of meetings hosted by ACE. The Big Six are often able to cooperate successfully because they agree on broad principles but work on different issues, issues that may be of interest to only one association. Nonetheless, there is tension and competition among these associations because their different constituencies are sometimes at odds with each other. Especially in regard to the priority they give various policy issues, the interests of public institutions sometimes conflict with those of private ones, four-year institutions sometimes conflict with two-year, research universities with liberal arts, urban institutions with rural, etc. (See chapter 7 regarding different institutional issues and approaches.)

In addition to policy differences, turf battles are another reason for the periodic conflicts among the Big Six. Each of the Six needs to claim credit for policy advocacy and achievements in order to justify its existence to its members. Although ACE's chosen instrument policy lets the association with the most at stake take the lead on a policy issue, it is not always clear who has the most at stake, and those with a lesser stake may still feel sufficient concern to want to be part of the action. A staff member in the Big Six lamented, "There is a lot of competition for the hearts and minds of our constituents, and for members of Congress. The degree of competition drives me crazy."

Personal relationships are also a factor, and rivalry among association staff sometimes lends tension to their interactions.[9] One of the public officials commented, "There is terrible in-fighting among the government relations people at One Dupont Circle. When I have meetings with them, half of the meeting is spent with them individually talking about the failures of the others." Similarly, one of the college presidents complained that "The associations spend all their time competing with each other instead of working together for the sake of higher education."

The competition is not just between associations but also between staff members because, for the most part, higher education lobbyists are people whose careers depend on their contacts and influence. Many higher education lobbyists come to their jobs with a Rolodex full of their contacts on the Hill and in the executive branch. The revolving door—with staff moving from government to interest groups and back again—exists in the higher education community, just as it does in other policy areas. In that respect, higher education is similar to other Washington policy communities (Heinz et al. 1993, 117; Walker 1991, 69; Schlozman and Tierney 1986, 287). For example, some of the current Big Six vice presidents for government relations came to their posts directly from higher education jobs in the federal government: ACE's Terry Hartle served on Senator Edward Kennedy's (D-Massachusetts) staff, NAICU's Sarah Flanagan was previously on Senator Pell's staff, and AASCU's Edward Elmendorf was assistant secretary for postsecondary education in the Department of Education.

During 1995–96 the associations were able to bridge the differences among types of institutions and thus present a united front in Washington to an extent that was unparalleled historically in the higher education community. Studies of other interest groups have shown that intense external conflicts typically lead to the development of stable coalitions within a policy community (e.g., Heinz et al. 1993, 324), and that has certainly been the case with higher education. With the arrival of the budget-cutting Republican Congress in 1995 and the perceived threat to federal higher education appropriations, the associations presented Capitol Hill with a consensus position whenever possible. In the view of one association leader, "Unity is strongest during periods of turmoil. It is harder to agree during periods of growth." Similarly, a college president commented, "The November election was a wake-up call that had a unifying effect on higher education."

ACE's role in coordinating higher education's voices was more critical during the 104th Congress, and the Big Six leaders recognized their dependence on ACE's consensus building function. Information from the interviews indicated that while tensions and differences still existed, the presidents of the Big Six (perhaps more than their staffs) were trying to be collegial and find common ground under ACE's umbrella. They recognized that their members believe they should be compromising and collaborating. According to an association board member, "There is little cat fighting among the associations now. One Dupont Circle has grown up. The associations rarely hurt each other. Atwell [ACE's former president] is good at keeping people under the tent. The new association leaders have been better at achieving consensus than the old ones were." However, in less stressful times it will probably be harder to maintain the collegiality that character-ized the interactions of the Big Six during the period of turmoil.

OTHER INFLUENTIAL ASSOCIATIONS

In addition to ACE and the other five major associations, many addi-tional groups represent higher education in Washington. Most of these more specialized associations are ACE members and work closely with One Dupont Circle; some are even located there. They vary in the extent of their federal relations activity, with some doing a lot and others doing little or nothing.[10] In response to questions about which organizations are especially active, the interviewees (i.e., association leaders, college and uni-versity presidents, and public officials) frequently mentioned many of the same associations.

The National Association of Student Financial Aid Administrators (NASFAA) is often mentioned because it has the largest institutional mem-bership base of any Washington higher education association and includes all types of postsecondary institutions, even proprietary schools. [11] Interviewees often noted the effectiveness of the National Council of Educational Opportunity Associations (NCEOA), which has usually suc-ceeded in protecting TRIO programs from budget cuts.[12] Additionally, they mentioned the United Negro College Fund (UNCF), which represents the private black colleges and is highly visible;[13] the National Association for Equal Opportunity in Higher Education (NAFEO), which represents the public black colleges; and the Association of Catholic Colleges and Universities (ACCU), which is one of the most effective of the several asso-ciations representing colleges on the basis of religious affiliation.

There are two student associations that observers consider influential, especially in regard to the 1995–96 lobbying on student aid. One is the National Association of Graduate and Professional Students (NAGPS), composed of graduate student unions and associations from hundreds of campuses. It does much of its organizing and mobilizing through electronic mail, and it is not headquartered in Washington. The U. S. Student Association (USSA) comprises state student associations and individual campuses and works most often on access to higher education.[14] Although it represents graduate students too, it sees itself primarily as representing undergraduates, including those in community colleges.

There is a large category of higher education associations representing faculty members in their fields of expertise, namely, the dozens of learned societies or disciplinary associations. Although most of these associations are also members of ACE, they have relatively little to do with it, rarely attend-ing its meetings or speaking up on policy issues. Most of them take policy stands less often than other Washington higher education associations, and the few that do engage in lobbying are mostly associations in the sciences.

An exception to this generalization is the Consortium of Social Science Associations (COSSA), which is a coalition of social science disciplinary associations and deals with a variety of policy issues. The American Association of University Professors (AAUP), while not a disciplinary association, also represents faculty interests, but its public policy concerns are restricted largely to issues involving academic freedom and faculty salaries.[15]

In addition to all these groups representing higher education specifically,[16] there are many other associations that include some percentage of higher education personnel. For example, the American Chemical Society and the American Physical Society, both of which are active on policy issues, are composed of chemists and physicists both within and outside of academe. Specialized associations representing biomedical research have been very active in recent years. Particularly prominent is the Association of American Medical Colleges (AAMC), whose members are medical schools, teaching hospitals, and other medical associations. It deals not only with medical education but also with research and patient care issues, usually working closely with other health-related associations both within higher education and outside it.[17]

There are a number of coalitions within the higher education community that handle specialized issues. Some of the groups are standing coalitions, such as the Coalition for National Science Funding (CNSF), which consists of science associations and others dealing with NSF. These standing coalitions usually have rotating leadership and no permanent staff. In addition, a variety of ad hoc coalitions spring up periodically to deal with crises on individual policy issues, and then fade when the issue has been resolved. They too lack paid staff, space, and other overhead expenses, so they have more flexibility than other types of associations. Two ad hoc associations, the Alliance to Save Student Aid and the Science Coalition, were particularly active and effective in the 104th Congress (see chapter 8).

There are also coalitions that bring higher education together with other policy communities, especially elementary and secondary education. One of them with individual institutional members is the Council for the Advancement and Support of Education (CASE), which focuses on tax issues, especially regarding charitable contributions.[18] Another association, the Committee for Education Funding (CEF), is a broad coalition of associations ranging from preschool to postsecondary. It provides the principal forum for discussion of issues between elementary/secondary and higher education representatives, and it strives to speak with a single voice in support of federal education funding.

The amount of interaction between ACE and these more specialized associations and coalitions varies. For example, ACE is one of the biggest associations in CEF, and CEF looks to ACE for information about higher education's positions. AAMC and the rest of the medical groups, on the other hand, have such specialized policy concerns that they have little to do with generic higher education issues, and their interaction with ACE is less frequent. Nonetheless, when these associations need help in building a consensus of higher education voices on Capitol Hill or in the executive branch, they typically come to ACE. Furthermore, many send representatives to ACE's Friday meetings where they too share information and learn from each other. Thus, ACE provides coordination for many interested associations and coalitions, yet there are many other specialized groups that make little use of ACE and consider its activities mostly irrelevant to their own concerns.

CAMPUS LOBBYISTS

In their study of other Washington policy domains, Heinz et al. wrote that many businesses and other institutions have found that federal policies affect them in distinctive ways, making it less likely that the services of the industry-wide associations will suffice. Therefore, many have decided to supplement those associations with representation of their own (1993, 30). That finding applies to higher education as well. Recently many colleges and universities have hired federal relations staff to deal with issues specific to their own institutions that the associations do not address. While there have been some federal relations personnel on the campuses for decades, along with a handful of Washington offices established in the 1970s, there has been a huge growth in the number of each in the last fifteen years.

The 1994 survey asked college and university presidents if their institutions have either a full-time or a part-time staff member in Washington, and 5 percent reported that they did. Specifically, 3 percent of the institutions said they have full-time staff, 3 percent have part-time staff, and 1 percent reported having both. The majority have had these Washington representatives for less than five years (see figure 5.6).

Figure 5.6
Duration of Washington Staff

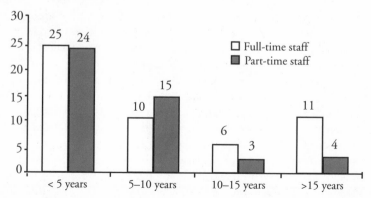

Source: 1994 Presidential Survey. The survey asked, "Approximately how long have you had a full-time or part-time staff member in Washington?" (Full-time *n* = 52, part-time *n* = 46; 12 respondents reported having both full-time and part-time staff.)

While the private universities were the first to become active in federal relations, virtually all of the AAU institutions have one or more full-time federal relations staff members now. There are more than a dozen universities with Washington offices, such as Harvard, MIT, Stanford, Michigan, and Vanderbilt. Some of those with Washington representatives and offices are "systems," such as the California State University system of twenty-one campuses, the University of California system of nine campuses, and the State University of New York system of sixty-four campuses. Because a Washington systems office has staff who represent several campuses, it often is perceived more like an association than a campus representative in terms of its clout. Campus offices in Washington cater to the needs of visiting faculty, administrators, students, and alumni/ae, often making contacts for them with public officials. These offices also handle requests from policy makers for information or even favors, such as football tickets.

In the last decade there has been a professionalization of higher education's federal relations. As one association vice president noted, "They are different from the old school, old faculty members who used to do federal relations for the universities." Most higher education lobbyists are people with public policy degrees, and many do not have much campus experience. They know how government works and are trying to make it work on behalf of the college or university they represent. As one member of Congress noted, "More of the lobbyists understand the political arena than understand higher education. Typically, associations and colleges hire people who understand one or the other, not both."

There are a few higher education representatives who are narrow specialists with expertise in one area of particular concern, but most representatives are broadly informed, taking back to their campuses a little information on a lot of topics. Most often the campus representatives lobby for appropriations for their institutions. Some representatives spend their time talking with executive branch program officers and following the *Federal Register* in order to keep track of all the federal grants competitions and other funding opportunities for their faculty, staff, and students. Other representatives try to obtain earmarked funds (as described in chapter 3), and the availability of these funds in the last fifteen years has increased the number of campus representatives in Washington.

Some association officials would prefer that campus lobbyists not come to Washington. One association official said they "muddy up the muddy stream." Another commented that the institutions with campus representatives are "getting ripped off, having to pay them to do a bunch of fluff" while the associations do the substantive work.

However, the majority of association staff are appreciative of the work done by campus representatives. If their presidents are coming to town, campus reps usually work with the associations on scheduling their lobbying and other activities, such as testimony before Congress, whereas institutions without Washington staff often rely on the associations to do it. Many campuses with Washington offices work closely with associations, especially on broad issues like student financial aid. Some campus representatives are part of the team when lobbying assignments are handed out. In recent years the coordination between the campus offices and the associations has improved. An association leader described campus lobbyists as "an extension" of his office, and another said, "We call on campus representatives and vice versa." As the SPRE story in chapter 3 showed, campus lobbyists may have an understanding of campus issues that the association lobbyists lack, so they make a useful contribution to decisions within the higher education community about positions on policies.

Sometimes campus representatives deal with issues the large associations are not addressing. A university president explained, "Our Washington office does different things from the associations. It deals with regional and state issues." A campus lobbyist commented, "The campus lobbyists are the workhorses for the associations, the foot soldiers. They do a lot of the strategizing." Speaking from the associations' perspective, the AASCU vice president for government relations described the relationship between AASCU and the campus representatives as mutually supportive: "Campus representatives double-team with AASCU on the broad interest issues. They complement each other. Major associations try to stay out of the way of the specialized representatives and associations when they are working on the interests of an individual institution" (Elmendorf interview, 1995).

HIRED GUNS

In addition to associations and campus representatives, there is one other regular set of Washington players in the higher education community, namely, the representatives of for-profit law firms, consulting firms, and lobbying firms, commonly referred to as "hired guns." These firms are very prevalent in Washington, and they are often staffed in large part by former federal employees from Capitol Hill or from the executive branch. The firms offer clients assistance with policy analysis and substantive expertise in the intricacies of specialized federal policy issues. The lawyers and policy analysts in these firms typically trade on their insider knowledge of the agency or congressional committee where they may once have been employed. In addition, of course, they trade on their personal relationships with the relevant federal employees, some of whom may once have been their co-workers or staff. Especially for those businesses, institutions, or groups without their own Washington representation, hired guns are important in offering assistance they cannot get elsewhere. However, even those who have their own representatives also find the specialized expertise and contacts of the hired guns very useful at times.

Hired guns are used by other policy communities, as well as by higher education, and to about the same extent; like other communities, higher education relies on its own associations much more than it relies on hired guns (Heinz et al. 1993, 67, 372). Heinz et al. describe two different types of hired guns: first, "heavyweights" who are "influence peddlers" with "political muscle" and special access, and second, "professional advocates" who do not have high visibility but have a thorough understanding of the technicalities of an issue (3–7). Colleges and universities hire the former primarily in their attempts to secure earmarked funds; they hire the latter for specialized expertise that their associations may not have.

The 1979 survey of the Washington higher education community (Cosand et al.) did not address the use of hired guns, probably because colleges and universities used them so infrequently when that study was done. The frequency of usage has increased over the last fifteen years, and survey data show that nearly one-fifth of the institutions now employ hired guns to deal with a special federal relations problem (see figure 5.7).

Figure 5.7
Use of Hired Guns
(*N* = 1554)

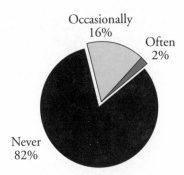

Source: 1994 Presidential Survey. The survey asked, "Has your institution employed a for-profit Washington law firm, consulting firm, or lobbying firm to deal with a special federal relations problem?"

The expanded use of hired guns may represent neither dissatisfaction with the federal relations work of the Big Six associations nor a challenge to them. Rather, it seems to represent the inherent limitations of general representation in an increasingly complex federal relations world. Hired guns rarely deal with broader higher education policy; they simply supplement the work of the Big Six and handle more narrow concerns. For example, hired guns may help a campus with acquisition of an FCC license for its radio station, or provide advice to an individual institution or even an association on a specific regulatory or tax issue. They also help guide institutions through the thicket of the federal grants competitions. One university president explained, "We were missing opportunities for research funding, so we hired a firm to tell us which research grants might be available so our faculty and staff could write more proposals." Since the 1994 election, associations and large universities sometimes have brought in Republican hired guns, to make up for the fact that their staffs consist mainly or entirely of Democrats. (This approach has not only been wise, it has also been obligatory. The new Republican congressional majority made a point of saying they preferred to meet with Republican lobbyists.)

Most often, colleges and universities have used hired guns to go after earmarked grants, and chapter 3 described Cassidy (formerly Cassidy and Associates), the best known of the lobbying firms employed for that purpose. In the 1980s and early 1990s, as the amount of earmarked funding for higher education increased, the number of hired guns grew accordingly. Many college and university presidents disapprove both of earmarked funds and of the hired guns who seek them. When asked if his university uses hired guns, one president retorted, "Almost never. I would wipe them off the face of the earth if I could. They get us into trouble, especially because of earmarking."

The major associations try to make the best of the fact that there are hired guns among the Washington representatives of higher education. For example, AACC's president said, "Colleges are using hired guns more now, so we try to work with them" (Pierce interview, 1995). In fact, however, there is very little interaction between the associations and the hired guns because it is usually the colleges and universities that hire them, rather than the associations. The hired guns do not ordinarily attend the Friday meetings of higher education representatives or any other regularly scheduled association meetings, so there is no real opportunity to inform them systematically about higher education's needs and concerns beyond what they have heard from their individual clients, or to learn from them about the Washington scene. The only ones who get the advantage of their expertise are their clients, and only on the issue for which they were hired. In terms of their daily interactions, the hired guns are not viewed as part of the Washington higher education community.

PROPRIETARY SCHOOLS

Thus far, this book has painted a picture of the higher education community as one characterized by relative harmony and cooperation. The associations try to work in a consensus fashion, the campus representatives are often partners of the association personnel, and most of the associations do not feel strong competition from the hired guns. The community engages in widespread information sharing and believes that a unified voice is the best approach.

That picture is not complete, however, because of the schism between colleges and universities on the one hand and proprietary schools on the other.[19] Colleges and universities are nonprofit institutions, while proprietary schools are for-profit enterprises resembling small businesses. There are 6,558 vocational institutions in the U.S. (*Chronicle of Higher Education*, 2 September 1996), most of which are proprietary schools. They differ from traditional postsecondary institutions, especially in the duration and breadth of their degree or certificate programs.

Since the passage of the 1972 Higher Education Act (HEA), Congress has chosen not to differentiate between proprietary schools and other postsecondary institutions in regard to provision of student financial aid, which is why a discussion of the higher education community must include mention of the proprietary schools. It was in 1972 that the student aid statutes began referring to *postsecondary* education, rather than *higher* education, in order to provide aid to proprietary school students.

Most of the larger proprietary schools, about 1,200, are represented in Washington by the Career College Association (CCA). Some observers believe that CCA is the "most sophisticated" lobbying group in postsecondary education (Waldman 1995, 138). CCA's lobbying tactics differ substantially from those of the rest of the higher education community, especially because CCA and some of its member institutions have political action committees (PACs). In keeping with their missions, their lobbying is more similar in approach to business and industry than it is to colleges and universities.

CCA's outlook often differs substantially from that of the other higher education associations. For example, most colleges and universities considered the 1992 creation of the SPREs a threat to their autonomy, an issue of major concern to them. CCA, on the other hand, welcomed Part H, the provision that would increase accountability, as long as it was applied equally to all of postsecondary education. In fact, CCA's former president said he had encouraged Congress to deal with the accountability issue, believing that protection from the "thieves and bandits" in postsecondary education was vital, and he continued to promote outcomes assessment and retention measures (Blair interview, 1995).

Although CCA is a member of the ACE Secretariat, CCA has not found ACE welcoming. Many CCA member institutions are not accredited by the regional accrediting associations and, therefore, are ineligible for ACE membership.[20] Furthermore, the other higher education associations, led by ACE, have tried to distance themselves from the proprietary schools on public policy issues. They worry about what one lobbyist called "the stench of fraud and abuse" the proprietary schools have brought to student financial aid. He went on to say, "Higher ed has had to fight lots of battles it would not otherwise have had." As a result, ACE and AASCU led the effort of the Big Six to try to make the proprietary schools ineligible for HEA Title IV student aid and also to move them jurisdictionally from the Department of Education to the Department of Labor. Additionally, ACE specifically disinvited CCA from participation in the Alliance to Save Student Aid (see chapter 8). All of this of course angered CCA's former president, who bemoaned the adversarial relationship CCA has with the rest of higher education and condemned the latter's "arrogance" (Blair interview, 1995). ACE has clearly chosen to keep the proprietary schools outside its umbrella.

CONCLUSIONS

At first glance it appears that much has changed in the higher education policy community in the last fifteen years. There are many more Washington representatives now, with new specialized associations and hired guns, and with more federal relations personnel from the campuses. The Big Six associations are cooperating more effectively than they used to, and the entire higher education community has more interaction, with broader coalitions and layers of coalitions. Like other communities, higher education may be described as "elastic and permeable" (Browne 1995, 205) because of the constant shifts in the number and nature of the players.

The community demonstrates remarkable stability and, in terms of organizational structure, looks just the way it always has. The Big Six are the same associations that dominated higher education lobbying fifteen years ago. The five associations other than ACE continue to serve specific types of institutions and represent their constituencies at Washington higher education meetings. There are many more higher education representatives now, which means the Big Six associations are no longer quite as unique and prominent as they once were. However, they still set lobbying strategies and tactics for the community, usually meeting together in a cartel-like fashion and excluding other associations from major decision making. In fact, one member of Congress characterized the Big Six as an "oligopoly."

The community's longstanding division of labor persists, with the Big Six dealing with broad policy issues and the specialized associations dealing with more narrow issues. The primary niche groups are those of control (i.e., private and public) and program (two-year, four-year, and research institutions), but there are also specialized niche groups involving service to specific student populations, such as demographic groups (e.g., historically black colleges), regional groups (e.g., Midwestern colleges), religious groups (e.g., Catholic colleges), and groups of students in professional programs (e.g., medicine and law). The niche groups are overlapping, as opposed to distinctive and mutually exclusive, and there are multiple alliances among associations as well as individuals. Most campus representatives handle campus-specific issues, as do most hired guns. The niche groups are characterized by cooperation, not by conflict or overt competition. Much of the cooperation in the higher education community is facilitated by structural factors, thanks to the role of ACE and the Big Six.

It is particularly striking that the role of ACE has remained the same in spite of the influx of many new Washington representatives. Just as was true fifteen years ago, and for decades before that, ACE is still considered to be responsible for the welfare of the whole community. It is the umbrella organization for its hundreds of sovereign association members, as well as for most of the rest of the higher education community. Although it may experience more frequent challenges, ACE still initiates many of the policy stands taken by the community, serving as the gatekeeper for key strategy meetings. Only the associations and coalitions dealing with specialized issues operate outside its purview, or with little involvement from it or the other five major associations. While they may have issue-specific differences, most college and university presidents regard ACE as the principal voice for higher education in Washington, and that view continues to be shared by the media.

Heinz et al. (1993) found in their study of communications networks and structures in four domains (agriculture, energy, labor, and health) that none of them has a hegemonic association that mediates and controls its federal relations. As William P. Browne points out, former hegemonic associations for these communities now limit their purview to a few issues on which they have some expertise, or they simply resort to playing a facilitation role, and doing consensus building on key issues (1995, 14–15).

ACE's role in higher education does not challenge these findings about the absence of hegemonic associations in Washington. There are limits to ACE's authority. As the association of associations, it convenes and cajoles, but it cannot impose its will on member associations. It is a confederation, not a federation, and rarely takes positions that are not endorsed by the other five of the Big Six. It tries to minimize internal conflicts, but as in the policy communities described by Heinz et al., individual colleges and universities, as well as the associations that represent them, "monitor policy issues themselves, develop more specialized interest coalitions, and pursue their own strategies" (1993, 375). The umbrella association has been supplemented by more specialized associations.

While ACE is not hegemonic, its role and the role of the Big Six more generally provide new insights into the structure and operation of Washington policy communities. All four of the domains examined by Heinz et al. have experienced a proliferation of representatives and a fragmentation of interests, just like higher education. Heinz and his colleagues concluded that, as a result, there are no longer single peak associations that integrate the demands of various segments and serve as the intermediary among contending interests.

These findings do not apply to higher education, for it has the Big Six, with five of these associations integrating the demands of specific types of colleges and universities, and with ACE acknowledged as the general intermediary. ACE has no competitors, and its agenda-setting, coordinating, and information-sharing functions enable it to play the role of an umbrella association quite effectively. That differentiates the higher education policy community from those studied by Heinz et al. and shows that its conclusions cannot be generalized to all other policy domains.

Size may be one reason why the findings of Heinz et al. do not pertain to the higher education policy community. Communities have fluid boundaries, with no clear delineation between their members and other players in the policy making process. Furthermore, the expansion in the type of issues

86

with which most communities deal has added to their elasticity (Browne 1995). Where one draws the community's boundaries may determine whether the principal association, if there is one, is truly an umbrella association; it is a question of the size and scope of a policy community. If one defines a community narrowly, to encompass only one industry, then a potential umbrella association has an easier role to play; if one defines a community broadly, umbrella associations have a more difficult role.

Each of the four domains examined by Heinz et al. (agriculture, energy, labor, and health) is comparable in scope to a Cabinet level department. The higher education community is not equivalent to these four because the jurisdiction of the U.S. Department of Education extends to elementary and secondary education and also includes the proprietary sector. ACE's umbrella provides only spotty coverage to proprietary schools, and it does not cover elementary and secondary education at all. Nonetheless, the higher education community is very broad and diverse in its composition. It includes both small, poor, public, two-year, rural colleges and huge, wealthy, private, urban universities, as well as everything in between. There are more than 3,600 colleges and universities and more than 200 associations representing them in the Washington, D.C., area alone. While the diversity of the community makes ACE's coordinating role difficult and its umbrella status unusual, the structural features of the domain have remained intact for decades, unchanged by the proliferation of Washington players.

This book began with a question about the effect of growth in the Washington higher education community; in the course of interviews, public officials were asked, "Does the fact that there are now more higher education representatives in Washington lead to greater success for higher education?" Most of these officials experienced the changes themselves. On the basis of their memory of the higher education community in the past and their perceptions of it now,[21] the vast majority of them answered that they do not believe its additional lobbyists make it more effective. A typical comment was, "The number of higher ed people doesn't make any difference. In fact, having too many individual institutional representatives has hurt the effectiveness of the associations. . . ." Some officials commented that, instead of quantity, the impact of lobbying is dependent on its quality: "Numbers help, but the quality and frequency of contact are the most important issues." One official said, "Multiple voices lead to less effectiveness, not more." A Department of Education official agreed, saying, "There are more players now, but they are no more effective. The environment has gotten tougher." Recent literature has questioned the value of so many Washington interest representatives (e.g., Salisbury 1990 and 1992; Browne 1988; Petracca 1992; Rauch 1994), and this book on the higher education community confirms the contention that more is not necessarily better. When it comes to keeping up with the interest group equivalent of the Joneses, strategy and tactics are more important than numbers.

Chapter Six

ORGANIZATIONAL MAINTENANCE IN THE BIG SIX ASSOCIATIONS

"Now that there is a common enemy, the associations have become more critical for us."
A college president after the 1994 election of the budget-cutting Congress

This chapter examines membership incentives, especially the role of federal relations, in the Big Six associations. The Big Six are a special breed of association, and there are several terms that can be used to characterize them. Most importantly, the Big Six are *institutional associations,* because their members are colleges and universities, not individuals. Jack L. Walker's study of various types of interest groups distinguishes between those in which the members are "autonomous individuals, whose decisions to join groups are all their own" or "organizational representatives, who join groups to represent an institution" (1991, 64). The members of the Big Six are clearly the latter, and it is the presidents of their member colleges and universities who serve as the organizational representatives.

The Big Six may also be called *occupational associations* because the presidents represent the institutions that employ them. The term *trade associations* applies to the Big Six as well. However, the Big Six differ from other trade associations in the common usage of the term since that term is most 'often applied to those in for-profit industries or businesses, as opposed to those in nonprofit professions like churches, hospitals, government agencies, and colleges or universities. Furthermore, trade associations are established principally for political advocacy even though many also provide other services. Higher education's Big Six lack the tax status necessary to make lobbying their principal activity.

Another term that applies to most occupational associations but that is not quite accurate for the Big Six is *professional association.* Many professional associations engage only rarely in politics (Schlozman and Tierney 1986, 41–44). For the Big Six as well, federal relations is only one of the services they offer their members; it is not their sole activity. Like the Big Six, professional associations are composed of people with the same kind of training and expertise. However, the members of professional associations are individuals who may not have the same employer. For example, chemists from many universities and many industries are members of the professional association called the American Chemical Society. The Big Six, on the other hand, represent only colleges and universities, not industries or other professions, and there is usually just one institutional representative per association (i.e., the president).

Because the Big Six are institutional associations with individual presidents as representatives, they provide both collective institutional benefits and also selective individual benefits. This chapter differentiates between the collective and selective costs and benefits of Big Six membership. It describes the role that federal relations plays as a membership benefit and its effect on members' satisfaction with their affiliations. It also explains the nature of members' involvement in association decision making and then describes the factors influencing their renewal decisions. In so doing, it adds to the literature on organizational maintenance in institutional associations and shows how they are similar to and different from other types of interest groups.

MEMBERSHIP COSTS AND BENEFITS

There is a rich body of literature on interest group membership incentives because, for established associations, maintenance of a strong membership base is the first prerequisite for self-preservation (Wilson 1973, 10). In order to survive, associations must provide incentives for new members and convince their current members to renew their affiliations.

Economist Mancur Olson (1965) contended that each interest group member undertakes a personal cost-benefit analysis before joining or renewing a membership commitment. The "exchange theory" of interest group membership, developed by Robert H. Salisbury (1969), took that idea one step further and conceptualized the relationship between the leaders and members of an interest group according to an economic model in which the interest group leaders *sell* benefits, and the prospective members *buy* those benefits for the price of affiliation with the group. According to this model, the benefits offered by the entrepreneurs and organizers of an interest group to customers and members must be of sufficient value to outweigh their costs of affiliation. Hansen defines costs as both dues and demands on members' time (1985, 82); Knoke specifies that costs also include effort and psychological engagement (1990, 226).

For individual college and university presidents, who are the organizational representatives for the Big Six, the most substantial membership cost may be their own time. There are multiple constituencies demanding presidents' attention: faculty, students, administrative staff, board members, alumni/ae and other donors, community representatives (including local government and business people), state policy makers, and others. Some presidents have a special interest in the work of the national associations, especially federal relations, but many do not. Nonetheless, as the organizational representatives for the Big Six associations, the presidents are expected to participate in some of the associations' work and, presumably, attend some of the meetings. This expectation is more important for smaller groups like AAU than for larger groups like ACE or AACC, which have more members to call upon.

For colleges and universities, as institutions, the most substantial cost of being a member of any of the six presidentially based higher education associations is simply the dollar cost of membership, which can range from a few hundred to many tens of thousands of dollars a year. (The 1995 dues structure of the Big Six is provided in note 7 of chapter 1.) In addition to Big Six dues, institutions are likely to pay dues to other higher education associations so that their employees can meet and learn from others who hold the same roles (e.g., chief financial officers or members of governing boards). Fees for all of these affiliations add up, costing colleges and universities large sums of money. One university president mentioned that his institution spends more than one million dollars on annual association dues (which include many more groups than the Big Six, of course). With this wide variety of associations, and with the financial constraints facing most colleges and universities, the costs of membership may seem especially onerous.

To defray the costs of membership, all interest groups offer a variety of incentives to attract members, and the amount of competition for members obviously influences decisions about which incentives to offer. Naturally, leaders feel more pressure to offer substantial benefits if they experience difficulty enrolling and retaining members (Walker 1991, 68). With the exception of AAU (which is an elite club of research universities and does not admit some institutions that are eager to join), none of the other major associations has tapped its full market share. Therefore, the Big Six work hard at attracting new college and university members and at retaining those who have previously joined. Institutional associations like the Big Six differ from other types of associations in their pool of prospective members. The number of institutions is limited, as are the funds they can spend on promoting association memberships. One gets the sense in interviews with the leaders of the Big Six associations that the size of their membership is a matter of constant concern to them.

If an organization offers a variety of membership incentives, it is more attractive to prospective members (Knoke 1990, 220). The promotional material of the Big Six associations shows that they offer an array of institutional and individual incentives, with ACE offering the largest number. Among the collective, institutional incentives provided by the Big Six are resource centers for data on their college and university constituency, and linkages with business, elementary/secondary education, and other sectors outside of higher education.

The leaders of the Big Six believe that, although their associations offer a variety of services, their federal relations work is a major incentive for membership. In that respect, the Big Six are like many other associations (Salisbury 1984, 69). Federal relations is an economic benefit for members because the associations help to improve the condition of member institutions through their lobbying. Whether the issue is an increase in appropriations or a decrease in regulations, substantial economic rewards can come from an association's influence on federal policy decisions. Even when associations have no particular influence, they can provide value to members by offering information about policy matters under consideration (Salisbury 1992).

College and university presidents consistently agree that the federal relations work of the Big Six is important, and many want the associations to emphasize it more than they do. In the 1979 survey of presidents (Cosand et al.), 80 percent of the presidents said they believed that the Big Six should give federal relations a higher priority. Given the increases in the Big Six government relations staff over the last decade, it is clear that they are emphasizing federal relations more than they did in the past. In 1994, when the presidents were asked whether their primary association "should give a higher or lower priority to federal relations," more than half said they are satisfied with the current prioritization of federal relations, which is a significant change from 1979. However, federal relations continues to be of particular concern to the presidents. In 1994, 47 percent said they want their primary associations to put a higher priority on it, and almost no one (fewer than one-half of one percent) thought that a lower priority would be preferable. In other words, members were nearly unanimous in their support for substantial emphasis on federal relations by the Big Six.

In the 1994 survey the presidents were also asked whether they thought that ACE, the umbrella association, "should give a higher priority to federal relations." There is a significant positive correlation between the preferred primary association priority and the preferred ACE priority.[1] That is, those who desire that the primary associations give considerable attention to federal relations are likely to have the same expectations of ACE. However, the presidents' preference for higher priority is much stronger with ACE than with their primary associations, as nearly half (46.6 percent) of the respondents reported a preference that ACE place a "somewhat higher" priority on federal relations and one-fifth (21.1 percent) preferred a "much higher" priority (figure 6.1). In other words, more than two-thirds of the presidents want ACE to emphasize federal relations more than it does. That finding corresponds to the conclusion reached by the *Report of the ACE Review Committee,* which was written in preparation for the search for a new ACE president in 1996. It said, "Virtually all of the interviewees named ACE's coordination and governmental relations roles as their highest priority for ACE" (American Council on Education 1996, 10).

Figure 6.1
Preferred Federal Relations Priority for Primary Association and for ACE

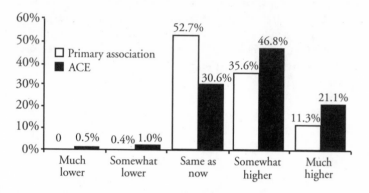

Source: 1994 Presidential Survey. The survey instructed, "Indicate the extent to which your primary association [or ACE] should give a higher or lower priority to federal relations." (Primary association *N* =1387, ACE *N* = 1311)

Another aspect of presidential satisfaction with the association's federal relations is the extent to which chief executives think their association is representing their own institutional interests. Data from the 1979 survey show that the associations were not perceived as representing all of their members adequately (Cosand et al. 1979). Interestingly, members' views on this topic have remained constant over the last fifteen years. The majority then and now think member institutions receive equal representation from the Big Six. As one president said, "I think they [the associations] do a reasonably good job of representing diverse institutions." Another commented, "I believe [my association] represents all appropriately, if not literally equally." Nonetheless, a sizable minority of presidents still disagree with that view (figure 6.2). In response to an open-ended survey question about what type of institution their primary association "mostly represents," 29 percent of the presidents took the time to write down the kind of institution they thought their primary association represents more than others. More than half (56 percent) of those responding indicated they believe the associations mostly represent the needs of "large" institutions, with one-quarter of respondents specifying "prestigious" institutions and one-fifth specifying "urban" ones. One president commented, "The glamour schools tend to be taken as the model and their plans/needs used to define [association] positions and philosophy."

While some members are not pleased with aspects of the representation they receive from the Big Six, presidents generally consider the federal relations work of these associations to be effective. They were asked in interviews about the policy achievements of the Big Six, and in many cases they referred to specific legislative or other accomplishments that they credited to an association's federal relations work. One president said, "Congress listens to higher education because of the associations." Another commented, "In general, they perform a useful function." A third wisely noted, "The effectiveness of the associations depends upon the issue."

On the whole, college presidents are very positive about the federal relations of their primary associations, with nearly every president (94 percent) saying they are effective (figure 6.3). A great majority think that ACE is effective as well, and more than two-thirds of the presidents consider all of higher education effective in regard to federal relations (figure 6.4). Although the presidents are generally positive about all aspects of their Washington representation, the degree of their endorsements vary. They consider their primary associations more effective than ACE, and both their primary association and ACE more effective than the Washington higher education community as a whole.

Figure 6.2
Primary Association Member Representation
(*N* = 1395)

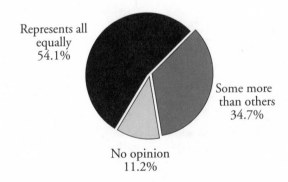

Represents all
equally
54.1%

Some more
than others
34.7%

No opinion
11.2%

Source: 1994 Presidential Survey. The survey asked, "In regard to federal relations, do you feel your primary association represents the needs of all its member institutions equally, or do you feel it represents some institutions more than others (e.g., rural or urban, large or small, public or private, etc.)?"

Since academics as a group frequently engage in critical analysis, it is surprising to find the overwhelmingly positive appraisal of the associations by college and university presidents. In the course of interviews, several Washington higher education lobbyists and policy analysts outside the Big Six expressed skepticism or cynicism about these survey results. One association

Figure 6.3
**Federal Relations Effectiveness: Assessment of Primary Association
(N = 1392)**

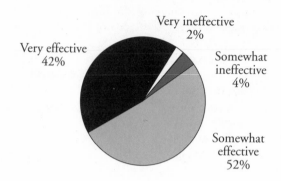

Very ineffective
2%

Very effective
42%

Somewhat
ineffective
4%

Somewhat
effective
52%

Source: 1994 Presidential Survey. The survey asked, "How effective is your primary association in regard to federal relations?"

Figure 6.4
Presidential Assessment of Federal Relations Effectiveness

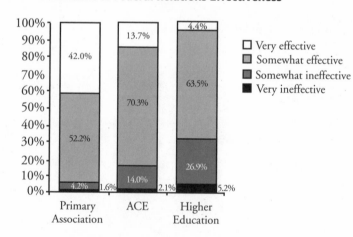

☐ Very effective
▨ Somewhat effective
▨ Somewhat ineffective
■ Very ineffective

Source: 1994 Presidential Survey. (Primary association N = 1392, ACE N = 1340, Higher education N = 1505)

staff member commented that the presidents' perception simply indicated that they are "inattentive" and more interested in personal benefits from association membership than they are in federal relations. Although there were few presidents who criticized the associations in their survey responses, those who did expressed their views strongly, saying, for example, "They [the associations] are part of the problem rather than part of the solution. They act like sheep and bow to federal dictates. . . ." Another said, "The intrusive and controlling nature of federal activities demonstrates the ineffectiveness of the associations." A third commented, "We [colleges and universities] are not exerting the influence we should," and a fourth said, "[The associations are] mostly irrelevant to our needs." Some presidents commented specifically on the large number of associations and their overlapping functions, saying for example, "Too many associations and too much fragmentation. They should streamline and merge and cut out duplication." Notwithstanding these few exceptions, the data clearly show that almost all the presidents think the Big Six are effective at federal relations.

Probably because most college and university presidents consider the Big Six effective, the majority of institutions rely solely on them for Washington representation. As one college president put it, "I'd hate to think where we'd be without our association." One-third of the institutions' presidents reported using the Big Six in conjunction with the services of other offices, groups, and firms (figure 6.5). A number of the presidents pointed out in interviews that their reliance on the Big Six saves them the cost of more expensive Washington representation, such as hired guns or their own federal relations staff, so they have a real incentive to use the Big Six. Of the presidents whose institutions have their own Washington staff, less than one-fifth said they have them because of insufficient help from the associations.

Figure 6.5
Reliance on Washington Representatives for Federal Relations
(_N_ = 1449)

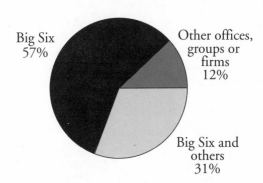

Big Six
57%

Other offices,
groups or
firms
12%

Big Six and
others
31%

Source: 1994 Presidential Survey. The survey asked, "To represent the interests of your institution in Washington, do you usually rely on one or more of the Big Six, on other offices, groups, and firms, or on both?"

In all types of interest groups, not just higher education associations, the importance of political benefits, as compared to other kinds of benefits, seems to vary for individual members. For some, political benefits are sufficient reason for membership; for others, political benefits must be supplemented by additional services (Hansen 1985). Competition among institutional associations often propels them to offer selective benefits to individual organizational representatives as well as collective benefits for the institution itself (Walker 1991, 91).

Association board members, who are the college and university presidents who were interviewed, expressed a strong interest in the selective political benefits they personally receive from the Big Six. They value the opportunity to testify before a congressional committee on higher education policy issues, or to have private time to talk with the president of the United States when he speaks at the association's annual meeting. Many of them noted the benefit they derived from the associations' provision of reliable, timely information, "They return my phone calls and provide me with information when I need it." Some presidents said that, for them, the federal relations work of the Big Six was a time saver. For example, one president said, "I let the Washington associations worry about federal relations because I have to spend most of my time on state relations."

The associations also provide other kinds of incentives for the presidents that are more selective and individual, like conferences and training programs for professional development, publications, and a forum for discussion of academic and other higher education issues. Most presidents value these benefits as career advancement opportunities. Information is a common selective benefit offered to association members (Berry 1977), and the Big Six try to provide a great deal of reliable information in a timely manner. In interviews, college and university presidents commented on the value to them personally of the selective benefits they receive from the Big Six, including information and an early warning system about Washington politics.

An early article on organizational incentive systems categorized the types of benefits an interest group may offer to attract and retain members. It described *material* or economic incentives, *solidary* or social incentives, and *purposive* or political incentives (Clark and Wilson 1961, 134–35). One would not expect social benefits to be the motivating factor in an institutional decision to join an association (Walker 1991, 87). Nonetheless, the social interactions of organizational representatives within their institutional association may gradually become an important reason for them to want to retain their affiliation, as is true of other kinds of interest groups as well (Rothenberg 1992, 116). In an institutional association the value to organizational representatives of camaraderie within the profession as a selective individual membership incentive may grow over time.

College and university presidents clearly value the social benefits that the Big Six provide. In interviews they mentioned the satisfaction of networking and sharing information with peers at association gatherings. They talked about their need for "camaraderie" and "mutual support" in this "lonely role." A large number said they especially value what they learn from their colleagues at association conferences and informal gatherings. For example, one president said that the association meetings let her find out "how tall I am and how we fit into the broader scheme of higher education." The presidents reported that social benefits are equally or more important to them personally than the federal relations benefits to their institutions of association membership.

The literature says that during periods when a group's public policy gains are threatened, political benefits take on more significance for members and prospective members than they do at other times (Truman 1951; Berry 1997, 70). Members then feel a greater need for associations that will provide them with effective representation (Hansen 1985, 93; Walker 1991, 92), and they may be less concerned about other types of member benefits than they are ordinarily. The costs of membership seem less onerous, and members are willing to pay more dues and devote more time to participation on behalf of the association in order to protect the benefits they value. The more endangered the benefits may be, the more easily the members may be activated to join and participate (Chong 1991, 88).

Not surprisingly, the importance to college and university presidents of the federal relations work of the Big Six associations seemed to increase after the November 1994 election. When the new Republican congressional majority began reviewing domestic discretionary spending to look for ways to cut federal appropriations, higher education programs were prominent on their lists. The interviews with college and university presidents in the spring of 1995 showed that, after the election, the members were relying on the federal relations activities of their associations more than ever.

Institutional and individual interests differ, so there are different cost-benefit calculations regarding association membership (Salisbury 1984; Walker 1991, 66). It was clear from the interviews with college presidents that most of them view federal relations as only one of the major benefits provided by their primary association, and in most cases they said it was not their number one reason for joining.[2] However, during the 104th Congress, the political benefits of Big Six membership took on new significance for the presidents.

MEMBER PARTICIPATION

While there has been little written about membership participation in institutional associations, a substantial body of literature can be found on membership participation in other types of interest groups. A democratic model is the standard against which interest groups are typically judged; the aura of a democratic structure provides respectability and legitimacy (Truman 1951). Consequently, most groups strive to demonstrate "a formal veneer of democracy" (Rothenberg 1992, 259) that makes the members feel their voices are heard and lets the staff operate with some information about member preferences. An additional advantage of this veneer, even if it is truly superficial in nature, is that it lets the group leaders tell policy makers that they speak for the membership as a whole. Policy makers are more likely to pay attention to association leaders who say that their positions and preferences reflect member views (Kingdon 1984, 55).

For most organizations the reality of the governance system is very different from a representative democracy. Many studies have shown that organizations tend to be governed in a manner that precludes significant participation on the part of members. In 1915, Robert Michels wrote *Political Parties*, the book in which he noted that the democratic goals of the West European Socialist parties were in sharp contrast to the oligarchic internal organizational structures of those parties. Citing his famous "iron law of oligarchy," Michels concluded that all organizations have the same tendency toward a nondemocratic, rigid hierarchy, with the leadership assuming responsibility for group decision making and policy positions.

Although Michels was describing political parties, his conclusions also apply to many interest groups. For example, Jeffrey M. Berry's (1977) study of public interest groups found that an oligarchic organizational pattern was clearly the norm. As Michels noted, the reason for the prevalence of an oligarchic governing system is its efficiency. The leaders have greater knowledge about the issues under consideration and more expertise in regard to the organization's core activities. Because they are relatively few in number, they can make decisions in a more timely manner. Furthermore, the members of an organization may show little interest in the decision making process and, in fact, may refuse to devote time to absorbing relevant information (Cook 1983) and then resist decision making when the leaders ask for their guidance. Some of the members may have joined the organization specifically because they do not want to make decisions themselves and prefer to rely on the expertise of the group's leadership.

As long as the leaders carry out the will of the membership, the symbols of democracy seem to suffice, whether or not that democracy operates in fact. Rothenberg's description of Common Cause provides a good example of the way that a member-based organization actually operates. The activist members' views have special authority, and they typically do the agenda-setting for the organization, sometimes based on the leaders' proposals. The rank and file members, whose information and interest level are lower, nonetheless retain the right to veto the major policy decisions and to maintain the status quo. The leaders themselves orchestrate the whole process and implement the policy decisions that are made by the activists and ratified by the rank and file. In the course of implementation, the leaders emphasize certain issues, craft tangible objectives, and determine the means necessary to achieve the desired ends (Rothenberg 1992, 187). This division of labor works well.

Like other membership-based interest groups, the Big Six seem to operate on the model of a representative democracy. That model is most likely to take hold in an association if certain conditions are met. Those conditions include the opportunity for periodic turnover in leadership; well-informed, sophisticated members who participate in committees and policy decisions; and general agreement between leaders and followers about collective goals (Knoke 1990, 14). All of these conditions apply to the Big Six.

In the Big Six associations there is a general expectation that institutional members will make the key policy decisions, that every member's voice will carry equal weight, and that the leadership will be elected by the institutional representatives, i.e., the presidents (Bloland 1985, 4). In fact, however, most of the Big Six associations operate like Rothenberg's (1992) description of Common Cause: that is, the activists and association leaders do agenda-setting in conjunction with the activist college and university presidents, the rank and file member presidents approve key decisions, and the association leaders do the implementation and exercise other discretionary authority, especially in regard to use of resources. In these associations, as in others, rank and file member presidents can be effective at exercising their prerogative to veto key policy decisions only if they are relatively well-informed. Association leaders make decisions about how they will structure their communications and the resources they will use for communication purposes.

The Rothenberg description of the rank and file's right to exercise a veto applies to the members of the Big Six. As one association leader put it, "We try to have consensus among members to the extent possible before taking a stand. We are always more successful when there is consensus." The association personnel went to great lengths to explain that they are not "runaway staff" and that their associations try to avoid taking stands on issues on which there is significant disagreement among members. However, before members can take a stand, they have to be informed, so the Big Six association leaders use a variety of methods to inform and involve members in federal relations work. Most of the presidents cited the association's annual membership meeting as a time when federal relations was discussed and association positions were explained and debated. They also mentioned special workshops on federal issues that were held at other times of the year, as well as communications such as newsletters, e-mail, and faxes, some of which come in the form of "action alerts."

It behooves association leaders to spend time and resources communicating with their rank and file members to keep them as informed as possible. If members become detached, they feel less sense of involvement with the organization and, ultimately, less commitment to membership (Knoke 1990, 167–68). Not surprisingly, therefore, when Schlozman and Tierney conducted interviews with 175 Washington representatives of politically active associations, they found that 42 percent of them considered their communications with members to be as important as their communications with public officials (1986, 143–44).

In the Big Six there seems to be little distinction between being informed and being consulted. When they send information to a college president about a public policy issue, no matter how routine, the leaders expect to hear opinions from members about the policy stand they prefer. Many of the association communications with members say that the association "proposes to do the following. . . ," knowing that members will respond if they disagree with the proposal. College presidents are not reticent, and when they receive notice that their association is considering, or taking, a position with which they disagree, they pick up the phone and call the association president to complain. As one president explained it, "This is a two-way street." Most of the association staff referred to frequent phone calls with member presidents, as if the dissenting calls came in on a regular basis, and several of the association personnel described angry letters and calls from member presidents, especially to the association chief executives and government relations officers. When asked about how members express their dissent with a policy position, one of them said, "I get phone calls at 11:00 at night calling me an SOB."

The Big Six almost never do systematic member surveys. NAICU is an exception to this rule since it now conducts frequent member surveys on different policy issues; for example, it recently finished one on accreditation. AASCU also has an elaborate system for tapping into member sentiment on policy priorities. It has a college president in every state who serves as the communications link between the state's member institutions and the national association staff. In addition, the government affairs people at AASCU develop a policy booklet each year, listing the issues on which the organization will work, and the stands it plans to take. The draft policy booklet goes to all members for their concurrence before being put in final form, and the AASCU leaders believe that, once the booklet is finalized, they understand most of their members' views and do not have to go back to them with frequent policy-related questions. The policy stands taken by AASCU in its booklet are mostly general in tone, such as support for appropriations increases for various programs.

Interest group leaders usually consider organizational maintenance as they make decisions about which members' views to give special attention. Members' views are rarely given equal weight. Those members who typically get special consideration are the activists and the major contributors, especially those who might leave if their views are not heard (Rothenberg

1992, 188, 260, 264). Activists often have joined an organization because of the opportunity for participation (Wilson 1973, 236). Activists tend to be more knowledgeable about group issues than nonactivists (Cook 1983, 12), so their involvement in key decisions is more useful than would be that of the rank and file who know less about the association's issues. Using the exchange theory, one can say that, for activists, extra opportunities for participation, and extra clout in decision making are selective incentives given as compensation for the costs of the extra effort the activists expend on the association's behalf.

In the Big Six, the activists who contribute more than other members and whose views carry more weight are the member presidents who serve on the association boards. The boards articulate members' views for the association leaders and have primary responsibility for agenda-setting, although some of the associations also have commissions and ad hoc advisory groups with special responsibility for federal relations, to supplement and inform board decision making. The board elections are the time when the democratic trappings of the Big Six are most in evidence. Most of them have a nominating committee made up of some of the current board members, and the general membership then vote on the slate presented by the nominating committee.

Board members said in the course of interviews that association leaders make sure they are well informed on federal policy issues, and they have the opportunity to get the attention of the leaders and highlight their own concerns. As one president said, "My membership [in the association] is especially important to me now that I am the board chair and can help set the agenda." According to the college and university presidents, there often is considerable board discussion and opportunity for dissent on federal policy issues. Many said the association leaders listen carefully to their views, trying to reach a consensus and take the stand agreeable to the largest number of association members.

The leaders of the Big Six associations rely on their boards to make key decisions because, with the exception of AAU (where the membership is small enough to be able to gather, debate, and choose policy positions as a group), the other associations are too large for general discussions. Therefore, the association leaders use board members both formally and informally to sound out reactions to policy options. As one association president put it, "If our poll shows an absence of consensus, I take the matter to the board." Another association president described his decision making process on federal policy issues as consisting of phone calls to key board members. Many of the associations take polls on policy issues by sending e-mail or telephone questions to their board members before taking a stand. The board member with the most influence is usually the board chair, and if there is an executive committee for the board, its members get special attention.

Naturally, the association personnel do not always and cannot always accede to the wishes of their board members on every federal policy issue. Two comments by top association staff were particularly striking as an indication that they retain the final decision making authority. One said, "Sometimes we change positions in response to phone calls and letters, but rarely." Another said, "Sometimes there is nothing the members can do to convince me I'm wrong about a policy position."

Nonetheless, the college and university presidents who serve on association boards, in the course of interviews, never referred to sharp disagreements with association leaders. In fact, they generally commented positively about the extent to which they were able to put items on the board agenda and influence debate. They did, however, discuss the differing views of the institutional members on various issues, and the need, as board members, to lobby other members to promote their own positions. One of them responded to a question about whether the college presidents' comments affect the policy decisions of the association by saying, "Members get out of the associations what they put into them. Membership is not a passive role. It is not a passive relationship." If members disagree with the direction in which the association is headed on a policy issue, it is incumbent upon them to lobby their board colleagues and change the association's plans. The presidents mentioned a variety of instances in which the boards had succeeded in changing the association's direction on federal policy issues, and the general sentiment from the presidents on the boards was that they felt well-consulted on federal relations issues.

In the course of the interviews, the association leaders were asked whether they listen more carefully to some member institution presidents' views than to others, as the literature indicates happens in most associations (e.g., Rothenberg 1992, 188, 260, 264). They all responded positively, with one leader saying, "I *hear* some institutions' views more than others, but I *listen* to all equally." Association leaders presented a variety of factors that lead them to hear some member presidents more than others. They tend to listen to presidents of large and/or urban institutions that will be significantly affected by pending legislation or policy issues. Because public institutions have been more concerned with state issues, associations have tended to be particularly attentive to private institutions, which have traditionally focused more on federal issues. That is changing, however, as presidents of public institutions increasingly are as concerned about federal issues as their private school colleagues.

Some institutions' presidents receive special attention from the associations because of their special characteristics. For example, long-serving presidents are more often heard than new ones, as are presidents who are especially knowledgeable about federal relations. Some presidents may be called upon because of professional expertise in a specific subject area. Other presidents are heard because of their locations; they may be in a region that is relevant to specific policy decisions, or perhaps they are constituents in the district or state of an important member of Congress.

An attractive political benefit of association affiliation is the opportunity to make a public demonstration of commitment to particular policy goals (Cook 1984, 425). Having made that public demonstration of support, members can devote their own time to politics, and the associations will facilitate their work. On the other hand, if the members do not want to spend their own time on political activity, they can rely on associations to do the work for them.

After the 1994 election, association personnel reported that institutional presidents' political activity had increased. In response to the interview question "Are college/university presidents any more active in federal relations than they used to be?" association staff commented that they have seen a major change in the presidents' degree of responsiveness. "Their level of interest, their attention span, their turnout are all greater now." According to one association leader, the same phenomenon occurred when Ronald Reagan was first elected president in 1980. There was a similar activism among college and university presidents in response to threats to higher education funding at that time. Thus, in times of threat as well as other times, there appears to be no particular difference between membership involvement in institutional associations, as compared to other member-based interest groups.

MEMBERSHIP RENEWAL

It would seem that those members who are satisfied with the benefits they receive from an interest group would renew their affiliation, and those who are dissatisfied would terminate it. The surprise occurs when those who are dissatisfied choose to remain nonetheless. Even for public interest groups, a substantial portion of the membership sometimes makes that unexpected choice (Cook 1984, 421).

At the most basic level, one can test the satisfaction of members of an institutional association in the same way one would test member satisfaction in other associations, that is, by looking at membership rates. A review of the 1995 membership data for the Big Six, in comparison with the 1980 data, shows an overall increase in the number of institutional members of each of the associations (see table 6.1).

However, none of the Big Six is able to tap all eligible members, and the number of colleges and universities has grown during this fifteen-year period. Therefore, these data do not show the extent to which current member institutions resign and new ones join. The information about movement in and out of the associations can be understood better by reviewing college presidents' answers to survey questions. Nearly half (46 percent) of the presidents said their institutions have joined one of the Big

Table 6.1
Institutional Members of Big Six Associations, 1980 and 1995

	1980	1995
AACC	947	1100
AASCU	330	410
AAU	50	60[a]
ACE	1700	1772
NAICU	683	840
NASULGC	135	182

Source: The associations provided this information about numbers of institutional members. In some cases, 1980 figures are approximate.
[a] Two of the AAU members are Canadian universities.

Six in the last ten to fifteen years, but only a small number (17 percent) said they had discontinued membership. It is clear, therefore, that the six associations have had more members join than resign, and overall they have grown substantially during the last fifteen years.

The 1994 survey asked presidents if they were committed to continuing their membership in their primary association. Nearly everyone (91 percent) responded positively, just as they did in 1979 (87 percent). While their commitment to continuation was higher for primary associations than for ACE, a very large majority (78 percent) expressed their commitment to continuation of ACE membership as well (see figure 6.6). Members also voiced their satisfaction with the associations in other ways. When asked if the institutional benefits of membership in their primary association were worth the present costs, a very large majority (82 percent) responded positively. Since a similar proportion (79 percent) gave a positive response in 1979 (Cosand et al.), it is evident that there has been no change in the overall satisfaction rate for institutional members of the Big Six over this fifteen-year period. In 1994 a substantial number of members (64 percent) felt that the institutional benefits of membership in ACE were also worth the costs (see figure 6.7), indicating that the satisfaction rate with the Big Six is consistently high. As one president said, "The associations are a terrific value." Another noted, "They're doing well with a difficult task. If they tried to expand operations to do better, and significantly elevated fees, they would lose members."

Federal relations has an effect on continuation decisions; there is a significant relationship between presidents' views of their primary associations' federal relations efforts and their decision to renew their affiliation. Almost all of those presidents who thought their primary association was effective in regard to federal relations also said their institutions planned to continue their memberships. The rating of federal relations effectiveness is

Figure 6.6
Commitment to Continued Membership in Primary Association and ACE

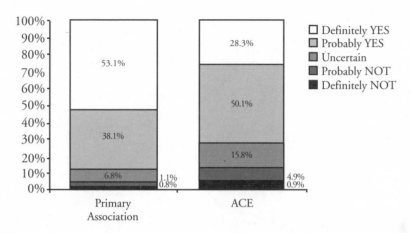

Source: 1994 Presidential Survey. The survey asked, "Are you committed to continuing your membership in your primary association/ACE?" (Primary Association *N* = 1395, ACE *N* = 884)

Figure 6.7
Membership Benefits: Worth vs. Costs

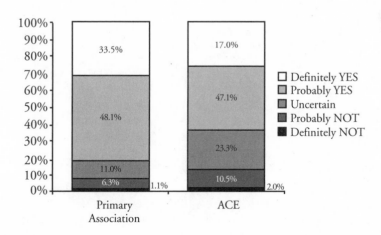

Source: 1994 Presidential Survey. The survey asked, "Are the institutional benefits of membership in your primary association/ACE worth the present costs?" (Primary Association *N* = 1396, ACE *N* = 904)

significantly related to the perception that benefits of the association are worth the costs,[3] which is quite highly correlated with the reported commitment to continued membership in the association.[4] All of the presidents who thought the benefits were worth the costs also said their institutions planned to renew their memberships.

Member institutions whose presidents believe that their primary association does not place appropriately high priority on federal relations are less likely to continue membership. The preference for federal relations priority has a significant negative correlation with the evaluation of primary association effectiveness regarding federal relations.[5] That is, those who prefer a higher federal relations priority are significantly less likely to rate their primary association as highly effective. Federal relations priority also has a smaller, but still significant, negative correlation with the assessment that association benefits are worth the costs.[6] These findings suggest, then, that those who feel that federal relations does not have enough priority in their primary associations also are more likely to question the value they receive from the associations.

When specifically asked about their reasons for withdrawing from a Big Six association, presidents of the majority of institutions that have actually withdrawn said they did so for budgetary reasons. A president said, for example, "Our very tight budget created reductions; this was one." Very few said they withdrew because the association inadequately represented their own institutional interests (see figure 6.8). Several presidents volunteered the information that after withdrawing, their institutions hurried to rejoin as soon as they could afford it. A typical comment was "We rejoined AASCU when finances improved."

Figure 6.8
Reasons for Leaving Association
(N = 251)

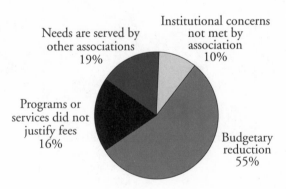

Needs are served by other associations 19%

Institutional concerns not met by association 10%

Programs or services did not justify fees 16%

Budgetary reduction 55%

Source: 1994 Presidential Survey. The survey asked, "Why did you withdraw from one of the six major associations?"

There is a difference between members' commitment to institutional associations, as opposed to other types of membership interest groups. According to Robert H. Salisbury, the strength of membership ties in non-institutional groups is more fragile, while commitment to membership in institutional associations is more "durable and persistent" (1984, 75). That finding holds true for the Big Six. Three-fifths of those presidents who thought the benefits of their primary association were not worth the costs, or were uncertain, planned to renew their membership anyway. Furthermore, a large majority of those who did not think their primary association was effective also planned to continue their memberships (see figure 6.9), and an overwhelming majority of those who said their primary association represented some institutions more than others also planned to continue (see figure 6.10). It is clear that, for most institutions, nonrenewal is not a possibility except when they simply cannot afford the association dues.

There are a number of reasons why dissatisfied members would choose to leave an association. One of them concerns the "free rider" option, which Mancur Olson (1965) described when he wrote about the irrationality of most people's affiliations with interest groups. He said that, with certain exceptions, the impact of one more member on the effectiveness of most large interest groups is negligible and does not compensate for the

Figure 6.9

Relationship between Views of Effectiveness and Commitment to Continued Membership in Primary Association
(N = 1381)

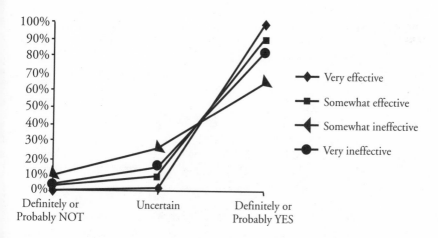

Source: 1994 Presidential Survey. The survey asked, "How effective is your primary association in regard to federal relations?" and "Are you committed to continuing your membership in your primary association/ACE?"

Figure 6.10
**Relationship between Views on Member Representation and Commitment to Continued Primary Association Membership
(N = 1229)**

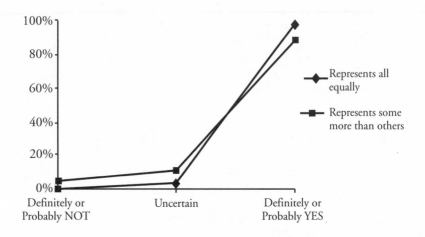

Source: 1994 Presidential Survey. The survey asked, "In regard to federal relations, do you feel your primary association represents the needs of all its member institutions equally, or do you feel it represents some institutions more than others (e.g., rural or urban, large or small, public or private, etc.)?" and "Are you committed to continuing your membership in your primary association/ACE?"

monetary and other costs to the individual who decides to join. Olson contended that rational people typically decide to join an interest group only if the group can provide tangible benefits to its members that are "separate and selective" in nature "so that those who do not join the organization . . . can be treated differently from those who do" (51). If an interest group fails to provide such benefits to its members, Olson maintained that it is more rational for them to be free riders—contributing nothing but enjoying the benefits provided by others' contributions to the interest groups' policy achievements. The free rider option is particularly attractive for potential members of groups that are engaged in public policy advocacy because the benefits of policy changes typically accrue to members and non-members alike.

While the prospect of being a free rider may be appealing in an economic, cost-benefit sense, there are powerful disincentives that serve to keep some dissatisfied members in a group they would otherwise choose to leave. The disincentives are unrelated to public policy outcomes. For example, Dennis Chong (1991) discusses the impact of reputational concerns on an individual's choice between being a free rider or engaging in collective action to achieve a public good. He points out that there will be future selective benefits for those who participate because their comrades will reward them for cooperation in the work of the association by involving them in subsequent activities. Similarly, there may be ostracism and damage to the reputations of those who do not participate in group projects, so social pressures make nonparticipation a less appealing choice (31–72). Since one's peers may view withdrawal from an association as the neglect of civic duty, "sense of guilt" may be the catalyst that prompts certain types of people to participate in the association (Wilson 1973, 26). Some members' support for specific goals may make them "consider the free-rider option morally reprehensible" (Moe 1980b, 118).

The disincentives to being a free rider figure strongly for dissatisfied members of the Big Six. ACE and AACC are large enough so that it is unlikely that an institution's absence from their membership rolls would be obvious, but colleagues would be more likely to notice withdrawal from other Big Six associations.[7] The comments of association board members showed that many of them want to avoid the stigma of withdrawal and think it is important to fulfill their institution's responsibility to the higher education community through membership in these major associations. They assume that their counterparts who lead other colleges and universities share the same views. For example, one president said, "Peer pressure keeps institutions in the associations. Presidents have a vision of collective responsibility on behalf of all of higher education in spite of their individual financial constraints. If colleagues know that a president is considering withdrawing from an association, they can appeal to that president to support the common good, and their argument is usually successful." Another president said, "Institutions have a civic responsibility to remain in the association. Everyone benefits, and if you don't pay, you are freeloading. It would look bad to peers not to be in the association."

Other presidents said that when institutions do not pay their dues, they are "getting a free ride" and they incur the displeasure of those who do pay their dues. They said it is "not fair" for an institution not to pay its dues, and they commented that it is a simple matter of "decorum and good taste" to be a member. Thus, presidents find unattractive the option of being a free rider in their institutional association for the same reasons that individuals typically worry about being free riders in other types of interest groups. Furthermore, given that budgetary constraints are the major reason for college and university withdrawal decisions, presidents may feel that nonparticipation would be a public sign of institutional fragility.[8]

An additional reason for remaining in an association that does not serve one's needs may be the absence of alternative groups. One or more interest groups may exercise a monopoly within a given policy community (Hirschman 1970). Therefore, the structure of a policy community determines which membership options are available. Some members remain not out of loyalty, but rather because the associations are the only source of desirable professional benefits for individual organizational representatives, such as participation in key conferences or engagement in the profession's collective federal relations efforts. When there is an occupational group that offers vital professional benefits, those benefits serve the objective of organizational maintenance for the group in the same way that personal material benefits typically do in other types of groups (Walker 1991, 93).

Although the Big Six are hardly a monopoly, they dominate higher education policy advocacy. They deal with every type of public policy concern, while the other associations deal with specialized policy issues. Most of the Big Six have a larger, more comprehensive membership base than those of most other associations. Furthermore, although the Big Six include other associations in many of their gatherings, they exclude them, and even their own satellite groups, from the highest level strategy sessions.

Because the higher education community relies so heavily on the Big Six for federal relations, there are not many feasible alternatives for dissatisfied association members. It was obvious from the interviews with college presidents, even those who are dissatisfied, that they consider these associations to be the most important higher education players in Washington. When asked about other spokespersons for higher education, the presidents often mentioned a name or two from one of the more specialized associations in Washington, or from various prominent universities, but they usually mentioned different names. There was no agreement on who the principal spokespersons for higher education are beyond the leaders of the Big Six. Some interviewees expressed nostalgia for the days when a Hesburgh (former president of the University of Notre Dame) or a Hutchins (former president of the University of Chicago) would express views on public policy issues of national concern and command national attention and respect. However, as Rita Bornstein (1995) notes, "It is the rare president who has the time, expertise, and independence to establish a leadership role in national affairs. The college presidency has become more complex in scope and administrative responsibility and is circumscribed by the pressures of multiple, fractious constituencies. When presidents do speak out, their voices often are lost in the cacophony of opinions, informed and uninformed, that swirl around public issues" (57). The result is that Big Six leaders, especially the president of ACE, now serve as the major voices for academe on public policy issues, which makes membership in the Big Six associations more attractive.

It is difficult to create competing entities to challenge or supplement the Big Six, and there seem to have been very few instances in which any group of college presidents has tried to do so. That did happen in 1976 when NAICU was formed by members of the Association of American Colleges. (The latter group still exists under the name Association of American Colleges and Universities, but it is no longer engaged in federal relations.) That precedent has made the Big Six cautious whenever satellite groups have sprung up within them.

Yet there are a number of satellite groups within the Big Six now. The Annapolis Group, currently consisting of ninety selective liberal arts colleges, considered splitting off from NAICU when it formed a few years ago. That alternative is no longer likely, and in fact, NAICU's President Warren now attends meetings of the Annapolis Group. NAICU has other affiliated satellite groups, such as the Council of Independent Colleges (CIC). Similarly, in the 1980s some of the AASCU and NASULGC members formed their own association, the Coalition of Urban and Metropolitan Universities. The Coalition serves large research and doctoral universities located in large cities, as well as doctoral and master's institutions located in suburbs or small cities. Most of the impetus for its creation came from the latter group because those institutions felt they were not sufficiently visible within the national associations. The Coalition has about fifty members. More than twenty of them, the large, urban, research universities, also belong to a more informal group called the Urban 13, which has a twenty-five-year history and meets irregularly (Holland letter, 1996). For NAICU, AASCU, and NASULGC, as well as the other Big Six associations, there are delicate issues involved in determining how best to deal with satellite organizations, which often meet in conjunction with a Big Six annual meeting, and how much support to provide them.

While the threat of defection or "exit" is the most obvious way that members can try to reshape an organization, it is not the only way to express dissatisfaction. Albert Hirschman (1970) showed that a major option is "voice," that is, protests to the association's leadership or more general protests designed to improve the association. He noted that "the voice option is the only way in which dissatisfied customers or members can react whenever the exit option is unavailable" (33). Because members of highly political organizations tend to be loyal and are likely to remain in a organization regardless of the incentives and services offered (Knoke 1990, 134–35), voice may be particularly important for them, especially for activist members. Activists are usually the members of an association who are the most loyal and satisfied (Cook 1984, 423), which makes sense from an exchange theory standpoint. They make more sacrifices of their time and effort on behalf of an association, and they get more out of it. If they become dissatisfied with their association, they have more to lose by abandoning their membership. The voice option appeals to them because they are the ones who are most likely to think they can make a difference when they speak up. They worry that the association would go from bad to worse were they to leave. The most loyal members may stay longest and exercise voice most loudly because they consider exit a poor alternative. As Hirschman noted, "As a rule, loyalty holds exit at bay and activates voice" (78).

Dissatisfied institutional presidents in the Big Six do express their concerns. The board members reported that when dissent occurs, it typically centers around specific issues, with similar types of members banding together. In 1979 a women's slate of ACE board candidates was submitted to the membership in addition to the slate proposed by the nominating committee, but now there are a large number of women on the ACE board, and no alternative slates have been proposed since that first one. One way the Big Six have accommodated and co-opted dissidents has been through the formation of councils or other internal subgroups representing specific elements of the membership. For example, most of the associations now have a special subgroup for women and another for minorities (or minority-serving institutions), and some have one for rural institutions, or for liberal arts missions, or for any additional special interests that need a voice. These subgroups can lobby the association leaders to make sure their particular public policy concerns are not overlooked.

If individual presidents become sufficiently dissatisfied with their associations, they have the option of avoiding the association meetings, or, as institutional members, they can send one of their vice presidents in their place. This is not a hard choice for college presidents because their time is at a premium, and any excuse to free up some of it may seem appealing. To try to head off a decline in presidential involvement, however, some of the Big Six associations have "presidents only" sessions at their major meetings.[9] Not surprisingly, the Big Six associations pay close attention to the number and stature of their meeting attendees.

While alternative organizations have not been formed to challenge the Big Six in the last twenty years, and while there have been unusually few public displays of membership dissatisfaction, that does not mean that the boards have been uniformly pleased with association leadership. Between 1991 and 1993 there was a turnover in the leadership of five of the six associations (all but ACE), and a few institutional presidents said that some of these leadership changes were quietly encouraged by board members. Most of the new leaders seem to have good support from their members, and some are perceived to be doing especially well with federal relations. Institutional presidents made it clear in interviews that they consider association leaders' effectiveness in federal relations to be a major determinant of success in their job performance. Accordingly some of the Big Six leaders noted that they spend the bulk of their own time on public policy issues, and federal relations dominates their own agendas.

CONCLUSIONS

This examination of the Big Six demonstrates the similarities and differences between institutional associations and other kinds of membership groups. The exchange theory which applies to individual membership groups operates on two levels in institutional associations; there are both individual and institutional costs and also individual and institutional benefits. Organizational representatives to the Big Six, i.e., college and university presidents, differentiate between collective benefits they believe their institutions need and selective individual benefits they personally value, but associations must take care to provide both in order to attract and retain members. Many presidents consider their own social and professional benefits the principal membership incentive. That is true even when federal relations ostensibly is the primary reason for institutional membership.

The democratic model of association governance serves as the standard for an institutional association, just as it does in an individual membership association, and there are the same variations in levels of member participation. If the associations provide attractive individual benefits, the presidents are more likely to play an active role, which is important because the level of presidential participation is an indicator of an association's health. Associations encourage presidents to attend meetings and serve on their boards, and most of the association boards play an active role in policy decisions. However, overall these institutional associations have no more than the "formal veneer of democracy" (Rothenberg 1992) which typifies individual membership associations.

Just as in individual membership associations, institutions feel that their associations sometimes place less emphasis on their needs than on those of other members. Even when the association is tilting toward other types of institutions, however, it is clearly awkward for institutions to resign their memberships. Budgetary pressures are the only reason for withdrawal that most presidents consider legitimate. There is a social cost to withdrawal, and peer pressure minimizes the number of free riders. As a result, it appears from the higher education experience to be more unlikely for an institution to resign from an institutional association than for an individual to resign from other kinds of interest groups. Thus, institutional memberships in institutional associations seem to have a special durability.

The leaders of the Big Six believe their federal relations activities are a major membership incentive. College and university presidents agree, and there is a strong relationship between commitment to membership renewal and presidents' views of the effectiveness of their associations' federal relations work. While few institutions resign from Big Six associations for reasons other than financial exigency, it is the presidents who think there is inadequate priority for federal relations who are most likely to resign. The presidents' satisfaction with the Big Six was evident from survey results showing that nearly every one of them consider the associations' federal relations to be effective. Of the small number of presidents whose institutions have chosen to hire their own Washington staff, very few attributed their choice to insufficient help from the associations.

Even before the Republican revolution of November 1994, nearly half the presidents wanted the associations to emphasize federal relations more than they did. After the start of 1995, the threat to higher education funding prompted presidents to say that the associations' federal relations took on new significance for them as a membership incentive. In that time of turmoil, the federal relations role became the associations' major role. The Big Six had a strong mandate from the presidents to take the lead on higher education advocacy in Washington; it was clear that most colleges and universities were relying on them to serve as their principal advocates. Nonetheless, different types of institutions had different views, as demonstrated in the next chapter.

Chapter Seven

FEDERAL RELATIONS DIFFERENCES AMONG INSTITUTIONS

co-authored with Gertrude L. Arnold

"When the higher education community is fractured, law-makers do whatever they choose."
A lobbyist for a specialized association

The Washington higher education community is characterized by diversity. It represents many types of colleges and universities, each of which has different policy priorities and different approaches to advocacy. The variety of types of institutions makes it especially difficult for the community to present a united front in Washington and speak with a single voice. This chapter concerns the differences among types of institutions in regard to Washington representation. It describes the priority the leaders of the higher education community put on consensus building, and the reactions of public officials. Then it details the similarities and differences among various kinds of institutions in regard to federal relations strategies. The institutions are categorized according to the Carnegie classification system, as described in chapter 1, with special emphasis on comparisons of public and private, two-year and four-year, and research and other institutions. The findings support the conventional wisdom that control (i.e., public or private) is the principal factor differentiating institutions, but they also show where and to what extent size and Carnegie classification play a role in shaping institutional attitudes and practices.

VALUE OF CONSENSUS

In his discussion of the causes of cooperation and specialization among the interest group members of a policy community, Jack L. Walker (1991, 68–73) notes that occupational groups are more likely than citizen groups to specialize and focus on specific policy niches. It is natural for occupational groups to coordinate activity with the rest of their policy community; they understand it is counterproductive to devote their energies to conflict with similar groups (Browne 1988, 39; Walker 1991, 73). Associations avoid conflict and try to coordinate their activities without overlapping

(Browne 1990; Heinz et al. 1993; Gray and Lowery 1996a and 1996b). A division of labor usually emerges within the policy community, and an umbrella association can shape and oversee that division of labor. This is easiest to achieve if each association occupies a relatively narrow policy niche, or to use the Gray and Lowery (1996b) term, if each association has a narrow "niche width."

There are at least two factors that can undermine cohesion and consensus within a community. The most obvious is policy conflict; a particular public policy decision may affect different members of a community in different ways. Therefore, the community may be split in its views about which issues merit the use of resources, and which positions to take. It may even be the case that a win for one part of the community in the competition for scarce resources constitutes a loss for another part.

A second factor that can undermine cohesion within a policy community is a high degree of competition for members among its component interest groups. Because most associations are dependent on member dues, they try to take credit for policy successes to enhance their reputations, make better appeals to new members, and more effectively retain their current ones (Heinz et al. 1993, 384; Stewart 1975, 125). Sometimes associations engage in "public posturing" (Browne 1988, 193) and take credit for advocacy efforts in which they actually participated very little. In addition, they may compete for leadership of the community's policy initiatives. Both situations create fissures that make coordination more difficult. While institutional associations seem to feel fewer competitive pressures than membership groups do, they may have more pressures than they acknowledge (Gray and Lowery 1996a, 104).

Cohesion is an important resource in convincing government officials to listen as a community tries to influence policy agendas, decisions, and implementation (Kingdon 1984, 55; Laumann and Knoke 1987, 387), and the united front must include all authoritative decision-makers (Hamilton 1977, 223–29). John Kingdon points out that "if a group is plagued by internal dissension, its effectiveness is seriously impaired" (1984, 55). A balkanized policy community lets policy makers follow their own policy preferences, so it is not unusual for them to craft legislation that divides a community, to play one part of it off against the rest.

In their study of four policy domains, John P. Heinz and his colleagues (1993) describe their component parts. Each domain, or community, has several niche groups, or networks of actors who most often share the same specific policy concerns within the community. While the niche groups are relatively stable, they join shifting internal and external coalitions as policy issues change. The coalitions are never fixed because, as Edward O. Laumann and David Knoke pointed out, corporate actors, like individuals, have multiple identities and interests, some of which may be divergent and contradictory. They noted that there is no single "master identity" for insti-

116

tutions, just as there is none for individuals (1987, 396). David B. Truman (1951) wrote that individuals' multiple memberships (or potential memberships) in interest groups serve as the political balance wheel in the United States. In the same way, the fact that a single institution has multiple identities and association affiliations helps to mitigate the conflicts that might occur within a policy community.

While the policy community studies of special significance in the social science literature have concerned occupationally based groups, especially profit-sector groups, higher education is different because it is part of the nonprofit sector. Higher education has its own niche groups, or internal networks, just as other communities do. Scholars who have written about higher education policy have usually commented on the divergence of views among types of institutions and the ways that public policies affect different kinds of institutions differently (e.g., Gardner, Atwell, and Berdahl 1985; Breneman and Finn 1978; Finn 1978; Bloland 1985; Stewart 1975). They have also noted that rifts between niche groups, especially public vs. privates, have intermittently threatened to disrupt higher education's efforts at unity.

The ethos of consensus building

Higher education, like every policy community, has a special culture and self-image that shape its federal relations structure and lobbying strategies in unique ways. The higher education community puts a particularly high priority on consensus building. That priority is evident in the well-defined association structure that overlays and integrates the community through a system of overlapping memberships across networks. Higher education's principal niche groups constitute the organizing principles for five of the major associations, each of which attracts and articulates the positions of two niche groups, as demonstrated in figures 1.1 and 5.4. The multiple identities of individual institutions are reflected in their choice of association memberships (see chapter 5), and their overlapping memberships facilitate the development of consensus positions.

A principal reason that the community devotes so much energy to development of consensus is that association leaders believe it to be an effective approach to advocacy. One association head affirmed that "it is critical to come in with one voice" when lobbying. A higher education lobbyist connected loss of consensus with political vulnerability, explaining, "The Hill . . . tries to divide us, but when we do not have consensus, we are 'self-canceling.'"

Many campus presidents understand the importance of achieving policy consensus. In response to a question on the 1994 survey about the associations' current presentation of issues to federal policy makers, the presidents were evenly divided about whether the associations typically arrive at a compromise and present a unified higher education position, or

117

acknowledge the conflicting interests and present different positions. For example, one president commented, "They [the associations] seem to be working more cooperatively than in the past," while another saw the situation differently and said, "They avoid the tendency to water down disagreements on policy." However, when asked whether the associations "*should* recognize the conflicting interests and present the different positions to the federal government" or "*should* arrive at a compromise and present a unified higher education position to the federal government," nearly twice as many presidents said they favor the compromise approach (see figure 7.1).

Figure 7.1
Presidential Views on Consensus, 1994

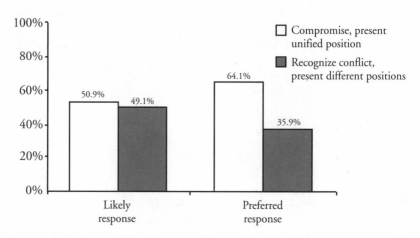

Source: 1994 Presidential Survey. The survey asked presidents what the associations "*now* are most likely" to do "when different associations have different positions on an issue," and what "they most often *should*" do in this situation. ("Likely" *N* = 1380, "Should" *N* = 1408)

Presidents' belief in the value of consensus has grown over time, as shown by a comparison of their views in 1979 with those they held in 1994. When Cosand et al. (1979) conducted their survey of college and university presidents fifteen years ago, about half of the presidents thought the associations should arrive at a policy compromise when there was a difference of opinion on a policy issue. The other half thought the associations should present different positions to the federal government. The 1994 survey data indicate that there has been a substantial change in presidents' views on this strategy over the years, with many more favoring consensus now (see figure 7.2).

Although the degree of unity varies by issue, of course, it is unusual for such a diverse community to put a high priority on consensus building. A

118

Figure 7.2
Presidential Preference for Consensus, 1979 and 1994

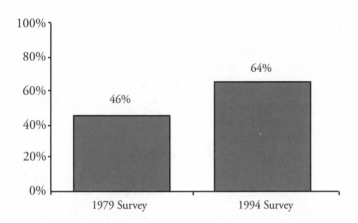

Sources: Cosand, Gurin, Peterson, & Brister 1979; and 1994 Presidential Survey. The surveys asked, "In general when different associations have different positions on an issue, do you think they most often should arrive at a compromise and present a unified higher education position to the federal government, or recognize the conflicting interests and present the different positions to the federal government?" Figure depicts percentage of "compromise" responses. The 1979 survey had 1284 respondents, although the number responding to this item is not included in the report; 1994 N = 1408.

director of government relations noted, "Our attempt to strive toward one position is our defining characteristic." In that respect, higher education's Washington culture replicates the culture of the campuses, where historically there has been collegial decision making and shared governance. The process of shared governance means that academic decision making typically follows a democratic, participatory model. The consensus building process is usually lengthy and arduous, and its hallmarks are attenuated debate and thorough testing of ideas. The myriad of faculty committees, the duration of their deliberations, and the slow resolution of major campus controversies are well-known trademarks of academic institutions.

The academic culture pervades the Washington higher education community[1] because the presidents of major associations are all academicians, usually former college presidents. The presidents typically earned Ph.D.s in the disciplines, rose through the ranks from assistant professor to full professor, and then accepted administrative positions as department chairs and deans before moving on to the presidency of a college or university. When they assume association presidencies, they bring to Washington the values of their former campuses, including a collegial decision making process, and that process is applied to the relations both within and among associations.

Below the top leadership level, the Washington government relations staff are not always enthusiastic about applying campus norms of participatory democracy to the Washington policy making process. Typically the staff are recruited because of their experience on Capitol Hill or in the executive branch, and many of them have spent little time on the campuses and have little patience for campus mores. Some staff commented on the difficulty of using a democratic decision making process in Washington. They noted that public policy making on Capitol Hill, for example, does not proceed at the slow pace of the campuses, and they bemoaned the difficulty of consulting widely and hammering out a consensus position fast enough to allow them to be players in the policy making process. A university lobbyist explained, "Higher ed is crippled by not being courageous enough to take positions that will alienate some members. . . . It brings habits of collegiality and consensus building to Washington, where those attributes do not fit. They hurt our ability to move quickly and deal with short term problems and opportunities. At the One Dupont Circle meeting they just go around the room and let everyone say something and by the time they're done, there is no action plan. Everyone is afraid of offending everyone else. Few people are brave enough to go out on a limb. Higher ed may get left in the dust because of its slow responses."

Higher education's proclivity for collegial decision making has been longstanding. Even in 1962, when Babbidge and Rosenzweig described the process that associations went through to secure members' approval before they could comment on legislation, they noted that the collegial relationship of the associations dictated that they remain silent if they disagreed with each other's positions (110–13). Similarly, in 1969, Harlan Bloland described the tendency of the associations to censure any member of the higher education community who was overly and independently aggressive in regard to policy advocacy, rather than waiting for the whole community to take a stand (158).

The fact that there are many more players in Washington now means that it takes even longer to touch all bases and come to consensus. Association staff and campus representatives talked about the increase in volume of communication among them. They said there are more informal communications than ever, and the number of meetings has grown, as well as the number of attendees. As one of the specialized association lobbyists put it, "You spend half your life in meetings now. . . ."

The large number of meetings cannot always accomplish consensus. An exasperated association official said, "Higher education's difficulty is coalescing internally. One Dupont Circle is a fudge farm because, within twenty-four hours after the associations make an agreement, some college will protest they weren't consulted, and it comes unglued. The associations seem to be lined up and going in the same direction, and then you say, 'Forward, march,' and they go off in four different directions." However, one lobbyist disagreed about that being a problem and said, "It is best to give the Hill forewarning about whose ox will be gored on each issue, or who will be happy or unhappy."

Public officials' views

The majority of public officials say that higher education typically presents them with consensus positions, as opposed to differing positions. However, they lack a common perception about the value of that approach and have often provided conflicting advice to the higher education community (Gladieux 1978, 272).

Many public officials contend that consensus positions are effective in producing the policy outcomes that the higher education community desires. For example, in response to the question, "Are there times when it is better for higher education to present you with information about the different positions of different types of institutions, or is it better to present a unified position?" some interviewees urged compromise, saying that speaking with "one voice" is "important," even "more powerful." They said they understood that diverse viewpoints exist within higher education, but an executive branch official contended that the higher education community "should compromise and get its act together anyway." Similarly, a congressional staff member argued that in a period of "very scarce resources . . . the specter of a divided higher education community fighting amongst itself for a part of a smaller pie will, I am afraid, result only in everyone losing."

Other public officials noted that understanding the differing positions and viewpoints within higher education certainly makes their own jobs easier, even if that is detrimental to the higher education community's overall objectives. A former congressional staffer with considerable policy influence said, "[Hearing different viewpoints is] good for policy makers. It gives them lots of choices and options, but it is not good for higher ed."

There are also public officials who question the utility and accuracy of consensus positions. ACE's letters to members of Congress on behalf of the higher education community by definition represent the lowest common denominator. A Senate staff member commented, "Unified positions get so watered down that Congress doesn't get the benefit of the discussion that went into them, and higher education's joint letter, when it comes out, is not sufficiently enlightening." Arguing in the same vein, another public official pointed out that "unity doesn't help if it's not accurate." Preferring that differing elements in the community "take separate positions and stick to them," he asserted that "a more rational higher education policy would result."

Despite adopting a consensus position in public, some institutions continue to pursue their own interests in private. "Too often a group will proclaim unity while they're in my office, and then one or two people will come back later with their own separate agendas that they didn't tell us in the first place," reported another Department of Education official.

Other public officials feel that the issue of differing views or consensus positions is simply a matter of timing. They want to hear differing perspectives early in a policy debate, but as the policy outcomes are better specified, they appreciate consensus. For example, a member of a House committee staff said, "I like to hear different views, but I need compromises eventually."

Finally, there are a few public officials who applaud higher education's differing views and say they prefer to hear a straight story about institutional divergence, at least occasionally. For example, the assistant secretary of postsecondary education said, "One voice doesn't accurately reflect the diversity of education. If higher ed always spoke with one voice, the perception of higher ed would be different. Higher ed maintains its integrity by giving honest views and therefore, because they are honest, the views of the differing sectors may vary. The image of higher education is better because they are not solely banded together because of greed, as the banks are, for instance" (Longanecker interview, 1995).

Nonetheless, it is clear that the Washington higher education associations and most public officials agree that, when possible, the community should adopt a consensus position. Given the diversity of higher education, however, that objective is difficult to achieve.

INSTITUTIONAL DIFFERENCES

Issues dividing the higher education community

Higher education officials understand that the federal budget pie is getting smaller and is usually a zero sum game, so one policy community's gain necessitates a loss for some other community. Since the early 1990s, Congress has divided the federal budget into three separate pools for appropriations purposes. The first pool is defense spending, and while some universities receive Department of Defense money for research, this is a not a principal source of funding for most institutions. The second pool is domestic entitlement programs, such as Social Security, which provide benefits to all individuals who qualify. This second pool provides higher education with funding in the form of federal loans, which are subsidized and guaranteed for students and have no limit on size. The third pool, discretionary domestic programs, is the part of the federal budget from which the majority of higher education programs come. It is for this third pool that the various parts of the higher education community must compete, and they compete not only with other domestic funding requests but also with each other. Therefore, a higher education lobbyist advocating more research dollars may be competing not only with lobbyists for other domestic priorities, like environmental protection and social services, but also with fellow higher education lobbyists who are advocating more student financial aid.

The problem is exacerbated by the fact that a single congressional committee may have to weigh the requests of different parts of the higher education community. For example, the Labor, Health and Human Services and Education Appropriations subcommittee deals with both the Department of Education and NIH. Therefore, it may find itself weighing higher education lobbyists' requests for Education's student financial aid programs against their requests for NIH research funding—and unable to appropriate money for both. Similarly, NSF clients in the higher education community may find themselves competing with colleagues who are NASA clients, since both lobby the Veterans Administration/Housing and Urban Development Appropriations subcommittee, which has responsibility for the two agencies. A single higher education association or institution may champion both NSF and NASA support but be forced, because of the agencies' placement in a single subcommittee, to set priorities.

Given the zero sum game, it is fortunate for the higher education community that there are few matters on which a win for one type of institution means a clear loss for another type. One example of such an issue, however, is tuition sensitivity in Pell Grants, which has occasioned a long-standing debate between four-year institutions and two-year colleges about whether the Grants should be tied to the cost of tuition. Four-year institutions want their students to receive larger Pell Grants to compensate for their higher tuitions, while two-year colleges, which have the lowest tuitions, prefer that all students receive grants of the same size, regardless of tuition level. Technically, the 1992 Higher Education Act amendments did tie Pell Grants to tuition levels by providing that if the grants rose above $2,400, some of the additional funds would go only to those students at higher priced institutions. However, in 1995–96 the maximum Pell Grants barely got over $2,400, so the tuition-sensitive part of the legislation was never triggered. The result was that this contentious issue for the higher education community was not a divisive factor during the 104th Congress.

While the higher education community infrequently faces issues which divide it into winners and losers, there are occasionally issues on which different parts of the community disagree. During the 104th Congress, one such issue was direct lending; AASCU and NASULGC were the Big Six associations that supported the measure when the rest of the community was divided. In regard to national service legislation, it was NASULGC, with its land-grant focus, that was the primary proponent, while other associations worried about the impact of national service funding on other forms of student aid.

Many policy issues affect different institutions differently and, therefore, take on varying degrees of priority for associations as they decide which ones to highlight in their lobbying. For example, community colleges have their own set of priorities. Pell Grants are especially important to them because their students receive over one-third of the Pell money, so AACC works hard on that issue. Since those colleges educate more immigrants than other institutions do, AACC puts resources into opposing legislation that threatens legal immigrants' aid eligibility. The same goes for aid to part-time students and job training programs, both of which are critical to community college students. Since these colleges educate more welfare recipients, AACC opposes welfare reform legislation that jeopardizes recipients' completion of education and training programs. On the other hand, AACC is not particularly concerned about research funding because two-year colleges receive almost none of it.

Research and doctoral universities have very different priorities. In regard to student aid, they lobby for federal fellowships for their graduate students, along with fellowship tax exemptions, and they too advocate undergraduate financial aid. However, for them, all other issues pale by comparison with the significance of research funding. Especially for AAU and NASULGC institutions, funding from NIH, NSF, and the Department of Defense is absolutely vital, and all research universities work to enhance their return on research investments. Since it is the research universities that most benefit from humanities funding, NEH typically has more support from AAU than from other associations. Universities with teaching hospitals are in a class by themselves in regard to lobbying priorities. They are threatened by health care reforms that do not take into account the extra costs of educating physicians, and the AAU institutions with medical centers work hard to communicate their special needs in concert with associations specializing in health care issues.

Private institutions have their own special concerns. Because most of them rely on private contributions more than most public institutions do, they expend more effort on advocacy for tax breaks for charitable donations. Private research institutions worry about indirect cost rates perhaps more than public universities do. NAICU was the association that was most vocal about the threats to institutional autonomy inherent in the SPRE legislation because its church-affiliated colleges are especially concerned about separation of church and state. (AAU, whose elite research universities also wished to avoid oversight by state bureaucrats, was very active in opposing the SPRE legislation too.) NAICU is typically the association most interested in the availability of student loans since its institutions' students are likely to borrow large sums to attend college.

Different associations and institutions may differ on which issues to highlight when they have the ear of public officials. The association(s) most concerned about a particular issue will take the lead on it while the others usually provide tacit support. The higher education community does not always achieve consensus on its positions, as noted in chapter 5, but when there are disagreements within the community, the general rule is "no surprises." Each association is expected to inform others when it plans active opposition to one of their positions.

Institutional views on consensus

Not surprisingly, presidents of different kinds of institutions have varying views of the importance of consensus. To understand the variation associated with institutional size and control, survey data were recoded into six combined institutional types ranging from "small private" to "large public." Data analysis shows that presidents of private institutions, both large and small, are much more likely to prefer presenting different positions, rather than a unified higher education position. Presidents of large private institutions are consistent with those from small private schools in their attitudes toward achieving consensus (see figure 7.3). Nearly half of the respondents in these two segments reported a preference for voicing divergent views. As one president noted, "The diversity of our institutions must be stressed; otherwise we will continue to get cookie cutter federal policy." However, presidents of medium-size private institutions closely approach the views of publics of all sizes, with nearly two-thirds backing the compromise position. All sizes of public institutions prefer presenting a unified position to the federal government. One of their presidents reflected the majority sentiment by saying, "Higher ed should grow up and cooperate." Another urged, "Let's work together and make our voices heard!"

Figure 7.3
Presidential Preference for Consensus, by Institutional Size and Control (*N* = 1380)

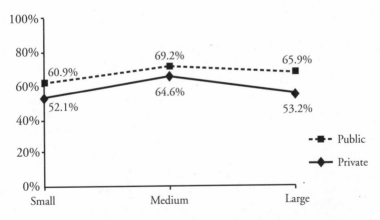

Source: 1994 Presidential Survey. The survey asked presidents what the associations "*now* are most likely" to do "when different associations have different positions on an issue," and what "they most often *should*" do in this situation. Figure depicts percentage of "compromise" responses.
(Small = < 1,000 full-time equivalent students [FTEs]; medium = 1,001 to 5,000 FTEs; large = > 5,000 FTEs)

Research universities have a great deal at stake in federal relations because federal funding for research, especially in science and health, has such a large impact on them. Among large research institutions (those enrolling more than 5,000 students), support for consensus was voiced by 58.5 percent of the public, as compared to 50 percent of private research university leaders who responded. By Carnegie classification, research institutions are more likely to favor presenting different positions to the federal government than other institutions are (see figure 7.4). One of their representatives said public officials should hear about differing views right from the beginning because "they find out anyway. It's just like your mother; she always finds out."

Figure 7.4

Presidential Preference for Consensus, by Carnegie Classification (*N* = 1389)

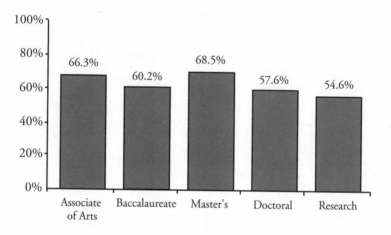

Source: 1994 Presidential Survey. The survey asked presidents what the associations "*now* are most likely" to do "when different associations have different positions on an issue," and what "they most often *should*" do in this situation. Figure depicts percentage of "compromise" responses.

The type of institutions that prefer the strategy of presenting different positions to the federal government are those that are either less numerous or have less political clout. They worry that a unified higher education position will not sufficiently represent their interests. For example, private institutions have less interest in consensus probably because they have less clout. Public officials are more likely to be concerned about the welfare of public institutions since they are supported with tax dollars. Similarly, the smallest and largest higher education institutions show less favor for a consensus view than those in the middle, which is a reflection of the fact that they are

126

simply outnumbered. Since 17.1 percent of the colleges and universities said they enroll fewer than 1,000 students, and 29.3 percent enroll more than 5,000, the majority of institutions have enrollments somewhere in between. As for the research institutions, they constitute only about 125 of the 3,600 institutions, which means they too are outnumbered. No wonder that institutions of these types are less enthusiastic about presenting policy makers with a unified view. The unified view is most likely to represent the interests of the majority of institutions.

ACE is widely regarded as the major voice for higher education, the association that best articulates consensus positions for the entire community. Of presidents surveyed, 60 percent confirmed that they think ACE speaks for all of higher education. Some presidents disagreed. For example, one said, "ACE is regarded a bit like the United Nations and treated with polite neglect." That view was unusual, however, since most presidents' comments ranged from "ACE is the leading group," to "ACE is the one voice for all of higher education," to "ACE is influential because it is the largest and covers all sectors." When evaluating responses according to institutional size, control, and two- or four-year status, no significant differences appeared. However, presidents who report that ACE is their primary association for federal relations were far more likely to agree that ACE is the major voice for higher education than those whose primary affiliation is with any of the other Big Six associations (see figure 7.5).[2]

Figure 7.5
Agreement that ACE is the Major Voice for Higher Education, by Primary Association
(**N** = 1276)

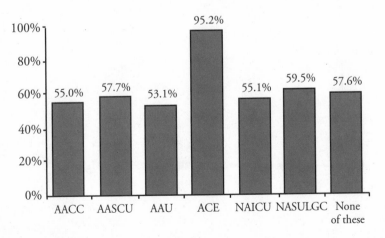

Source: 1994 Presidential Survey. The survey asked, "Do you consider ACE to be the major voice for higher education in Washington?" Figure presents percentage of "Yes" responses.

Washington staff

Most colleges and universities rely on campus-based federal relations staff and the major higher education associations to convey their views to Washington policy makers. In addition, some employ for-profit Washington law, consulting, and lobbying firms, and a few have established their own Washington offices. According to survey responses, only 5 percent of colleges and universities have Washington offices (or are part of a system that does), and the ones that do are mostly large, public institutions with programs beyond the associate degree level. They typically have more resources for Washington staff. By Carnegie classification, research and doctoral universities tend to place staff in Washington more than others do because they have greater need to monitor federal regulations and pursue research funding.[3] They benefit from supplementing association lobbying with their own because, as one research university president put it, "We are most effective dealing one-on-one with our own congressional delegation."

Eleven community colleges report having Washington staff, but these are rare exceptions, since state and local government relations often demand more frequent and immediate attention from two-year colleges. Baccalaureate-granting colleges (mostly private, and mostly small or medium-sized) are least likely to employ Washington staff, undoubtedly because of budgetary constraints (see figure 7.6). These institutions rely very heavily on Washington associations. One of their presidents explained, "Smaller institutions need more help."

Figure 7.6
Federal Relations Staff in Washington, by Carnegie Classification (*N* = 1410)

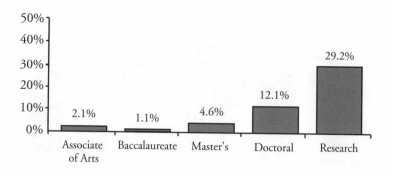

Source: 1994 Presidential Survey. The survey asked, "Do you have a full-time staff member in Washington?" and "Do you have a part-time staff member in Washington?" Figure depicts percentage of combined "Yes" responses, counting each institution only once.

Hired guns

The use of hired guns, that is, employing the expertise of for-profit law, consulting, or lobbying firms, is at least an occasional practice of one-sixth of the survey respondents. Only thirty-three institutions (2.2 percent) reported having used a Washington firm "often," while the overwhelming majority indicated they never have done so. Both control and size are factors, as more than half of the large, private universities report using hired guns at least occasionally, as compared to one-fourth of the large, public institutions (see figure 7.7). By Carnegie classification, research and doctoral institutions, which are the ones most likely to have the greatest involvement in federal policy issues, are the ones most likely to use hired guns. In contrast, just one in ten associate of arts or baccalaureate-granting institutions have employed a for-profit Washington firm for federal relations. One of the presidents whose institution does use hired guns explained, "Because we have no Washington office, we use them for earmarks." (Chapter 5 describes other reasons for using hired guns.)

Institutional PACs

The questionnaire asked presidents whether their institution has a political action committee (PAC) for federal relations. Among the responding institutions, only eleven reported having institutional PACs. All are

Figure 7.7
Use of Hired Guns, by Institutional Size and Control
(*N* = 1496)

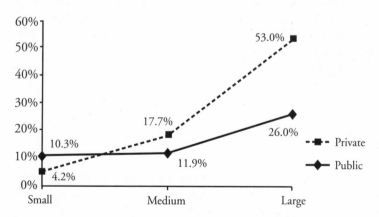

Source: 1994 Presidential Survey. The survey asked, "Has your institution employed a for-profit Washington law firm, consulting firm, or lobbying firm to deal with a special federal relations problem?" Response options were "Yes, often," "Yes, occasionally," and "No, never." Graph depicts percentage of combined "Yes" responses.
(Small = < 1,000 full-time equivalent students [FTEs]; medium = 1,001 to 5,000 FTEs; large = > 5,000 FTEs.)

public colleges or universities enrolling at least a thousand students. Two are doctoral institutions, two are master's level institutions, and the remaining seven are associate of arts colleges.

Research universities are much more likely than others to have Washington offices and to employ hired guns to monitor and influence public policy, but they clearly have made a deliberate choice not to create PACs. They are the institutions most likely to have the resources for PACs, yet they have elected not to pursue that strategy. One large university president said, "Congressional delegations are independently lobbied [by individual institutions] to a sufficient degree already." Another pointed out, "The PAC game is too hard to win. Big dollars from other industries. We can't play in that league." Presidents of all types of institutions also expressed their disapproval of PACs, saying, for example, "Its just more special interest lobbying and there needs to be a move away from it; we'd be adding to the problem." Another said, "I oppose all PACs. Two wrongs don't make a right." There were many idealistic statements like the following: "In its purest form higher education must remain above politics or it becomes a vessel of and for politicians." One president summed up the general opposition to institutional PACs by saying, "Increased costs. Doubtful benefits. Philosophically opposed." (See chapter 8 for a more detailed explanation of the higher education community's reaction to PACs.)

Association PACs

Just as institutional PACs have found limited support, few presidents support the establishment of PACs by the Big Six associations. When college and university presidents were asked whether the six major higher education associations should utilize PACs to "make campaign contributions to congressional candidates and incumbent members of Congress," their opposition was clear. Five out of six (84.7 percent) agreed that the associations should not have PACs. One of them commented, "PACs would underscore the fact that they [higher education associations] are special interest groups. Why brag about it?" Another said, "Our interests are too diverse to formulate one PAC position." Some thought, "The associations have a freer and more open access to the political framework in D.C. without PACs." Practical presidents also noted, "Funding would probably come from increased dues [at a time when] most colleges are experiencing budgetary problems."

Associate of arts institutional presidents responded more positively than their colleagues about PACs (see figure 7.8), with more than one fifth (22.7 percent) indicating support.[4] That is probably due to the fact that proprietary schools, which sometimes compete with community colleges for students and resources, have long used PAC contributions to achieve their policy objectives. As one president said, "We are not as effective as the proprietaries because we don't spend the necessary money."

Figure 7.8
Support for Association PACs, by Carnegie Classification
(*N* = 1493)

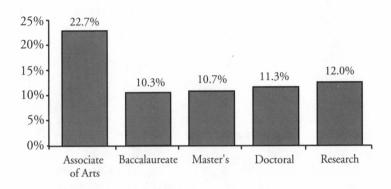

Source: 1994 Presidential Survey. Regarding the six major higher education associations, the survey asked, "Do you think they should have PACs?" Figure depicts percentage of "Yes" responses.

Among institutions with Carnegie classifications other than associate of arts, support for Big Six association PACs was consistently low, ranging from 10.3 percent to 12.0 percent. Additionally, there was a small but highly significant difference according to institutional control, with private presidents marginally less likely than public to oppose association PACs.[5] This finding is reinforced when the responses are analyzed according to primary association membership (see figure 7.9). While no association approaches majority support, AACC and NASULGC members are much less likely than their counterparts to oppose PACs.[6]

Reliance on the Big Six

When asked whom they rely on to represent their interests in Washington, nine out of ten presidents (88.3 percent) said they count on the Big Six. While more than two-fifths (42.8 percent) also rely on other resources, nearly three-fifths (57.2 percent) rely on the associations alone. That proportion increases to nearly two-thirds when considering only institutions having no Washington staff. Even those with Washington staff talked about using the associations as "an early warning system," and one president commented, "We don't rely on the associations to pursue specific institutional interests; we only rely on them to pursue our broader interests."

The differences in institutional choices appear not to be affected by size of institution, but control is an important element. Private institutions

Figure 7.9
Presidential Support for PACs, by Primary Association
(*N* = 1408)

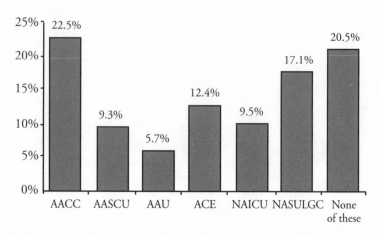

Source: 1994 Presidential Survey. Regarding the six major higher education associations, the survey asked, "Do you think they should have PACs?" Figure depicts percentage of "Yes" responses.

appear to mobilize a broader range of resources than their public counterparts, reporting a significantly different pattern of representation.[7] Just half rely solely on the Big Six, while more than one-third also use other "offices, groups, or firms," which typically means they use specialized associations or hired guns or both. Among public colleges and universities, a large majority (61.9 percent) count on the Big Six for Washington representation, with more than one-quarter (28 percent) also employing outside help. A small group (10.1 percent) indicate reliance only on other associations and firms, not utilizing the Big Six at all (see figure 7.10). In summary, then, more public institutions than private tend to rely solely on the Big Six associations for federal relations assistance, while more private institutions rely on a combination of the Big Six and other offices, groups, and firms. As institutional size increases, so does the likelihood of having Washington staff.

The Big Six associations perform many membership services in addition to federal relations, as explained in chapter 6. When presidents were asked whether they thought that ACE and their primary association "should give a higher priority to federal relations" they expressed a strong preference for higher priority in regard to ACE (see figure 7.11). More than two-thirds (67.9 percent) preferred that ACE give federal relations a higher priority, which makes sense in view of the reliance on ACE to serve as the voice for higher education. Regarding their primary associations, fully half (52.7 percent) of the respondents preferred that the priority remain the

Figure 7.10
Public and Private Institutions' Reliance on Washington Representatives for Federal Relations
(*N* = 1435)

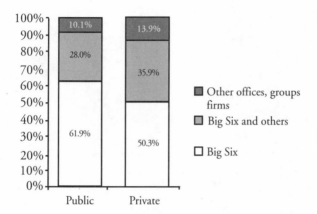

Source: 1994 Presidential Survey. The survey asked, "To represent the interests of your institution in Washington, do you usually rely on one or more of the Big Six, on other offices, groups, and firms, or on both?"

"same as now," with less than one-half (46.9 percent) preferring higher priority. Only 1 percent preferred that the associations, including ACE, assign federal relations lower priority. One university president's comment that "We need more visible leadership on higher education issues in Washington" was representative of the views of most others.

Presidential familiarity with federal issues

To gauge the familiarity of the presidents with federal policy issues, the questionnaire asked them about their level of information for the views they expressed in the survey. From three response alternatives, 51.2 percent of the presidents selected "informed opinion," while 27.7 percent chose "general impression," and 21.1 percent claimed "intimate knowledge." The survey data show that as institutional size increases, so does self-reported presidential familiarity with federal relations activity.

In a comparison of means, responses of public presidents did not differ significantly from those of private presidents. However, when institutional type (distinguished by both size and control) was considered, some interesting differences emerged.[8] Large private institutions report a significantly higher level of presidential expertise than large public institutions.

Figure 7.11
Preferred Primary Association and ACE Federal Relations Priority

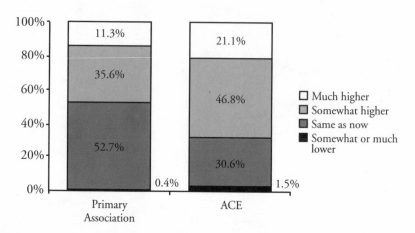

Source: 1994 Presidential Survey. The survey instructed, "Indicate the extent to which you think that your primary association/ACE should give a higher or lower priority to federal relations." Response options were "much higher than now," "somewhat higher than now," "same as now," "somewhat lower than now," and "much lower than now." Responses for "somewhat" and "much" lower were combined. (Primary association $N = 1387$, ACE $N = 1311$)

Additionally, medium-size private institutions report a significantly higher level of presidential expertise than medium-size public institutions. Presidents of small institutions do not appear to differ by institutional control in their self-reported familiarity with the survey issues (see figure 7.12). They are the least informed group, and one of them answered the survey question with a request for more information, saying "How can one find out more specifics about these associations?" Another said, "As a new president I know nothing about all this."

By Carnegie classification, it is clear that presidents of research universities rate themselves as most informed, followed closely by doctoral, then master's, then baccalaureate, and, finally, associate of arts institutions (see figure 7.13).

Thus, the degree of college and university presidents' self-reported knowledge about federal relations varies according to both control and institutional size: the larger the institution, the more knowledgeable the president. As a general rule, presidents of large and medium-size private institutions perceive themselves as more knowledgeable than public institution presidents of comparable size. Perhaps that is because the public institution presidents have to devote more time to state government relations, which can mean they have less time for federal relations.

Figure 7.12
**Presidential Federal Relations Expertise, by Institutional Size and Control
(*N* = 1469)**

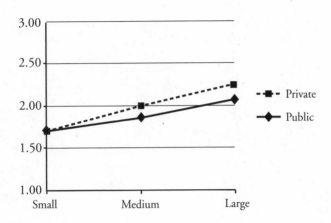

Source: 1994 Presidential Survey. The survey asked, "On what did you base the views you expressed in this survey?" (1 = General impression, 2 = Informed opinion, 3 = Intimate knowledge)

Figure 7.13
**Presidential Federal Relations Expertise, by Carnegie Classification
(*N* = 1480)**

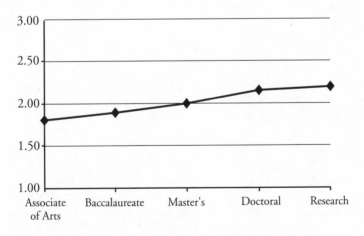

Source: 1994 Presidential Survey. The survey asked, "On what did you base the views you expressed in this survey?" (1 = General impression, 2 = Informed opinion, 3 = Intimate knowledge)

CONCLUSIONS

To understand a policy community dominated by institutional associations, it is useful to conduct an analysis of attitudes and activities distinguished both by institution and by association. The data analysis in this chapter shows that institutions, like individuals, have multiple identities and policy interests, some of which may be divergent and contradictory. Furthermore, there are also multiple identities within the associations. Even the Big Six associations do not have internal consensus since each represents more than one type of institution (i.e., both two- and four-year, both public and private, or both research and other types). As the AACC president noted, "On a given issue, there might be more cleavage within the community colleges than between the community colleges and the others" (Pierce interview, 1995). The multiple and overlapping institutional and associational identities, or niche groups, no doubt help to mitigate conflicts that might occur within the higher education policy community if it were structured differently.

Overall, the data show that institutional complexity is closely associated with the degree of involvement in federal relations. Larger institutions with research and doctoral emphases use the widest array of approaches, probably because they have the most federal funding and regulation, as well as greater resources to pay for federal relations activities beyond their Big Six memberships. The fewer resources an institution has, the more likely it is to rely solely on the Big Six for federal relations assistance. Smaller institutions with more narrowly defined roles (baccalaureate and associate of arts colleges, for example) are less likely to create their own Washington presence. Similarly, most of the presidents of these institutions say they have less federal relations expertise than those from master's and doctoral institutions.

These findings confirm the importance of the federal relations role of higher education associations, especially for smaller institutions. Most do not have the resources to establish offices in Washington or to hire for-profit lobbying firms. While their local congressional delegation may serve many of their needs, they also rely heavily on the Big Six associations to monitor policy issues for them and speak on their behalf to the federal government.

Reliance on the associations is complicated by the issue of consensus. While the majority of presidents still consider consensus to be the best approach to federal policy makers, some are willing to act independently on behalf of their institutions, potentially undermining the unified position favored by the majority of their colleagues. The types of institutions that are most likely to act independently are, not surprisingly, the ones that believe the community's unified positions do not always represent their own interests. Unified positions less frequently represent the institutions that are not in the majority or that lack good political connections.

Conventional wisdom has always said that institutional control, either public or private, is most often the determining factor regarding both institutional perspectives and their choice of lobbying tactics. Analysis of data from the 1994 survey of college and university presidents confirms that wisdom but also indicates that institutional size and Carnegie classification significantly affect particular attitudes and approaches. The most noteworthy finding may be that there is less variation among institutional attitudes and approaches than one might expect. Though leaders of different types of institutions have different views on specific policy issues, the higher education community shares a remarkably uniform outlook in regard to strategies for federal relations. Given the value of a unified approach, this finding bodes well for future higher education advocacy.

Chapter Eight

THE CHOICE OF LOBBYING TECHNIQUES

"Higher education couldn't organize its way out of a paper bag."

Congressman John Kasich (R-Ohio), chair of the House Budget Committee, as reported by David Warren, president of NAICU, at the beginning of the 104th Congress

As members of the new Republican congressional majority were sworn into office in January 1995, they began working on ways to balance the federal budget by cutting domestic spending. Higher education appropriations looked like an easy target, and it was clear the Republican leadership did not expect colleges and universities to wage an effective lobbying campaign to maintain their funding. As one observer put it, "Higher ed has always been 'Amateur Hour' in Washington." Shortly after the 1994 election, John Kasich, chair of the House Budget Committee, told the president of the National Association of Independent Colleges and Universities (NAICU) that he thought the higher education community was in disarray and made the disparaging "paper bag" comment that appears in the epigraph to this chapter (Warren interview, 1995).

This chapter describes new techniques that the higher education community adopted or piloted in 1995–96 and contrasts those techniques with ones it relied upon in the past. It is possible to generalize about higher education lobbying because the members of this policy community typically make similar decisions about which strategies and tactics to use or avoid. An analysis of higher education lobbying demonstrates the nature of this policy community's reaction to a major challenge, i.e., what it does more of, or differently, because of the challenge. The challenge in this instance was the change in party control of Congress and the Republicans' plans to restructure higher education policy and cut appropriations. This chapter shows how lobbyists handled the congressional sea change.

CHOICE OF LOBBYING TECHNIQUES

There are many studies of interest group lobbying techniques in the social science literature (especially political science), some of which contrast the lobbying techniques of individual policy communities (e.g., Heinz et al.). Others classify interest groups and explain how different types of groups go about influencing the political process. For example, Jeffrey M.

Berry (1977) did a pioneering study of the lobbying of public interest groups, Jack L. Walker (1991) surveyed voluntary associations, and David Knoke (1990) studied professional societies, recreational organizations, and women's associations.[1]

In a particularly extensive study of Washington interest group activity,[2] Kay Lehman Schlozman and John T. Tierney (1986) described the explosion of groups in Washington in the 1970s and 1980s, with many more interests represented, and many more individuals engaged in advocacy. In their interviews with Washington representatives, they asked whether "the massive increase in pressure activity" was accompanied by "an expanded use of various kinds of weapons in the organizational arsenal" (1986, 156–57). They reasoned that the previous decade had been a period of rapid change and, for many groups, a period of substantial political upheaval. Consequently, they were interested in understanding how groups respond during periods of turmoil, and particularly whether they do more or proceed differently. Based on their data, they concluded that political turmoil leads to more political activity. However, each type of group typically pursues the same lobbying techniques it used previously; they simply do more of the same.

Different types of interest groups lobby differently (Schlozman and Tierney, 1986; Gais and Walker, 1991). Schlozman and Tierney divided interest groups into four categories (i.e., corporations, trade associations, unions, and citizen groups)[3] and showed, for example, that corporations typically choose techniques that differ from those of citizen groups (1986, 431). Reviewing their data, Thomas L. Gais and Jack L. Walker (1991) noted that nonprofit sector citizen groups often lobby by conducting protests or demonstrations, talking to the media, publicizing voting records, and mounting grassroots campaigns.[4] They also pointed out that profit sector associations, such as corporations and the trade associations that represent them, are more likely to alert Congress to the effect of bills, help draft legislation and regulations, and shape the implementation of policies.

Citizen groups, also known as *public interest groups,* are ones "whose primary purpose is the pursuit of collective goods that will not selectively and materially reward their members" (Berry 1977, 10). These groups believe the policies they advocate constitute a compelling moral cause that will benefit the public at large (Walker 1991, 34; Schlozman and Tierney, 1986, 45; Heinz et al. 1993, 63). Among the best known examples of citizen groups are environmental groups, civil liberties groups, and those concerned about campaign finance reform. All are part of the nonprofit sector.

Another part of the nonprofit sector that has received little attention in the literature on lobbying techniques is that made up of occupationally based nonprofit associations. Higher education associations fall into this category, as do the associations of professionals in hospitals, museums, elementary and secondary schools, and transportation authorities, as well as groups of professionals who are salaried employees in governmental and other nonprofit organizations (Walker 1991, 60). All are organized around an economic interest or livelihood and therefore appear to have more self-interest than citizen groups when they lobby. Occupationally based non-profit associations usually lobby much the same way that citizen groups do (Gais and Walker 1991, 117–19).

The choice of lobbying strategies and tactics depends in part on a group's determination of what might work best, given who is currently in power (Browne 1985). If there is a change in the majority party in Congress, for example, it is possible that changes in lobbying techniques may also be appropriate. Other contextual factors also affect a group's choice of techniques, including the nature of the policy issue(s), the options legally available to the group, the degree of opposition it faces, the extent of its resources, and its experience with what has worked in the past (Schlozman and Tierney 1986, 161). This chapter will examine each of these contextual factors before turning to a description and analysis of the higher education community's lobbying.

CONTEXT FOR HIGHER EDUCATION LOBBYING

Nature of the policy issues

The nature of its policy issues influences a group's choice of lobbying techniques. Higher education groups are much like citizen groups in their conviction that their needs are in the national interest and should not be considered a special interest. Even a century ago, the president of the first higher education association, in his 1895 annual address, said that higher education was "united for the purpose of mutual aid and the promotion of common interests, which are public interests" (Hawkins 1992, 31). Similarly, in his historical study Hugh Hawkins writes, "Few educators wanted to admit that the world of teaching and learning constituted a *special interest*. They saw that world as an unquestionable good for the entire society. Even when the associations sought influence by means resembling those of a textile manufacturer's alliance or a labor union, they expected politicians and public administrators to grant the indubitability of education's social benefit" (124).

College and university presidents still think of themselves as championing a public good. For example, one president said, "Higher education is significantly different from other sectors and special interests. It is not self-serving, it is other-directed, it serves society; and it does little special interest pleading. Higher education can usually be regarded as more of a public interest than a special interest." Another president also sounded this public-good theme by stating, "Higher education is preparing the next generation. It is assisting the nation and the world. It is addressing the ills of the country and helping those who need to better themselves in our society. Education is a necessary and legitimate good in our society." A third commented, "Higher education has the moral high ground. We are not selling products for our own profit." Another simply said, "We wear white hats."

Many higher education association officials share the institutional presidents' view that higher education is special and, therefore, should be treated differently from other policy communities. Said one association official, "Members of Congress mostly respect higher education more than they respect other sectors." Another official commented, "Members of Congress think we are acting in the public interest. They think we are creating and transmitting knowledge that is essential for economic growth. They know that the U.S. system is second to none and is an enormous national resource." A third association official remarked, "Higher education is an official good. In principle, legislators don't want to hurt higher education."

These characterizations of higher education refer to the community's advocacy of student financial aid, scientific research, and other major policy issues involving colleges and universities. They do not refer to individual institutions lobbying for earmarked funds. Earmarks have the characteristics of other special interest legislation; they benefit a specific institution or group of institutions, excluding others, and are legislated quietly, out of public view. (See chapter 3 for more information regarding higher education earmarks.) Individual lobbying for earmarks makes higher education look like other special interests. Earmarked funding for higher education is a relatively new phenomenon. It grew in the late 1980s and early 1990s, reaching an all-time high in fiscal year 1993 and constituting a significant share of higher education appropriations. As one member of Congress put it, "Higher education does two types of lobbying. One is generic, pro-education lobbying and is usually done by coalitions of institutions and associations. The other is purely selfish, i.e., lobbying by a single institution for earmarked funding for its own use."

Opposition

A second factor influencing a group's choice of lobbying techniques is the nature of the political opposition it faces. Most interest groups confront multiple adversaries as they lobby. A few scholars (e.g., Knoke 1990, 209–10; Gardner, Atwell, and Berdahl 1985, 56) have found that groups facing opponents actually fare better in the policy making process because they are more likely to mobilize their members and participate in coalitions and because the controversy leads to more visibility for their issues. However, most scholars have come to the opposite conclusion. Most say groups with opposition have to be more careful about presenting complete and accurate information to policy makers (Wright 1996, 187–201), and they note that groups pursuing policies with no opponents will fare better than those that have some (Heinz et al. 1993, 346). The more extensive and effective the competition, the less likely a group's success (Schlozman and Tierney 1986, 396).

Historically, the question for most legislators has been how the government should go about supporting colleges and universities, not whether they should be supported. There has usually been bipartisan support for higher education, not ideological polarization. As former Senator Paul Simon (D-Illinois) noted, "Over the years members [of Congress] have liked to be associated [with higher education]. There was no downside" (1996 interview). However, as higher education recently has come to be regarded less often as a societal investment, and more often as a personal benefit,[5] there has been more contention about higher education policy, and it has received a lower priority on the public agenda.

Higher education has appeared to go from being viewed as a *distributive* policy to a *redistributive* one, which has affected the likelihood of contention over higher education policy making. Distributive policies are ones that appear to have only winners, not losers, while redistributive policies seem to transfer government subsidies to one group at the expense of another group (Ripley and Franklin 1982). It is easier for interest groups to influence legislators as they are making distributive policy decisions than to do so for redistributive ones, especially since the former tend to be less ideologically controversial and less visible to the media and the general public (Lowi 1979; Petracca 1992; Ripley and Franklin 1982; Schlozman and Tierney 1986). The fact that many of the most significant issues in higher education policy making, such as grants for scientific research and various aspects of student financial aid, are complex issues involving considerable technical expertise has also helped keep them out of public view.

As noted in chapter 4, the contentiousness about higher education policy was considerably aggravated by the Republican leaders' attitude toward academia, coupled with the desire in Congress to reduce the federal domestic discretionary budget. Public officials point out that higher education is like all policy communities in having competition in the appropriations process, since all are competing for the same dollars. Given that most of the federal budget is allocated for entitlements and defense, higher education, of course, is pitted against other domestic funding priorities, like Head Start and the environment, for the remaining discretionary dollars.

Nonetheless, most policy makers say that higher education has no real adversaries in the policy making process. One said, "Few people would want to be portrayed as anti-higher education. Everyone claims to be for the ultimate goal of higher ed even when they argue against student aid or other higher ed programs. Another commented, "Nobody talks bad about higher education except about the cost of college tuition." A third agreed that "no one opposes higher ed, although they may disagree on what the right level of funding for it should be." A more worrisome comment, however, came from a public official who contended that "Higher education is not visible enough to have enemies."

Legal status

An interest group's lobbying choices are also shaped by its legal status. With the exception of proprietary schools, all of postsecondary education is a nonprofit enterprise, with 501(c)(3) status. That is also the case with all of the major higher education associations. This nonprofit status makes them tax-exempt, and it also means that, according to the Internal Revenue Code, they cannot devote a *substantial* amount of their activities or resources to attempts to influence legislation. The Lobbying Disclosure Act defines *lobbying* as oral or written communications to high level executive or legislative branch officials regarding the selection of federal officials or the formulation, modification, or adoption of federal legislation, regulations, and programs. Since this definition does not include informing or educating policy makers, those activities are acceptable under the Code. In any case, all higher education associations engage in myriad activities apart from federal relations.

What the associations cannot do because of their tax status is participate or intervene in political campaigns on behalf of or in opposition to candidates, though individuals within those organizations have the same rights as any other citizens. For example, they can form political action committees (PACs) with their personal funds. Organizations can also adapt to the restrictions on their political activities by creating affiliated arms with 501(c)(6) status that are registered as lobbying organizations.[6]

On January 1, 1996, the new federal Lobbying Disclosure Act (LDA) went into effect. It does not affect the legality of federal lobbying activities, but it does broaden the definition of lobbying beyond the one in the federal tax code and requires that activities above a certain level be disclosed semiannually. While the law does not single out higher education, it says that organizations must register if they have any staff who devote one-fifth or more of their time to lobbying and also spend at least $20,000 on lobbying every six months. In addition, lobbying activities on behalf of the organization must be reported.

Higher education associations and institutions struggled with the new legislation, deciding whether or not to register as lobbyists. Given the confusion about the law, there was a lot of variation in their decisions. For example, while three of the Big Six higher education associations registered right away (the American Council on Education, the American Association of Community Colleges, and the National Association of Independent Colleges and Universities), the other half (the Association of American Universities, the American Association of State Colleges and Universities, and the National Association of State Universities and Land-Grant Colleges) did not. Similarly, about two-thirds of the universities with a

Washington office registered initially, while one-third did not. Public universities, like the University of Michigan, were more inclined to register than were private institutions, like Princeton University, for example (Lederman, *Chronicle of Higher Education*, 8 March 1996).

An interesting aspect of the legislation is the provision that there is no need to report faculty or students who lobby on their own behalf, as opposed to their lobbying at the request of the institution. That provision perhaps recognizes that lobbying by college or university administrators may have very different objectives than faculty and student lobbying. Simply put, administrators lack control over faculty members and students.

Potential resources

Resources influence the extent and nature of the lobbying techniques chosen by interest groups. In his seminal work on interest group influence, David B. Truman (1951) stressed the importance of access to policy makers as a political resource. Access is a prerequisite for a group wishing to influence policy making, or at a minimum, learn about upcoming policy changes (Salisbury 1992, 100, 359). Special access means a group is likely to have special influence (Berry 1997, 227). Representatives of higher education institutions typically benefit from relatively easy access to legislators, thanks to their prestige, their numbers, their economic impact, and their geographical distribution.

In spite of the decline in public faith in institutions of all types, and the frequent criticism of higher education in particular, prestige continues to be an important resource for the higher education community. The public's confidence in colleges and universities remains fairly high.[7] The presidents of these institutions command special respect, as evidenced by a survey of job prestige in which the public ranked them second (below doctors, but above astronauts) in a list of 740 occupations (Williams, *Chronicle of Higher Education*, 4 December 1991). Since a substantial part of the presidents' job involves promotion of their institutions to various constituencies, they tend to be articulate spokespersons and good lobbyists for higher education more broadly.

There are also economic incentives for legislators to listen to higher education advocates. These institutions are major economic engines within their communities and have a substantial impact on the communities' well-being. Furthermore, colleges and universities are numerous. The institutions themselves are spread across every congressional district and every state, with higher education personnel among the constituencies of all members of Congress, including key committee chairs.

For all these reasons, higher education has ready access to legislators, and high level representatives of colleges and universities can usually get a hearing from members of Congress and other public officials.[8] The fact that officials have a basic familiarity with higher education, thanks to their own college experiences and those of their family members, also facilitates the advocacy process.[9] Furthermore, because of the nature of the higher education enterprise, its representatives have useful policy information, and presentation of specialized information to public officials is an effective way to wield influence (Wright 1996).

What has worked in the past

Finally, a major factor influencing an interest group's level of political participation and choice of lobbying techniques is what has worked for it in the past. In the twenty-five years since it was called the worst lobby in Washington (Gladieux 1978, 266), the higher education community has gradually come to understand the necessity of fuller participation in the political process. There are still rumblings from some quarters about how it should not have to stoop to political involvement, and there are still occasional comments about *lobbying* being a dirty word. Nonetheless, the leaders of the higher education community have come to accept political participation as a necessity.

On large issues, interest groups usually expend considerable resources and pursue all available strategies (Heinz et al. 1993, 360). However, an analysis of the higher education community's lobbying techniques prior to the 104th Congress shows that while it used some very frequently, it tried others less frequently or not at all. Higher education representatives typically used the same techniques most commonly used by other policy communities to inform public officials about their needs and preferences. As one association leader put it, "Our real job is to avoid letting big policy changes have unintended consequences that end up knee-capping us." With that objective in mind, higher education representatives routinely testified at hearings, contacted public officials directly, engaged in informal contacts with officials, presented research results, sent letters, attempted to shape the implementation of policies, consulted with government officials to plan legislative strategy, inspired letter-writing or telegram campaigns, shaped the government's agenda, and helped draft legislation, regulations, rules, and guidelines. Nearly all types of Washington organizations use these same techniques (see table 8.1). The higher education community simply lobbied the way the largest number of other groups do and usually avoided other kinds of techniques. In other words, it has taken a cautious, low-key approach to lobbying.

The extent to which higher education associations, and their member colleges and universities, engage in these common lobbying practices has grown through the years as more higher education associations have participated in the political process and more campuses have sent representatives to Washington and hired lobbyists or consultants. Although the major associations are usually headed by former university presidents, in recent years their government relations staff and campus representatives in Washington have often been people with a master's degree in public policy and previous experience on Capitol Hill or in the executive branch. As one lobbyist noted, "The campuses are smart enough to hire Hill Rats." These are people who are well-schooled in lobbying, and their use of various techniques is the result of conscious choice, not a lack of expertise.

Table 8.1
Use of Lobbying Techniques by All Types of Washington Organizations

Lobbying Technique	Extent of usage %
Testifying at hearings*	99
Contacting officials directly*	98
Informal contacts*	95
Presenting research results*	92
Sending letters to members*	92
Entering into coalitions with other organizations	90
Shaping implementation*	89
Planning legislative strategy*	85
Helping to draft legislation*	85
Inspiring letter-writing campaigns*	84
Having constituents contact	80
Mounting grassroots lobbying	80
Contributing financially to campaigns	58
Publicizing voting records	44
Running ads in the media	31
Contributing work or personnel to campaigns	24
Endorsing candidates	22
Engaging in protests	20

Source: List of lobbying techniques excerpted from Schlozman and Tierney 1986, 150. Table depicts percentage of all types of Washington organizations using each technique.
*Major higher education lobbying techniques prior to 1995.

Going into the 104th Congress, it was clear that higher education lobbying was affected by perceptions regarding past successes. When college presidents were asked just prior to the 1994 election, "In general, how effective do you consider all of higher education to be in regard to federal relations?", more than two-thirds indicated they consider higher education effective (see figure 6.4). Furthermore, comments from Washington public officials and higher education leaders frequently underscore the extent to which the community has succeeded in commanding public resources over the years. People commented on how well higher education usually fares in the appropriations process, even in bad times, and many talked about the bipartisan support that higher education has enjoyed.

That is true in spite of the fact that higher education has long since lost some of its exalted status. For at least a decade there has been a steady flow of reports and books about the decline in quality of American higher education, as well as charges of mismanagement and other improprieties (for which, see chapter 3). Since the views of members of Congress reflect public opinion, it is not surprising that the 1992 Higher Education Act (HEA) held some important disappointments for the community, especially in regard to accountability and reporting regulations. The disappointments were serious enough so that when five of the Big Six associations changed leadership during that period, the negative aspects of the 1992 Higher Education Act were probably a catalyst for some of the changes. The higher education community experienced additional regulatory and funding threats in 1993–94. Nonetheless, as the 1994 election approached, the associations had a fresh set of well-regarded leaders, and most college presidents said they saw no need to adjust their lobbying techniques.

Then came the wake-up call from the 1994 election, which resulted in a set of Republican congressional leaders determined to restructure higher education policy and reduce its funding. In response, the higher education community's approach to lobbying became increasingly varied and spirited, with its lobbying in the Second Session of the 104th Congress, in 1996, more aggressive than in the First Session, in 1995.[10] What follows is an analysis of higher education techniques, showing how practices during the period of turmoil diverged from the historical approach.

LOBBYING IN THE 104TH CONGRESS

Political advertising

Until 1995 the higher education community almost never chose to do political advertising. In that respect it was unusual because organizations have used political advertising campaigns throughout this century; it is not a novel political tactic (Tierney 1992, 206). Although some groups are constrained by the high costs of electronic media (Berry 1977, 250), most believe that political advertising can influence public opinion and activate the public to communicate with policy makers. As Kay Lehman Schlozman and John T. Tierney point out, "The public can be a natural ally—and increasingly in this electronic age, a created ally" (1986, 396). Many policy communities create ad hoc associations which do political advertising and try to raise the public's consciousness and support when the community's interests are threatened (Berry 1977, 250).

Given the enormous number of people who are enrolled in higher education programs, employed by colleges and universities, and supportive of their objectives, political advertising could be a useful strategy for the community. Nonetheless, about half of the institutions' presidents agreed in the 1994 survey that their associations did not and should not purchase advertising in newspapers or other media to express association opinions on policy issues. Some pointed out that members of Congress are already knowledgeable about higher education themselves, unlike other policy topics such as transportation or agriculture. For example, one college president said, "Everyone in Congress went to college themselves, and their children go to college, and they have served on our boards of trustees. Members of Congress are all interested in higher education, and all of them consider themselves experts already."

Without their member institutions' clear endorsement of the use of media to influence public opinion, it is not surprising that the major associations have rarely used such tactics.[11] Their most noteworthy effort to do political advertising occurred in the early 1980s when the Reagan administration was trying to cut student aid and eliminate the newly created Department of Education. An ad hoc coalition was formed by NAICU and the Council for the Advancement and Support of Education (CASE), along with twenty-five other associations, in December 1981. The Action Committee for Higher Education (ACHE), as it was called, did intensive political advertising, with leadership from both government relations and public relations staff in the associations.[12] Students were heavily involved in the lobbying effort as well. ACHE distributed a press kit, plus an 800 number for supporters to call. However, its efforts were made to appear amateurish when a telephone company error led callers to the 800 number of a hotel registration desk, rather than to information about lobbying on behalf of student aid (Wentworth interview, 1995). Nonetheless, academic leaders and members of Congress judged ACHE's efforts to have been effective because the Department of Education survived and Congress refused to cut student aid further in 1982. Congress then began consideration of funding restoration and increases in 1983 (C. Brown 1985, 10). ACHE not only contributed to the favorable policy outcome, it also emboldened the higher education community and made it more visible and collegial (C. Brown 1985, 95–98).

When student financial aid again was threatened in 1995, Robert Atwell, then president of ACE, compared it to the early 1980s and said, "I believe the budgetary pressures on us will be as severe as those we faced in the early years of the Reagan administration, and we will have to be at least as vigilant and aggressive as we were at that time to meet this challenge" (*Higher Education and National Affairs*, 21 November 1994).

As before, the higher education community responded by creating an ad hoc coalition for political advertising. This one was called the Alliance to Save Student Aid, and it was organized primarily by David Warren, president of NAICU,[13] along with Robert Atwell, president of ACE, for the sole purpose of protecting existing levels of student aid. The two associations joined forces to create the Alliance, which they financed with $300,000 in contributions from thirty other higher education associations. The lobbying efforts of the Alliance to Save Student Aid differed substantially from previous higher education lobbying; it was much more aggressive and visible, with more wide-ranging tactics.

The Alliance to Save Student Aid began by hiring a Republican public relations firm to conduct polling and focus groups. The results showed more widespread support for student aid than the higher education community had anticipated. In fact, the polling revealed that public support for federal student aid was second only to public support for Social Security: 92 percent supported current funding levels for Social Security, and 89 percent supported current funding levels for student financial aid. However, the focus groups showed that most parents and students did not understand that their financial aid, both loans and grants, usually came from the federal government. Thus, it was clear that an education campaign would be necessary and that the public was likely to be very receptive to higher education's message.

With that political intelligence in hand, the Alliance devised a media strategy, with press kits and press conferences, especially targeting the regional House Budget Committee hearings. The Alliance also created an 800 number to inform callers about the status of legislation and connect them with congressional offices for advocacy. Additionally, the Alliance paid for newspaper ads and aired radio spots during drive time in the Washington area, as well as in the seven states of key House and Senate Budget Committee members. The Alliance also offered the media suggestions for op-ed pieces on student financial aid, and it characterized financial aid issues in simple terms, appropriate for sound bites, thereby generating substantial public awareness of the threat to student aid. Much of this information appeared in a handbook published by the Alliance entitled *Stop the Raid on Student Aid.*

Public relations firms, focus groups, 800 numbers, media buys—all these Alliance tactics were new for higher education. As NAICU President Warren emphasized, "The Alliance has changed the way we relate to the members of the associations and the way that the associations relate to Congress" (Warren interview, 1995). One of the Big Six vice presidents agreed, "The Alliance has been a big change in strategy for higher education. In fact, there is a systemic change in the way we are doing business now."

There was a second higher education ad hoc group established for political advertising at the start of the 104th Congress. Known as the Science Coalition, its purpose was advocacy of university-based research in science and engineering, with special emphasis on medical research. The Coalition was created by eighteen major research universities, mostly private ones, with their senior government relations and public affairs officers taking the lead.[14] Unlike the Alliance, the Coalition's budget was university-funded, rather than association-funded. It included among its members not only universities, science and engineering societies, and other higher education groups, but also corporations, voluntary associations, and prominent scientists. By 1996 it had grown to more than 370 organizations, institutions, and individuals (Blank, *The University Record*, 17 September 1996).

Like the Alliance to Save Student Aid, the Coalition employed a consulting firm for polling and focus groups, and its Washington strategies were message development and media outreach.[15] Its major 1995 achievement was an "advertorial," i.e., a letter and newspaper ad entitled *A Moment of Truth for America*, which advocated federal investment in university research. One version of the advertorial was signed by twenty-seven governors, both Republican and Democratic, and the other by fifteen corporate CEOs. Besides serving as a newspaper advertisement, it was used as a letter to all members of Congress. The Coalition also published a letter signed by sixty Nobel Prize winners expressing concern that budget cuts would hinder medical and scientific achievements. In addition, the Coalition took out advertisements in *Roll Call*, the Capitol Hill magazine, to explain the significance of university-based research and to point out that while the United States was cutting its research budget, Japan's research budget was being doubled. To educate members of Congress about the impact of federal funding, the Coalition also organized forums on science and technology in the spring of 1996 for both the Democratic and Republican Policy Committees (Blank, *The University Record,* 17 September 1996).

The Republicans were sufficiently concerned about higher education's aggressive new techniques to threaten retribution. One congressional staff member said, "We will start investigating how much colleges are actually spending on political issues. We are going to find out just what it has cost them to pay for every ad and what every 800 number call has cost them. We intend to use this information against them when we need to. We are watching what they do. We know that the money they spend on advertising just means that tuition will be that much higher."

Nonetheless, those who led the ad hoc organizations felt the results would be worth the risks. As NAICU's president put it, "All this is new for higher education and higher education is in it for the long haul" (Warren interview, 1995).

Protests and demonstrations

College campuses have long been the site of protests and demonstrations, with the civil rights and Vietnam protests of the 1960s having begun there before spreading beyond the campuses. Protests are a lobbying technique used by a sizable number of citizen groups and, as Jeffrey M. Berry notes, their purpose is always to gain publicity for a cause. The protest is judged a success if media decide to cover it because that leads to more public understanding of the protesters' point of view. Media coverage usually provides the protesters with leverage in the policy making process (1977, 233).

Given that student groups have often used civil disobedience on campus to pressure their institutions' administrators, it is surprising that they have so rarely organized protests and demonstrations in Washington to pressure public officials on higher education policy issues.[16] Student groups frequently demonstrate to express opinions on issues unrelated to higher education, but prior to 1995, the only time that most observers remember protests about higher education policy (specifically, student aid) was during the early years of the Reagan administration.

In the 104th Congress, during the debate on student aid, there were two active student organizations working with other major higher education associations in the Alliance to Save Student Aid: namely, the United States Student Association (USSA) and the National Association for Graduate and Professional Students (NAGPS). As one Big Six association president stated, "We have seen students (and their representative organizations) who are connecting with the associations for the first time." Another association leader said, "In the Alliance, the associations were the generals, but the students were the army. They were the ones who provided the numbers. They had the stories."

The activism of the student groups could be traced to the publicity given to congressional Republicans' plans to cut $18 billion out of the student aid budget. Usually students are largely unaware of the potential consequences as millions of dollars move into and out of various student aid programs. However, this time Speaker Gingrich and other congressional leaders were very vocal about their legislative plans, and the magnitude of the cuts got the students' attention—thanks in no small part to the leadership and resources provided by the major higher education associations.

The student groups took advantage of electronic message groups on the campuses and sent daily e-mail messages through the Internet. They mobilized students to conduct demonstrations, most often local in nature but sometimes on Capitol Hill, to protest the proposed cuts in student aid. In all, there were four rallies at which students packed congressional committee sessions and buttonholed individual legislators. The coordinator of grassroots development at NAICU told the story of student involvement in the Senate Labor Committee's "mark-up," or redrafting, of a bill that affected student financial aid in September, 1995.[17] It was a story with a happy ending: "Three to four hundred students packed the hearing room, and stood outside, and got TV coverage. *Congressional Quarterly* had a picture of them. Senator [Dan] Coats [R-Indiana] asked a rhetorical question during the hearing, and one of the students answered it. The bankers were taken by surprise by the students. Since the Republicans were committed to their votes before they went into the mark-up session, they voted just as they'd planned to do, and the students' position lost. However, the Republicans went back and told their leaders that they could not continue holding that position. The bill's language was changed on the floor and passed 99 to 0. It represented a several billion dollar reversal in policy" (Combs interview, 1996a). The student groups were pleased with the outcome. As the legislative director of USSA put it, "Our relationship with One Dupont has been strengthened. They respect us more and see we can mobilize the grassroots" (Adelsheimer interview, 1996).

According to many association lobbyists, the spirited participation of the two student organizations in the Alliance to Save Student Aid was probably the single greatest influence on congressional policy decisions. No wonder then that, shortly after one of the student demonstrations, a member of Congress introduced a bill to silence students by cutting student aid to universities providing funding to student groups that lobby. That bill, however, failed in subcommittee.[18]

Constituent contacts: college and university presidents

Political scientists have long contended that members of Congress are motivated first and foremost to ensure their own re-election (e.g., Mayhew 1974). They do that most effectively by responding to the concerns of their constituents, so it is common for interest groups to bring influential constituents to Washington (Tierney 1992, 211). Many observers have noted that all politics is local and that district issues guide national policy making (e.g., Browne 1995, 207). As Robert H. Salisbury explained, "Public policy tends overwhelmingly to be formulated in disaggregated district- or group-specific terms . . . it is less the national need for scientific research and more the advantages that redound to the areas around Boston, Palo Alto, Berkeley, Ann Arbor, Madison, St. Louis, and other locales where the research universities are located" (1992, 250–51). William P. Browne's 1995 study of agricultural policy making notes that constituent pressures have replaced interest group pressures as the major factor influencing the policy choices of members of Congress.

College and university presidents have always come to Washington to engage in advocacy on behalf of their institutions, and their lobbying has been effective (Helms 1993). In 1995–96 the Washington associations tried to mobilize their help much more often than previously. As a higher education lobbyist explained, "Now we need to do less talking and have our members do more talking, and that has been a big difference since November [1994]." Consequently, presidents for the first time were more visible on Capitol Hill than association personnel.

Even before the arrival of the 104th Congress, it was evident that federal relations had taken on increasing importance for college and university presidents, but during that period association leaders said presidents were better-informed and more active than they had been in the past. That impression is confirmed by survey data regarding the presidents' self-reported knowledge: In 1979 only 29 percent of the presidents reported that they had an "informed opinion" about federal relations issues (Cosand et al. 1979), but by 1994 nearly three-quarters of them (72.3 percent) considered themselves at least relatively well-informed, according to their survey responses. The survey data reflect the fact that in 1995–96 there were more college presidents spending more time on federal relations than ever before. As one Big Six association leader commented, "Presidents' level of interest, their attention span, and their turnout are all greater now."

The associations activate and mobilize their member presidents in a variety of ways. They feature speakers and conduct programs on federal relations at annual meetings and board meetings, they fill their publications with information about policy issues, and they mail updates on specific issues. Since the higher education community is well-connected electronically, associations often use e-mail as well as phone calls and faxes to notify presidents about issues that need their involvement. Sometimes associations encourage presidents not only to contact members of Congress before critical votes, but also to contact them after the votes to thank them for their support or to express the hope that they might vote differently in the future. Associations urge presidents to phone legislators or write letters, e-mail messages, telegrams, or faxes, and they especially encourage the presidents to make personal visits.

Some presidents complain that the associations send so many *action alerts* that they do not know when their intervention with local representatives or senators is really essential. They said they get so much federal relations information from their associations that they cannot possibly read it all, much less act on it. As one president said, "I get inundated by mail from AACC [the American Association of Community Colleges], both informative and inquisitive. They bombard me with faxes, and faxes are the world's worst invention." That response was not surprising, given that the major associations had begun hiring outside firms to send *blast faxes* (or *broadcast faxes*) to 1,200–1,400 people at the same time. In 1995–96 the presidents responded to these requests. For example, one Big Six association leader said, "We send the fax at two o'clock in the afternoon, and calls are coming into the congressional offices from college presidents by four o'clock."

Association personnel talked about the careful calculus of determining when it is really important to activate the presidents, and how. The presidents have a myriad of responsibilities, and their increased involvement in federal relations comes on top of growing demands in many other areas, thereby generating more work and more stress. Association leaders well understand that, as one of them put it, "You have to think about how many times you can go to the well and ask the presidents to contact members of Congress. You can only ask them so many times. They are busy people."

During 1995–96 it was clear that the Washington associations had to "go to the well" more than usual. Some presidents were initially unresponsive because, as one association official commented, "We have told the presidents time and again the sky is falling. We have cried 'wolf' too often and they're not paying attention." However, the magnitude of the congressional challenge quickly became apparent, and the associations kept repeating how high the stakes really were. An association leader's communication with the presidents explained, "This is a single elimination tournament. If we falter at any stage, we are eliminated." Many presidents responded aggressively, and some, such as MIT's President Charles Vest and the University of Michigan's then-President James Duderstadt, were in Washington every month.

Fortunately for the higher education community, there are college and university presidents who are constituents of every member of Congress. The associations especially target for mobilization those presidents whose congressional delegations occupy leadership positions, and they are often asked to express the views of their colleagues. For example, the presidents of Kansas and Vermont institutions were especially important during the 104th Congress because of the influence that Senators Nancy Kassebaum (R-Kansas) and James Jeffords (R-Vermont) had on higher education policy making. All sectors and types of higher education institutions were called upon, not just the elites. As one college president noted, "Members of Congress think that the elites don't really need federal help. Using [Harvard President] Rudenstine gets you in the door of a member of Congress but then he is not helpful in actually making the case for higher education [as a whole]."

Many public officials commented on how much more influence the presidents typically have than do association personnel. Republican staffers and members of Congress contended that the associations have a Democratic Party bias, which mitigates their effectiveness. Republicans said they prefer talking to college and university presidents, some of whom are "Rush Limbaugh clones," as one association leader remarked. Though one said that college presidents tend to lecture all listeners, which does not play well in Congress, most interviewees said that presidents are quite effective. Furthermore, members of Congress are responsive first and foremost to constituent requests, and lobbying by Washington government relations staff is always of less value.

Grassroots lobbying

Historically, higher education institutions and associations have rarely mobilized their various constituencies for grassroots lobbying. Grassroots lobbying is usually defined as efforts by government relations people in Washington to involve the folks back home in contacting their legislators for the purpose of influencing policy making (Schlozman & Tierney 1986,

185). Grassroots organizing is a particularly resource-intensive activity for Washington offices, so they reserve this effort for times when their interests are most threatened (Evans 1990, 269).

The potential number of people who could be marshaled for advocacy is huge. The higher education community includes not only college and university administrators but also large numbers of faculty, students, alumni/ae, trustees, and other constituencies. For example, there is potential support from parents whose children are in college, community leaders who value their local institutions, and businesses that rely on higher education for job training. However, institutional administrators have often been reluctant to run the risk of involving others in lobbying and have even discouraged association personnel from contacting them because their own public policy views and institutional priorities may not be shared by these other higher education players. Students, for example, are unlikely to support university requests to state officials for tuition hikes.

Some individual faculty members (as opposed to faculty associations) are heavily involved in politics. They may provide expert testimony on issues facing Congress, or spend their sabbaticals working on policy concerns in congressional offices, or even run for Congress themselves. However, those faculty members are rare. More numerous are the faculty who do lobbying on behalf of their own grants and projects. While the percentage who lobby is very small, it has grown in recent years as faculty have tried to generate or maintain research funding for themselves and their departments. Faculty in the sciences have been particularly active when their research budgets have been threatened by budget cuts, since they have the most at stake.

Nonetheless, most academics have no intention of lobbying and often ignore local and national politics. For example, even as Republican leaders considered eliminating the National Endowment for the Humanities (NEH) in 1995–96, most faculty humanists did not respond with communications to members of Congress.[19] As one observer put it, "For most academics, the art of relating the college or university to the political process is a mystery; even worse it is a mission they view with scorn . . . [and] the less they know about it, the better they feel" (Johnson 1981, 1). One association leader agreed, saying, "Faculty are very individualistic. They think they're purer than the political process. They're above it all. They are engaged in the life of the mind. Faculty have an apolitical style and set of values. They deal with reason and precision, neither of which are part of the political process. They don't provide much help. They think that One Dupont represents management, not faculty." Another association leader said, "The university faculty are truly disconnected from federal relations. They have no awareness of how things work; in fact, they disdain the process. They actively remove themselves." Although that is less true than it used to be, it is still more true than not.

For the most part, institutions are glad that their faculty have little interest in lobbying, and college and university administrators have infrequently asked faculty, as a group, to contact public officials on behalf of the institution. Even though faculty may be doing research that is relevant to policy decisions, it has been uncommon for institutions to ask individual faculty members to visit members of Congress or provide expert testimony to congressional committees.

When asked why his university does not try to activate its faculty for advocacy on behalf of their institutional employer, one president responded, "We don't trust them." The unease about faculty lobbying can best be illustrated by noting that at one institution, faculty are told to fill out a form and get permission if they want to lobby. Administrators have found that, although faculty usually agree with them about federal overregulation and under-funding of higher education, faculty views on public policy issues often differ from theirs. For example, when indirect cost rates were threatened in the early 1990s, university administrators were distressed to find that some faculty members told Congress it would be fine to eliminate the rates altogether. That was true even though administrators said their institutions could not afford to have faculty work on most federal research projects without the infusion of large indirect cost returns to cover overhead expenses. Given differences of opinion like that one, it is not surprising that faculty are rarely asked to lobby.

It has been still more unusual for college and university administrators to ask their students to lobby, even though their sheer numbers (about 14.3 million in 1995–96) could be powerful and students (like faculty) could give dry policy debates a human face. Nor do the major associations typically involve student organizations. While the spirited participation of USSA and NAGPS in the Alliance to Save Student Aid was credited with having a substantial impact on congressional policy decisions, the participation of these organizations in concert with the other associations is uncharacteristic of higher education lobbying. The institutions they attend almost never inform and mobilize them for lobbying on aid or other issues.

Similarly, although most colleges and universities have their own boards of trustees, administrators rarely call on board members for participation in higher education advocacy. That generalization applies less often to community colleges because their trustees are mobilized by the Association of Community College Trustees (ACCT), which works closely with AACC. The same partnership does not operate for four-year institutions even though the association that represents the trustees, the Association of Governing Boards (AGB), would be glad to have its 28,000 trustee members more engaged in public policy initiatives on behalf of higher education (Ingram interview, 1995). While trustees cannot replace college and university presidents as congressional lobbyists, trustees are often prominent com-

156

munity leaders who can represent their local higher education needs more authoritatively, and with less appearance of self-interest, than the presidents can (Helms 1993; Saunders 1981).[20] Furthermore, many of them have useful political connections. Nonetheless, with the exception of the Ad Hoc Tax Group's trustee network, major associations have usually refused to involve trustees in lobbying efforts. Their members worry that trustees may have opinions that are unrepresentative of those of administrators and faculty. Consequently, trustees are often a neglected resource (Crawford 1981).

Finally, although there are millions of college and university alumni/ae, they too are rarely mobilized on behalf of their alma maters. On the state level, the University of California system has organized some of its prominent graduates for advocacy, and other institutions like the University of Michigan have developed similar in-state networks. While these efforts are uncommon, it is even more unusual to see alumni/ae mobilized for federal lobbying. The University of Florida is one of the few institutions that does so. In 1993 a few universities called graduates, now industry leaders, to lobby for Department of Defense funding of university research. However, such efforts have been infrequent and targeted only at opinion leaders, not all college graduates. It has been unusual too for the various higher education sectors to identify congressional staffers among their alumni/ae and try to organize their assistance to serve institutional needs. It has mostly been small liberal arts colleges, especially Jesuit institutions, that have done so in the past.

During the Second Session of the 104th Congress, the Washington higher education community began to mobilize more of its constituents. Disciplinary professional associations sent e-mail or newsletter action alerts to faculty members, urging them to contact members of Congress at key points in the budget debates. The American Association of Medical Colleges (AAMC) helped bring together 130 medical and scientific societies (including hospital groups, physicians, and those in allied health fields), voluntary health groups, and academic and research organizations in the Ad Hoc Group for Medical Research Funding. Its objective was an increase in support from the National Institutes of Health (NIH) for biomedical and behavioral research. Similarly, faculty and others conducted lobbying efforts on behalf of the budget and programs of the National Science Foundation (NSF), especially through the Coalition for National Science Funding. The NSF Coalition comprises fifty-five organizations, including the American Physical Society, the American Mathematical Society, and the American Society of Cell Biology. They encouraged faculty to voice their support for NSF, and their call to action produced about ten thousand letters, phone calls, and e-mail messages to Congress. Other coalitions were equally active in lobbying the 104th Congress. In many cases they were organized around specific research topics, such as oceanographic research (Park 1996, *The*

Sciences, May/June; White 1996, *Technology Review,* May/June), or for advocacy of funding for specific agencies, such as the Department of Defense or the Department of Energy.

At the same time, NAICU began to encourage its member institutions to activate the more influential college trustees,[21] and there was discussion about creating a database of alumni/ae of private colleges and parents of students who attend those schools, for the purpose of mobilizing them in the future. Similarly, the Science Coalition announced its plan to expand the use of a "grasstops" strategy in which it more vigorously identified and mobilized key opinion leaders, including alumni/ae, donors, trustees, parents, and others, to promote university-based research to key members of Congress. It was evident by 1996 that grasstops and grassroots lobbying were becoming more acceptable to most constituencies in the higher education community.

Electoral involvement

Occupationally based nonprofit lobbies typically try to avoid too close identification with either political party, especially at election time (Heinz et al. 1993, 81). By contrast, many citizen groups, such as environmental and consumer groups, provide publicity for candidates' voting records and policy stands (often called "voter scorecards"), and they endorse candidates and contribute work or personnel to campaigns (Berry 1977, 238; Heinz et al. 1993, 81; Schlozman and Tierney 1986, 431).

To college and university presidents, partisanship seems risky. Presidents pointed out in interviews that their trustees and donors, as well as other constituents, are sensitive to partisan leanings and consider them inappropriate for an institution of higher learning. They noted that partisanship is likely to get a chief executive officer in trouble.[22] Rita Bornstein (1995) conducted a survey of private college and university presidents on their role in public policy issues and partisan politics.[23] She found that 74 percent of them thought presidents should not be involved. They say their biggest worries about political involvement are that it could offend diverse constituencies, have an adverse impact on fund-raising, and incite a negative reaction from their trustees (58). Public institution presidents avoid partisanship even more than private institution presidents. For example, the former president of the University of Texas at Austin wrote that "the president of a public university should not be politically active and certainly should not be closely identified with a political party or movement. You should be identified as independent and bipartisan, and you should maintain friendly and cordial relations with politicians of all parties" (Flawn 1990, 184).

Those observing the higher education community usually agree that it is most effective when its approach to federal relations is seen as bipartisan. For example, in the 1996 evaluation of ACE in preparation for the search for a new president, ACE's board specifically recommended that the association's government relations agenda be less partisan and that the association work more effectively with both parties (ACE 1996, 10).

During the 104th Congress bipartisanship was a real challenge for higher education leaders. On one issue after another they found themselves opposed to Republican congressional proposals but allied with the Clinton administration. President Clinton did his best to publicize higher education as a Democratic Party policy issue, and he courted the community by making the rounds of association annual meetings and sending cabinet secretaries as well. Yet the community tried to avoid overt partisanship; for example, a Democratic congressional aide described calls she got from lobbyists asking her to tone down the partisan rhetoric. They recognized that, to the extent possible, bipartisanship would be the best strategy.

While many interest groups publish voter scorecards, most higher education associations have avoided that tactic. An ACE lobbyist pointed out its complexity, noting that there are rarely outright congressional votes on higher education issues; rather, the issues are usually folded into bills with multiple topics (Hartle interview, 1996). Furthermore, different types of institutions put priority on different policy issues: for example, community colleges are more interested in job training bills than are universities, and universities are more interested than community colleges in funding for medical research.

Just as the higher education community has avoided voter scorecards, it has also avoided outright candidate endorsements. Nonetheless, just before the 1992 election there was an event that indicated a change in higher education's characteristically nonpartisan approach to elections: a group of 223 college presidents, administrators, and trustees advertised their personal (as opposed to institutional) support for candidate Bill Clinton in the *Chronicle of Higher Education* (28 October 1992).[24]

At the start of the 1996 election year, higher education began to involve itself further in electoral politics. In a January 1996 letter to university colleagues on behalf of the Science Coalition, President James Duderstadt of the University of Michigan and President Charles Vest of MIT advocated the use of local radio spots, communication with newspaper editorial boards, and generation of story placements in "the small to mid-sized newspaper markets typically found in the congressional districts of members whom we are trying to reach." For example, letters of thanks from universities to congresspeople who had championed university-based scientific and medical research were to be sent to their local newspapers—a boost during an election year. Meanwhile, some of NAICU's state affiliates, most of which have 501(c)(6) status, drafted candidate questionnaires to put candidates on the record about higher education issues. Nonetheless, since 1996 was a time when most national interest groups were particularly active in campaign publicity (e.g., choosing specific congressional races and running their own ads on behalf of a candidate), the higher education community still engaged in less political activity than many other interest groups.

Probably the most important election year activity undertaken by the higher education community was its spirited voter registration drives. Their purpose was to change the fact that in 1992 only slightly more than half (52.4 percent) of the 18-to-24-year-olds had registered to vote, and of those registered, many fewer than half (42.8 percent) had actually voted (*Chronicle of Higher Education*, 27 September 1996). NAICU's President Warren and AASCU's President Appleberry co-chaired the National Voter Registration Project, which was endorsed by the Secretariat (see chapter 5) and supported by thirty-eight Washington associations. It took advantage of the "Motor Voter Law," which was passed in 1993 to facilitate voter registration. NAICU published a handbook, *Your Voice—Your Vote: The National Campus Voter Registration Project Organizing Handbook*, which showed campuses how to set up voter registration drives, how to form steering committees of faculty, staff, students, and community representatives to lead the efforts, and how to organize nonpartisan educational events, such as voter forums, to inform the campus about political issues and candidates.

Although the Big Six's National Voter Registration Project initially tried to organize and spearhead the various student registration initiatives, ultimately there were many separate efforts. Different groups sprang up on the campuses, with local student leadership and, occasionally, some corporate or association sponsorship. During the fall of 1996 MTV's Rock the Vote campaign was probably the most visible voter registration effort on college campuses, especially because of its Rock the Vote and Choose or Lose buses, which went from campus to campus organizing get-out-the-vote activities and distributing materials. The MTV campaign was financed in part by MCI Communications. Together, they set up an 800 number (1-800-REGISTER) that allowed callers to respond on a touch-tone phone to a series of questions. The callers would then receive, in the mail, a federal voter registration form customized to their information and valid in forty-seven states, which they could check, sign, and mail to the location where they wanted to register. Rock the Vote and MCI Communications also set up a Web site that used the same procedure. This system was particularly helpful for students who wished to register at home while attending school in another state.

There were other student voter registration efforts as well. Among the groups registering students under the Motor Voter rules were the College Republicans, the College Democrats, and Youth Vote '96, a coalition of twenty youth groups (including USSA) concerned about issues such as the environment and consumer rights. At the City University of New York, the Barnes & Noble Bookstores, many of which are on college campuses, teamed up with a student group, the Student Voter Registration Fund, to try to register the system's 200,000 students. Voter registration forms were printed in the student newspaper, and Barnes & Noble contributed more than $100,000 for promotional materials. At Chatham College in Pittsburgh electronic registration was available for students. A group at the University of California at Berkeley arranged for students living in the residence halls to receive a voter registration card along with their room keys. At the University of Michigan the Voice Your Vote student group registered 6,500 people during the first five weeks of the fall semester.

Some student groups created voter scorecards; USSA, for example, compiled its voting record summaries both in February and again in October 1996, as the 104th Congress adjourned. It rated members of Congress mostly on financial aid issues but also included their views on immigration, welfare reform, employment nondiscrimination, and same-sex marriages. Among the other student groups with 1996 scorecards for congressional candidates were Campus Green Vote and the U.S. Public Interest Research Group (USPIRG). As a result of all these uncoordinated and student-based efforts, the higher education community was more involved in electoral politics than ever before.

After the 1996 election it appeared that about three-quarters of the campuses had experienced voter registration activities of one sort or another. Altogether, these efforts seemed to have led to the registration of more than one million 18–24-year-olds prior to the 1996 election (Combs interview, 1996b). Polls showed that President Clinton led overwhelmingly in that election among voters for whom education was the primary concern, and the majority of college-age voters cast their votes for him. Although Clinton did not beat Dole on every campus, there were some campuses, such as Stanford University, where he won the support of more than 70 percent of the student voters (*Chronicle of Higher Education*, 15 November 1996).

Coalitions: standing and ad hoc

Coalition building is one of the most useful lobbying techniques available, especially when there is strong organized opposition (Schlozman and Tierney 1986, 279; Berry 1997, 187–94; Hojnacki 1997, 84–85). It is a strategy that does not depend on resources and, in fact, can result in savings (Berry 1977, 254–55). It has many advantages, ranging from providing assistance for friends, to addressing member pressures for greater issue involvement, to gaining information from allies (Browne 1990, 496). Coalitions are particularly effective because they can shift flexibly in response to current policy concerns.

Coalitions are ubiquitous in Washington (Evans 1990, 262), but citizen groups and corporate interests are more likely than occupational groups to form them (Hojnacki 1997, 85). John P. Heinz and his colleagues commented on the variation in the extent to which different domains form coalitions and noted that some do it more and better than others (1993, 376). The more allies, the more effective a group can be, especially since allies can help focus policy makers' attention on the coalition's issues and get them on the agenda in the first place (Schlozman and Tierney 1996, 396; Browne 1988, 190).

The higher education community has always been very effective at creating internal standing coalitions, as evidenced by its Washington organizational structure and its umbrella association, ACE. However, historically, higher education has had fairly limited alliances with other policy groups. In 1976 an article on higher education lobbying commented on the community's need for coalition building (Murray, 86–89), and a 1979 survey of college and university presidents and Washington higher education leaders showed they wanted the community to build effective coalitions (Cosand et al. 1979). As one public official put it, higher education has "talked only to itself."

During the 104th Congress, higher education became especially adept at building coalitions that were ad hoc in nature. Ad hoc coalitions are a natural outgrowth of groups coordinating their efforts; they can create and finance new organizations as a way to advance their mutual interests (Walker 1991, 69). Their purpose is to deal with a current policy problem and then vanish when the threat subsides. The composition of each coalition is different, with short-term, constantly shifting alliances. They draw on different players in different configurations, each of which is geared to a specific policy issue.

The creation of ad hoc organizations stemmed in part from the institutional limitations of the Big Six, made apparent when they faced a policy crisis. Though ACE had traditionally been the leader in comprehensive higher education lobbying campaigns, the Big Six relinquished some of their leadership role to the ad hoc groups. Those who formed the Science Coalition, for example, did so specifically because they felt they could not count on the major associations to lobby effectively for university-based research funding.[25]

The ad hoc groups have advantages that the major associations cannot match. Associations like the Big Six gain their resources and clout by building a substantial membership base, but the larger and more diverse their membership, the more difficult it is to have consensus on policy issues. Each of the Big Six includes institutions of a variety of types (e.g., public and private, or two-year and four-year), so members are likely to disagree on some specific policy concerns. Since it is risky for these associations to take political action without general agreement, they often take no position at all. They frequently engage in the time-consuming process of polling their members before taking a stand. By the time a poll has been completed, the opportunity for political intervention may have come and gone.

The situation for ad hoc groups is very different. They are formed to accomplish specific policy objectives, and their members have already agreed to those objectives by joining the coalition. Consequently, ad hoc associations can maneuver more quickly than major associations to deal with crisis issues. Furthermore, ad hoc groups have another advantage: Their sole purpose is lobbying, and they benefit from a tax status that does not constrain them. Additionally, ad hoc coalitions are cost-effective. They lack staff, space, and annual meetings, so they have no overhead costs to pass on to member institutions.

As described above, some or all of the major presidentially based associations joined with student groups, professional or disciplinary associations, and others outside of academe to pursue advocacy jointly, as in the Alliance to Save Student Aid, the Science Coalition, and the National Campus Voter Registration Project. During the 104th Congress, there were also ad hoc monthly working groups to lobby for funding of various federal agencies, such as the Ad Hoc Group for Medical Research Funding for NIH, the Coalition for National Science Funding for NSF, and the groups supporting funding for various federal agencies. Although it operated without funding, there was also a National Direct Student Loan Coalition, a low-profile gathering of lobbyists engaged in the fight with the loan industry. In addition, there were ad hoc fledging organizations created just in case their issue became politicized. For example, supported by funding from several associations, ACE created the College Costs Working Group to gather and disseminate information from focus groups and surveys about college tuition costs. During the period 1995–96, ad hoc coalitions became the norm for the higher education community.

It is possible that the strategic choice to use ad hoc coalitions could also pose problems for the higher education community's federal relations. Astute Washington observers realize that it would be easy for higher education to pour its resources into ad hoc coalitions at the expense of major associations. Yet because the associations facilitate consensus building among different types of colleges and universities, any diminishment of their stature could precipitate more fissures within the higher education community. Right now, the overlapping jurisdictions and coordinating functions of the major associations promote consensus and often lead to a united stand on Capitol Hill. Furthermore, the Big Six handle many bread-and-butter policy issues that may be less visible but are still important to the community. If the community's resources were devoted primarily to single-issue ad hoc coalitions, the less visible issues could go unaddressed. Nonetheless, as long as coalitions do not supplant the major higher education associations, they appear to be a good approach to specific lobbying challenges. The new president of ACE said, when asked if the coalitions represent competition for the Big Six, that the right policy outcomes reflect well on everyone, including the major associations (Ikenberry interview, 1996).

The 1995–96 ad hoc coalitions were not unique; over the years higher education has had a long list of coalition partners. On student aid issues, especially before the advent of direct lending, there were coalitions between higher education and the banks and guarantee agencies. In regard to state funding issues, there have been coalitions with groups like the National Governors' Association (NGA), the National Conference of State Legislators (NCSL), the State Higher Education Executive Officers (SHEEOs), and the Education Commission of the States (ECS). Higher education advocates have often aligned themselves with the Independent Sector coalition, an umbrella group for more than 800 nonprofit organizations, such as the Salvation Army, the YMCA, health groups, religious groups, and charities. There have also been periodic alliances between higher education associations and the environmental lobby or the children's lobby, such the Children's Defense Fund. In addition, interviewees mentioned coalitions with unions like the American Federation of State, City, and Municipal Employees (AFSCME), as well as ad hoc coalitions with utilities, veterans' groups, the arts, transportation, telecommunications, aerospace contractors, civil rights groups, and scientific professional societies.

These ad hoc coalitions allow a division of labor. As an ACE lobbyist explained, the breadth of higher education issues frequently makes it necessary to rely on others, and higher education just stays in touch to make sure that its interests are represented. For example, the Independent Sector often takes the lead for the whole not-for-profit community on charitable contributions, the restaurant industry on benefits for part-time workers, and the communications industry on Federal Communications Commission (FCC) regulations.

In contrast to its relatively frequent use of ad hoc coalitions, higher education representatives have had fewer standing coalitions with external communities. Part of the reason is that they have chosen not to lobby on tangential issues, such as health care or welfare reform. In that respect, colleges and universities are similar to business firms, which also lobby on issues close to their particular business, as opposed to labor unions, for example, which may lobby on a broad range of social issues (Heinz et al. 1993, 59).

The most permanent coalition partner for higher education has been the elementary/secondary education community. In fact, from the outset, a key purpose of the twenty-five-year-old Committee for Educational Funding (CEF) has been to bring the two parts of education together, and ACE is a cornerstone of the CEF coalition. CEF's dues are based on numbers of players and size of operating budgets; its biggest dues payers are the National Education Association (NEA) and the American Federation of

Teachers (AFT). In contrasting NEA and AFT with higher education associations, an ACE official noted, "They are more partisan and rich and endorse candidates, and we do not."

CEF meetings are the place where the higher education and elementary/secondary groups learn about each other's views, though they devise strategy independently. An association official said, "The purpose of CEF is [for higher education and K-12] to avoid hurting each other or offending each other." One policy maker described their relationship as follows, "Elementary/secondary education is the covert antagonist in the competition for resources, but higher ed and el/sec do not bad-mouth each other. Each sector uses percentage increases in the other's budget to make an argument for catching up. Neither sector ever tries to hold the other one down." The president of CEF explained, "Congress alternates between support for one sector of education or the other. CEF helps to reverse that tendency and ask for funding for both parts of education. It tries to avoid the divide and conquer approach. . . . If the pressure is sufficient, the pie will grow for both parts of education." Department of Education officials have sometimes referred disparagingly to the representatives of major CEF affiliates as "the Blob," but CEF's president credits their work, in part, with thwarting the 104th Congress from making substantial budget cuts in education (Boyer interview, 1996).

The higher education community's standing alliances also extend to business and industry, with ACE's Business-Higher Education Forum being one of the best examples. The medical community has also maintained standing coalitions, such as Research America, a ten-year-old organization made up of academic and industry groups interested in biomedical research.

During the 104th Congress, leaders of the higher education community enlisted more allies than ever before. Nonetheless, there are many more standing coalitions that the higher education community could create. One congressional staffer bemoaned the absence of higher education in the traditional liberal alliance. He pointed out that the labor and higher education communities, for example, have many interests in common, but higher education associations have not formed coalitions with labor that would let the whole group work on all of each other's issues, rather than just on individual issues. Accordingly, prominent faculty members initiated some high profile meetings with labor union representatives in the fall of 1996, with the specific objective of encouraging more joint political action between higher education and labor.[26]

Another potential ally for higher education is the senior citizen community. Senator Pell specifically suggested more concerted effort by higher education to reach out to retired citizens, saying "It is essential that retired citizens see that education is essential to insuring that their retirement will be a secure one. They need to understand better that a healthy economy helps their retirement, and that education is the key to a healthy economy" (Pell letter, 1996).

Astute observers of the higher education community also suggested more outreach to mayors and city councils and school boards. As one pointed out, "Most colleges have a major influence on the economic activity of a community and could be mobilizing its members to be helpful." A college president said, "Other sectors have formed coalitions around economic interests; higher ed has not." Many interviewees cited the Science Coalition's letter from major corporate leaders as an example of the kind of alliance with other sectors that should be brought to bear more often.

In the midst of the battles with the 104th Congress, one of the Big Six lobbyists said, "We need continuing coalitions, but we are short-staffed and also we can't build coalitions in the middle of a fight." His comment speaks to the need to create standing coalitions during periods of relative calm, rather than waiting to ally during emergencies, such as that generated by the 104th Congress. However, the forces which dictate that the higher education community not become overly politicized also dictate that it not overtly support other communities in their battles and become more publicly and frequently involved in the political process. Nonetheless, it is clear from the experience of 1995–96 that the higher education community is moving toward more coalitions with other policy groups, and at least for now, most of them seem to be ad hoc in nature. In time, of course, ad hoc coalitions often take on permanence.

Political Action Committees (PACs)

Although higher education representatives have begun lobbying more aggressively in most other respects, their attitude toward political action committees (PACs) remains unchanged. The legitimization of PACs by federal laws and Supreme Court decisions in the 1970s made them a technique frequently utilized by other policy communities for gaining access to legislators (see, for example, Langbein 1986). In fact, it is very unusual for a prosperous, sophisticated policy community not to use PACs as a regular part of its lobbying operation. Partisan and ideological factors can lead to a spurious connection between money and voting (Wright 1996, 137; Evans 1990), but the distribution of PAC money does correlate highly with success on policy issues, as in the case studies of four domains done by Heinz et al. (1993, 349). Consequently, there has been an explosion of PACs, with several thousand of them providing campaign contributions to sympathetic challengers or helping friendly incumbent legislators get re-elected. PACs are typically utilized by corporations, trade associations, and labor unions, but less frequently by citizen groups (Schlozman and Tierney 1986, 431; Heinz et al. 1993, 81).

Higher education PACs are very unusual. There are several states in which college and university personnel do belong to PACs,[27] but these are focused on state lawmakers. In the 1980s AACC worked with community college presidents to form a PAC for congressional candidates, but they could not raise enough funds to make the PAC viable.[28] At the federal level, the only segment of the postsecondary community with PACs is the proprietary vocational school segment.

Individuals employed in higher education make campaign contributions out of their own pockets, probably in the same amounts as other educated citizens. However, because they have no PACs, their contributions are not specifically and identifiably credited to the higher education community, and they are small by comparison with those from other occupational sectors, including school teachers who contribute heavily through the NEA and the AFT. There are a few higher education association presidents whose salaries are inflated to allow them to make political contributions on behalf of their organizations,[29] and occasionally Washington higher education representatives help organize campaign fund-raisers for their best congressional supporters. However, the majority of college and university personnel rarely attend fund-raisers. One who did feel compelled to attend such an event negotiated a discounted price for showing up briefly and leaving before the meal was served.

While hired guns who represent higher education may make sizable contributions to members of Congress, their contributions are not credited to the higher education community. These representatives of for-profit law, consulting, and lobbying firms are Washington insiders who regularly attend fund-raisers. Even though it may be higher education dollars that they use for political contributions, it is the hired guns who get credit, not the higher education community. It is no wonder that a Washington association official said, "There is no retribution available to us if we don't get a vote. . . . It's like shooting blanks."

Members of Congress who serve on higher education committees well know that doing so will not win them the same funds for their next campaign that would come from involvement with other policy issues. One of them said she was told by congressional colleagues, "Don't work on higher ed issues because you won't get any campaign money." Another commented that he would have "gold stars on his forehead when [he] got to the pearly gates" thanks to all the effort he had expended on higher education, in spite of the failure of colleges and universities to provide him with funds for his re-election campaigns. He dubbed the higher education community "the worst cheapskates in the political business" and noted that several key legislators friendly to higher education had been defeated over the years because of inadequate campaign coffers.[30] As a result, some members of Congress refuse to serve on committees dealing with higher education, or switch committees as soon as they have the flexibility to do so.

The survey responses from 1994 show that college and university presidents are very clear about their reluctance to form PACs. They continue to believe in the value of what one association president disparagingly called "self-inflicted laryngitis" (O'Keefe 1985, 11). When asked whether the Big Six should have PACs, college and university presidents responded "no" overwhelmingly, and nearly two hundred of them took time to write in comments on the survey about why they do not want to create higher education PACs in Washington. Remarkably, only one president wrote a comment favoring PACs.

Two-thirds of the presidents (67.1 percent) agreed that "forming a PAC would diminish higher education's special status, moving it from a public interest to a 'special interest.'" Several presidents commented on the apolitical nature of higher education. One president said, "Forming a PAC would politicize higher education, to our detriment," while another remarked, "Political issues shouldn't be mixed with education." In a similar vein, a president said, "If we must pay our Senators and Congressmen to vote for education, our country is in real trouble."

While PACs may provide access to public officeholders, higher education has access already. One official commented, "The presidents are unusually lucky. They get calls back easily from members of Congress. That is not true of most average citizens." A congressional staffer concurred with that assessment, saying, "Members [of Congress] tend to trust and value visits and information from college presidents." The presidents themselves agree they do not need PACs to obtain access and be successful. As one president put it, "We don't depend as much on the strategy of financial contributions to accomplish our policy objectives. We strategically try to substitute information and public support for money." Another president similarly observed, "We have no PACs; we influence and persuade instead." One president linked access to public officials with the legitimacy of the ideas or issues advanced: "If we can't convince without money, it must not be justifiable."

Presidents also indicated a dislike of the hardball politics inherent in PAC contributions. One respondent said, "We have no hit list," while one other remarked, "We have [no PACs and, therefore,] fewer open wounds and no enemies list." A third president expressed opposition to the hardball nature of PACs by stating, "We are less strident. We use persuasion. We do not use blackmail."

Another aspect of the presidents' reluctance to form PACs is their concern that they could not create effective ones. Of those surveyed, one third agreed that, "The difficulties of forming and maintaining effective PACs outweigh the possible benefits that might be derived." One such difficulty involves the lack of financial support that presidents believe could be channeled to higher education's supporters. For example, a president suggested, "We could not support enough people to result in a coordinated or rational direction." Other presidents viewed this low financial support as potentially awkward, particularly when compared with the large sums of money raised by industry and other lobbies. One president remarked, "We can never have as much buying power as big business," while another said, "The small amount of money they could raise would be embarrassing!" Similarly, an association head said, "Higher education would just be spitting in the ocean."

Presidents also thought that PAC formation would be inappropriate because of the nonprofit, tax-exempt nature of colleges and universities. Some presidents did not seem to understand that associations could establish lobbying arms, and individuals on the campuses could form PACs with their personal funds if they chose to do so. One respondent remarked, "We are a tax supported institution. A PAC would be inappropriate," and another concluded, "It is a poor use of the public money given to us to educate students." Other presidents foresaw potential conflicts of interest with campus constituents and other institutional priorities. One president expressed the following opinion: "Donors and tuition-paying parents would have problems with this, even if personal rather than institutional dollars were used. They would conclude that executive salaries were raised to permit contributions, and they would be correct." Yet another president commented that "Universities would have to raise private funds, which would conflict with other fund raising."

Presidents also pointed out the difficulty of agreeing on PAC contributions, given the diversity of higher education institutions. One observed that "institutions are too diverse to be comfortable funding PACs that will seldom be promoting their institution's specific interests." Another president asked, "Because of diversity of institutions, missions, goals, issues, who would decide upon which candidate/program to support?" Diversity of institutional size and geography were particularly problematic for some presidents who were interviewed. As one put it, "PACs would represent large urban institutions at the expense of a small, rural institution, such as mine."

Additionally, they questioned the wisdom of creating PACs at a time when the public increasingly views PACs with disfavor. A president stated, "As PACs come under attack, the higher education lobby would be an easy and politically safe target." Other presidents suggested that the creation of PACs would be an act of especially poor political timing. Said one respondent, "The public would react negatively since PACs have a bad image." Another president commented, "It would be impolitic to form PACs just as public cynicism about them reaches a high point."

Finally, the majority of respondents said they deplored the existence of PACs in the political process and did not want to be associated with any move to increase their numbers. Representative comments included, "I have an aversion to PACs on principle," "[PACs are] too much like a bribe," "PACs are the problem, not the solution," "PACs are a form of corruption," and "PACs are not in the best interests of good government or our nation." One president suggested, "We ought to reform campaign finance, not contribute to additional abuse." Another president summed up his own idealistic views and those of his colleagues by saying, "I believe that PACs are not in the public interest. Therefore, higher education should not participate in this practice even if it will otherwise benefit us. The ends do not justify the means."

CONCLUSIONS

The story of higher education lobbying is the story of adaptability. Although representatives of the higher education community once engaged in little lobbying, and only with reluctance, in recent years they have adopted many techniques commonly used by other interest groups. Higher education lobbying became especially intensive in 1995–96, thereby supporting the finding that, during periods of turmoil, interest groups are likely to do more lobbying than usual (Schlozman and Tierney 1986). The change in congressional leaders and policy objectives served as a wake-up call and since the higher education community had a new set of association leaders, it was especially receptive to a new approach.

Unlike most groups, however, higher education expanded its lobbying practices not only in intensity but also in the array of techniques utilized; it was not just "more of the same." Established groups do occasionally, though rarely, alter their preferred lobbying strategies—but not usually without first having prolonged discussion and a series of policy failures (Gais and Walker 1991, 119). Going into the 104th Congress, higher education had not suffered a series of policy failures, so the fact that the community altered its strategies anyway makes it unusual.

In 1995–96, in addition to its usual techniques, the higher education associations made more use of campus-based resources. They had more college and university presidents lobbying on Capitol Hill, which meant that association personnel were less often on the front lines. Student organizations used the Internet to mobilize their members for demonstrations and coordinate lobbying with the major associations.

It is ironic that, after the number of Washington higher education representatives mushroomed, the community became increasingly reliant on campus-based resources for federal relations activities. Nonetheless, it was mostly Washington representatives who translated the issues and options for the campus-based groups and convinced them that aggressive action was necessary, and it was these representatives who devised strategies for the local college presidents, student groups, and others to carry out. The strategy was set in Washington even though the tactics were utilized by people based on campuses across the country.

Besides the campus players, the other striking feature of higher education lobbying during the 104th Congress was its reliance on ad hoc coalitions. Two of them, the Alliance to Save Student Aid and the Science

Coalition, both used polling and focus groups to gauge public opinion and then did political advertising and grassroots mobilization. A multitude of other ad hoc coalitions also employed these and other lobbying tactics, including voter registration drives on the campuses. Together, use of ad hoc coalitions and campus-based resources constituted a new paradigm for higher education lobbying in 1995–96. The community finally moved beyond "Lobbying 101" to a more spirited, sophisticated approach.

When interest groups are divided into categories in order to compare their lobbying techniques, it is apparent that different types of groups tend to lobby differently (Schlozman and Tierney 1986). Profit-sector organizations usually lobby with what Gais and Walker call "inside strategies." For example, corporate trade associations often help to draft legislation and have influential constituents contact members of Congress (1991, 117–19). These techniques depend on having substantial resources, such as a sizable staff, policy expertise, and access to influential constituents. Higher education representatives have begun to take better advantage of their resources, but their lobbying is still unlike the profit sector because they eschew the use of political action committees (PACs). They lack both the resources and the will to use PACs for federal lobbying.

In 1995–96, as higher education representatives began experimenting with new lobbying techniques, they chose to employ "outside strategies," that is, those that are more common to low-budget citizen groups (Gais and Walker 1991, 117–19) than to corporations. The outside strategies used by colleges and universities included media ads and voter registration drives. Student groups, without higher education association coordination, used additional outside strategies, especially protests and demonstrations, and voter scorecards (see table 8.2).

There is nothing inherently better or worse about the use of inside or outside strategies. They are simply chosen tactics, deemed to be most appropriate for an interest group's own history and characteristics and most helpful for organizational maintenance and for the degree of conflict it faces (Gais and Walker 1991, 120). The stakes are higher with outside tactics since, when misused, they can backfire (Evans 1990, 258–59). Groups choose tactics they think will be most effective in influencing the group currently in power (Browne 1985). In this case, the change from Democratic to Republican control of Congress meant that higher education representatives no longer felt like insiders, so their use of more outside strategies made sense, especially given the highly conflicted nature of their relationship with the Republican leadership. Nonetheless, higher education leaders maintained their longstanding refusal to use the most common inside strategy, and the one most characteristic of corporations, namely, political action committees (PACs). Their disdain for PACs and hardball politics is exemplified by one college president's assertion, "Higher education is not the National Rifle Association!"

Table 8.2
Use of Lobbying Techniques by Corporations and Citizen Groups

Lobbying Technique	Corporations %	Citizen groups %
Contacting officials directly*	100	100
Testifying at hearings*	98	100
Informal contacts*	98	96
Entering into coalitions with other organizations**	96	92
Presenting research results*	94	92
Shaping implementation*	90	92
Planning legislative strategy*	90	83
Sending letters to members*	85	86
Inspiring letter-writing campaigns*	83	83
Helping to draft legislation*	86	74
Mounting grassroots lobbying**	81	71
Having constituents contact**	77	58
Contributing financially to campaigns	86	29
Running ads in the media**	31	33
Publicizing voting records***	28	75
Contributing work or personnel to campaigns	14	33
Endorsing candidates	8	29
Engaging in protests***	0	25

Source: Excerpted from Schlozman and Tierney 1986, 431.
Note: Table depicts percentage of Washington organizations in each category using these techniques.
*Major higher education lobbying techniques prior to 1995.
**Additional higher education lobbying techniques in 1995–96.
***Lobbying techniques used only by student groups in 1995–96.

Contrary to Congressman Kasich's expectations, during the 104th Congress higher education learned to "organize its way out of a paper bag." Prior to the 1994 election, one college president asserted, in response to a survey question about new lobbying techniques, "I do not wish to politicize our work." Another commented, "Education already has adequate priority in the government arena." Thanks to the challenges resulting from the change in congressional leadership, most higher education leaders understand now that their work is already politicized and that the future of colleges and universities is in fact on the line. Observers agree that higher education has come a long way since the days when it was considered the worst lobby in Washington.

Chapter Nine

SUCCESS IN THE 104TH CONGRESS

"We won everything we ever dreamed of."
**A higher education lobbyist at the conclusion
of the 104th Congress**

As the historic 104th Congress came to an end, it could boast of numerous successes, including a two-year, $53 billion reduction in federal spending. However, some of the most coveted items in the "Contract with America" were left unfinished, including a balanced budget amendment and tax cuts. As for higher education appropriations, they were not reduced to the extent the Republican leadership originally had intended. The 1996 fiscal year budget turned out to be a victory for President Clinton, the associations, and the higher education community as a whole. Then the 1997 fiscal year budget brought even greater gains, building on advances made in 1996.

FISCAL YEAR 1996 LEGISLATION

The compromise budget package for the 1996 fiscal year was signed into law in April 1996. Only a few months before, the president's public approval rating had been at its lowest point ever, and his favorite higher education programs, national service and direct lending, had faced massive cuts, if not elimination. With nothing to lose, the president chose to highlight his opposition to congressional budget cuts by vetoing both of the continuing resolutions (CRs) in the winter of 1995–96, thereby shutting down the federal government on two separate occasions. The vetoes were Clinton's pivotal moments and proved to be his winning strategy. The tide began to turn when the public blamed the Republican Congress for the budget stalemate and applauded the president for holding the line on popular programs, including funding for higher education. The Alliance for Student Aid and the Science Coalition had uncovered the depth of public support for higher education funding through their polling and focus groups, and President Clinton capitalized on that support. With his change in political fortunes, President Clinton took the lead on student financial aid and other higher education programs. The 1996 fiscal year budget that finally emerged thus had the following provisions.

State Postsecondary Review Entities (SPREs)

The SPRE story came to a conclusion when Congress rescinded funding for the State Postsecondary Review Entity Program for fiscal year 1996.

The higher education community regarded the decision as a major triumph, the result of its prolonged pressure against the regulations.

A consequence of the SPRE legislation had been the mobilization of the Washington higher education associations (see chapter 3). While all the associations joined forces to defeat the SPREs, NAICU was a particularly critical player in large part because of its solicitation of support from members of the new congressional Republican majority. NAICU invited Speaker Newt Gingrich (R-Georgia) to its 1995 annual meeting and informed him about the SPREs. When he commented publicly that they sounded like an inappropriate federal intrusion on higher education, the assembled private college presidents rose to their feet with a standing ovation. Shortly thereafter, Representative William Goodling (R-Pennsylvania), chair of the House Economic and Educational Opportunities Committee, expressed agreement with Gingrich's position, so the funds for the SPREs were rescinded. The role of the Department of Education in implementing the SPRE legislation came to an end.

NAICU and the private colleges did not wage the SPRE battle alone; the major associations shared a common concern and collaborated to lobby against the legislation. The SPRE legislation helped bring them together, and the role of the associations in causing its eventual defeat was evident to most observers. For example, a chief Department of Education official commented that although the associations' action on the SPREs "was disproportionate to [their] importance . . . [the associations were] effective in their fight against the regulations." College and university officials were pleased with the associations' accomplishment and gave them credit for the success.

In addition to the mobilization of the Washington associations, and as an important aspect of it, there emerged during the SPRE debate an aggressive and visible role for college and university presidents. In reflecting on the implications of the 1992 Higher Education Act (HEA), the Department of Education official most responsible for the implementation of the SPRE legislation emphasized the involvement and impact of the institutions' presidents: "The 1992 Higher Education Act and our own activism engaged the associations and pushed the presidents into being more informed and involved in federal relations than they ever were before. Previously, prior to 1992, government relations people and student aid people did all the federal relations work. But since '92 the higher-level higher ed people have become involved in federal relations and there's much more discussion now" (Longanecker interview, 1995). The associations were ultimately successful, and the institutional presidents were certainly engaged.

One outcome of the SPRE story was likely to be a closer look at the possibility of enacting separate rules and procedures for the inclusion of proprietary schools in federal student aid programs. The proprietary schools understood how much was at stake for them and regularly contributed substantial amounts to both Republic and Democratic members of the key congressional committees. In the early 1990s President Robert Atwell of ACE had tried to remove the proprietary schools from Title IV (i.e., HEA student financial aid) because their default rate was typically higher than that of other types of postsecondary institutions. He had support from some association colleagues and some public officials who believed, as a Department of Education official did, that "It's too bad that the higher education community asks us to treat Harvard the same way that we treat any truck driver school." Nonetheless, Atwell ran into opposition not only from the proprietaries and some key members of Congress but also from some of the other associations. By 1996, after the higher education community had lived through the SPRE battle, it understood better the implications of the high default rates. Though the SPREs had been eliminated, the community had expended resources on the issue that could better have been utilized in other ways. Furthermore, the commitment to balance the federal budget signaled a permanent reduction in domestic discretionary resources, so it behooved higher education representatives to advocate funding for a more limited number of institutions, and the proprietary schools were the most obvious group to exclude.

Direct lending

While President Clinton continued his support for an expansion of the direct lending program, the 104th Congress alternated between proposals for a cap on direct student loans and their complete elimination. There was no consensus in the higher education community, so most of the associations refrained from taking a public stand. Some institutions did not favor the direct lending system due to concerns about their own capacity to handle the administrative workload or their doubt that the Department of Education could administer the new system effectively. Colleges and universities that were already trying direct loans mostly liked the new system and wanted it to continue. On balance, most institutions felt it was useful to have a direct lending system, at least as an alternative to the old system. A letter from three hundred of their presidents to President Bill Clinton, Senate Majority Leader Robert Dole (R-Kansas), and Speaker Newt Gingrich contended that direct loans had introduced healthy competition into the student loan industry and had led to better service and lower rates for students and the institutions they attended (*Higher Education and National Affairs*, 13 November 1995). The presidents of some colleges and universities, while favoring direct lending, were pressured to refrain from expressing public support for the new system by members of their boards affiliated with banks or guarantee agencies. Consequently, Senator Paul Simon (D-Illinois) said that when he received personal calls and visits from presidents urging his support for direct lending, they often asked that their entreaties remain confidential (Simon interview, 1996).

In the winter of 1995–96, President Clinton vetoed bills that restored several billion dollars in funding to education because he said they failed to satisfy his demand that the direct lending program not be capped. Finally, in late April 1996, six months into the fiscal year, congressional Republicans and the Clinton administration reached a compromise spending bill for fiscal year 1996, which contained no cap on the direct lending program.

Student financial aid

In November 1995, House and Senate conferees agreed to a cut in federal student loans that was significantly less than the Republicans had originally proposed. Nonetheless, that agreement was unsatisfactory to the Clinton administration. The president continued to insist that student aid programs be restored to 1995 fiscal year spending levels. Also, the president unveiled an aggressive education agenda in his 1996 State of the Union address. Clinton called for an expansion of the College Work-Study program, plus creation of new merit scholarships and enactment of a college tuition tax deduction.

The 1996 fiscal year budget that finally emerged with the president's signature in April 1996 was very different from the initial Republican proposals. It set the maximum Pell Grant award at $2,470, an increase of $130 over the 1995 maximum award of $2,340, while appropriating $5.7 billion to the program for fiscal year 1996. While there was a substantial decline in funding for the Perkins Loan program, the Supplemental Educational Opportunity Grant and Work-Study programs were funded at their 1995 spending levels. The higher education associations considered this a major triumph.

Affirmative action

The higher education community had felt threatened by the Equal Opportunity Act of 1995, proposed by Senator Dole and Representative Canady (R-Florida), to eliminate federal affirmative action programs. The issue was so complex and controversial that it did not advance beyond committee in the First Session of the 104th Congress. By the time the Second Session had begun, in 1996, Senator Dole was a formal candidate for the U.S. presidency, and in the spring of 1996 he became the expected Republican nominee. While the Republican Party platform continued to oppose affirmative action policies, Senator Dole himself no longer focused attention on that topic, and there was no further congressional action.

National service program

The 1996 fiscal year budget, rather than eliminating the president's national service program, AmeriCorps, provided the program with a decrease of 18 percent from the previous year. Republicans had worked hard throughout the 1996 fiscal year budget process to eliminate AmeriCorps, and in February 1996, the House Appropriations Subcommittee on Veterans Affairs and HUD (Housing and Urban Development) passed a spending bill that not only would have halted the enlistment of new volunteers but also would have terminated the positions of approximately a thousand current program participants.

Despite the widespread and intense Republican opposition, President Clinton made clear his willingness to fight for his popular national service program, and his vetoes of congressional continuing resolutions in the winter of 1995–96 stemmed, he said, in part from congressional attempts to cut this program. As Office of National Service Director Eli Segal later commented, "This program is too much the heart and soul of this president for it to be cavalierly brushed aside for someone's political agenda" (Segal interview, 1996). Against the backdrop of the Republican opposition, the relatively modest decrease in funding for AmeriCorps represented a major victory for President Clinton, who desired to focus on the program in his upcoming re-election campaign. It was also a victory for college and university students, who had lobbied on the program's behalf.

Research and agency budgets

NIH, unlike many other federal agencies that sponsor university-based research, received an appropriation in the 1996 fiscal year budget that was even greater than the president had requested. In separate appropriations measures, NIH won a healthy funding increase of 5.7 percent. As for NSF, its overall appropriation was less than the president had requested, but its research budget actually increased by 4 percent. The social and behavioral sciences division in NSF was not eliminated, as had originally been proposed. In regard to earmarked funding, for the 1996 fiscal year Congress slashed earmarks by 50 percent, from $600 million in 1995 to $299 million in 1996, a successful outcome in the eyes of the major associations.[1]

The NEH and NEA budgets met very different fates from those of NIH and NSF. Many congressional Republicans had pushed for the total elimination of both NEA and NEH for ideological reasons, but these plans were ultimately scrapped in favor of deep funding cuts. Ultimately, the 1996 fiscal year budget included a substantial 38 percent decrease in NEH funding, while NEA, which had been attacked even more vigorously than NEH, received a 41 percent budget cut. Nonetheless, supporters of both agencies felt fortunate they survived at all.

FISCAL YEAR 1997 LEGISLATION

The fiscal year 1996 budget outcome had a significant effect on the budget proposals that followed. After the intensely partisan battles over higher education in 1995 and the beginning of 1996, the 1997 fiscal year budget proceedings were surprisingly amicable. Republican budget plans introduced into the House and Senate in May 1996 differed dramatically from those introduced just a year earlier in that they did not call for the elimination of direct lending, the in-school interest exemption for federal student loans, or the Department of Education. Moreover, these budget resolutions called for moderate increases in the research budgets of several federal agencies, including NSF.

On September 30, 1996, President Clinton signed into law an omnibus appropriations bill, the 1997 fiscal year budget. The higher education portion of it was as conspicuous for its lack of partisan conflict as the 1996 fiscal year higher education budget was for its pervasive partisanship. In fact, House Speaker Newt Gingrich lauded the "bipartisan spirit" in which the bill had been drafted (Burd, *Chronicle of Higher Education*, 11 October 1996). A Republican congressional staffer put it less graciously, explaining that "Clinton beat the hell out of us. We funded every one of his priorities at the level he wanted. The higher education community won't know what to do with all the money they got."

The 1997 fiscal year budget raised the maximum Pell Grant award to its highest level ever, from $2,470 to $2,700. The various restrictions previously proposed by Republican lawmakers on legal immigrants' eligibility for student aid were not enacted, much to the relief of the major associations, especially AACC. The 1997 budget also increased funding for the College Work-Study Program by 35 percent, a record level, as well as increasing the TRIO Programs for disadvantaged students by 8 percent. The federal contribution to the Perkins Loan Program was restored to its earlier level, after the previous year's cut. While some duplicative or narrowly focused education programs were eliminated, the budget preserved a variety of federal fellowship, scholarship, and continuing education programs that had been targeted for extinction the previous year, especially the State Student Incentive Grant Program, the Jacob K. Javits Program,[2] and the Dwight D. Eisenhower Professional Development Program. In fact, rather than shutting down the Department of Education, as the Republican Contract with America had originally proposed, Congress increased its budget by 7 percent over the previous year. Congress also provided funding for NEA at the fiscal year 1996 level and increased the budget of NIH by 7 percent and NEH by 5 percent. Overall, federal R&D funding increased by 4.1 percent in a year when Congress had originally called for double-digit reductions, but an overall decline in R&D funding of 2 percent in real dollars from the 1994 fiscal year to the 1997 fiscal year showed that the research community had not accomplished as much as it had hoped (Samors, *DRDA Reporter*, 11 November 1996).

In a clear victory for the president, the 1997 fiscal year budget placed no caps on the number of institutions eligible to participate in the Federal

Direct Student Loan Program, and the president's request for administrative funding for the program was granted in full. (The direct loan budget was particularly noteworthy given that the one hundred banks providing the largest number of government-guaranteed loans had contributed $2.3 million to congressional opponents of direct lending in the 104th Congress.) While there was opposition to some of the president's pet programs, including AmeriCorps, for example, the 1997 fiscal year budget process was relatively generous and noticeably bipartisan in its treatment of higher education. As the new president of ACE noted, "In the closing days of this session, there was a race by both parties to see who could do the most for higher education, both student aid and research" (Ikenberry interview, 1996).

One of the chief factors contributing to this dramatic change of fortune for higher education was the kickoff of the 1996 presidential campaign. While few college or university presidents endorsed the Clinton candidacy, they did credit him with holding the line against the 104th Congress. Most members of the higher education community were grateful for the president's support of student financial aid, his reversal of the Bush administration ban on minority scholarships, his staunch defense of affirmative action programs (with the promise to "mend it, not end it"), and his support of NEH and NEA. They felt that, over time, Secretary Richard Riley had been helpful in restraining some of the regulatory excesses of the Department of Education; in fact, the Big Six sent the president a letter asking that he keep Riley on as Secretary in the second term. While college and university presidents noted that President Clinton had not provided the support for basic research, especially biomedical research, that they would have liked, they spoke highly of him nonetheless. ACE's president expressed the consensus of the higher education domain when he said, "This president has to be given very good grades as education president" (*Chronicle of Higher Education*, 1 November 1996).

More so than in previous presidential elections, the 1996 campaign was fought, in part, on issues involving higher education. Higher education was specifically mentioned at the Democratic and Republican National Conventions and in party platforms. For example, presidential candidate Robert Dole continued the Republican Party's longtime advocacy of eliminating the U.S. Department of Education. Meanwhile, Democratic candidate Clinton unveiled new proposals to make higher education more affordable, including the Hope Scholarship, a $1,500 tax credit to help pay for the first two years of college (for students graduating from high school with a B average) and a $10,000 tax deduction for a family's expenditures on postsecondary education. (These suggestions differed from customary higher education student aid in that they involved tax issues, not appropriations.) Clinton also suggested that 100,000 college work-study students be mobilized to provide tutoring for schoolchildren to help them learn to read. President Clinton made higher education a central component of his re-election message. His standard stump speech highlighted his support for "Medicare, Medicaid, education, and the environment," a phrase he repeated at every opportunity to the point where it became known as the M^2E^2 mantra.

In congressional races across the country, Democrats criticized Republicans for favoring cuts in federal student aid, while highlighting President Clinton's defense of student aid, direct lending, and the national service program.[3] The Republicans' attempts to cut federal student aid a year earlier became a political liability as Clinton and other Democrats accused them of undermining college accessibility and affordability for middle class Americans. Key Republicans were quoted as saying they did not oppose a federal role in education, and they held press briefings to explain that the 104th Congress had actually increased higher education spending, not cut it. They took special credit for having increased spending on university-based basic research, an expenditure favored more by Republicans (especially Representative John Porter (R-Illinois), a key sub-committee chair) than by the Clinton administration.

The 1996 election may well have been the first federal election in which funding for higher education played a prominent role. In the past, members of Congress have rarely gained much political benefit from their service on higher education committees or their support for specific legislation. The absence of higher education PACs meant that there were few monetary rewards to help them finance their next campaign, and the low visibility of higher education issues meant that they could rarely be a campaign theme. Yet the low yield that congressional candidates had derived from support for college and university appropriations changed dramatically during the 1996 election. It suddenly became politically attractive to support higher education funding, and longtime friends of higher education, both Democrats and Republicans, benefited during the election campaign. The effect was likely to be a change in congressional perceptions of higher education committee assignments. As one Big Six official noted, "It used to be an act of selflessness for a member of Congress to serve on an education committee because there were no political or financial gains. That changed with this election. Now there are political gains from supporting education."

All in all, the higher education community was pleased with the policy outcomes of the 104th Congress and congratulated itself on its handling of the advocacy process. For example, ACE's chief lobbyist said, "The effective work done by college leaders on Capitol Hill during the past year demonstrates that higher education can make a compelling case about the importance of this sprawling enterprise to the nation's well-being" (Hartle,

Chronicle of Higher Education, 28 June 1996). Similarly, President Ikenberry of ACE said at the close of 1996, "We did very well in the 104th Congress. We lost no major issue. Higher education may be in a stronger position now than it was two years ago" (Ikenberry interview, 1996).

Some parts of the community were more active and had better outcomes than others. The private college lobby was most effective in eliminating the SPREs. Through NAICU and ACE it also spearheaded the Alliance to Save Student Aid, and as a result, financial aid for students in all types of institutions fared well in the Congress. The research universities benefited from their Science Coalition, especially the letter and advertorial from CEOs concerning university-based research, which helped sustain the NSF budget. The medical lobby, through its multiple associations and coalitions, was credited with the quick turnaround in the NIH budget. Yet even if some parts of the community fared better than others, no single part of it was particularly disadvantaged.

BETTER PROSPECTS FOR THE 105TH CONGRESS

At the start of the 105th Congress an article in the *Chronicle of Higher Education* summarized the gains by saying, "Higher education is hot on Capitol Hill. More Americans cite education as their first concern than any other topic. Lawmakers of both parties know it's a can't-miss issue and scramble for a piece of it. President Clinton's proposed tax breaks for college costs, and this year's scheduled renewal of the law that governs most federal higher education programs, insure that college issues will be unusually prominent in the business of Congress in 1997" (Burd et al., 25 April 1997).

This is not to say that higher education would face smooth sailing in the 105th Congress. The 1996 election brought a Republican majority back to both houses of Congress, and it was the first time in sixty-eight years that Republicans succeeded in retaining control of Congress. There was a change in committee leadership, especially in the Senate, and the arrival of new staff unfamiliar with complex higher education issues. The new players in the 105th Congress injected an air of uncertainty into the process.

Furthermore, the scheduled reauthorization of the Higher Education Act in 1998 meant that, yet again, there would be substantial debate about student aid issues. The director of NSF said, "The long-term budget outlook for research and development in general remains grim . . ." (Lane, *Chronicle of Higher Education*, 6 December 1996). Similarly, ACE's Hartle noted, "The trends make clear that budget uncertainty will be with us for years to come" (Hartle, *Chronicle of Higher Education*, 28 June 1996).

Nonetheless, success breeds success. Thanks to the favorable legislative outcomes in the 104th Congress, the higher education community could go into the 105th Congress with less trepidation than it felt when the 104th Congress convened two years earlier. Given President Clinton's very public commitment to higher education funding during the fall 1996 campaign, it seemed unlikely that the Republican congressional leadership would again overread their electoral mandate in regard to higher education budget cuts. A Republican staffer admitted, "Whatever revolutionary fervor we had is gone now."

Chapter Ten

A NEW UNDERSTANDING OF HIGHER EDUCATION LOBBYING

"Times change, and the slope of the grade becomes steeper. Associations may be more effective than they were, but the issues are more complex and the environment is more difficult."

President Stanley Ikenberry of the American Council on Education

DETERMINATION OF INTEREST GROUP EFFECTIVENESS

Although a review of policy outcomes shows that the higher education community accomplished many of its objectives during the 104th Congress, one cannot conclude from those results that its federal relations were a success. Much has been written about what constitutes success for interest groups, but there are no generally accepted criteria.

Given the complexities and overlapping responsibilities of the various components of the U.S. governmental structure, it is next to impossible to ascertain whether input demands from an interest group have caused a specific policy outcome, i.e., to establish cause and effect. Current theories and data are insufficiently instructive (Knoke 1990, 193). Many students of the policy making process have concluded that interest groups have only limited influence, as evidenced by the absence of a particular pattern to policy outcomes (e.g., see Browne 1988, 211). Political activity, regardless of its quality or quantity, is not the same thing as political influence (Schlozman and Tierney 1986, 169), so it is difficult to assess the impact of activity on public policy decisions (Knoke 1990, 193; Berry 1997, 274). Tracing broad variables, such as political contributions, for example, shows that these alone are not the controlling factors. In any case, every policy outcome is issue specific, and the determining factors as well as the extent of group influence vary from one policy debate to the next (Heinz et al. 1993, 351; Hrebenar and Thomas 1987, 15–56; Schlozman and Tierney 1986, 395–98).

While the structure and activities of a policy community typically have some impact on policy outcomes (Heinz et al. 1993, 22), it is possible that decisions related to a community may sometimes be made without its involvement (Browne 1988, 192; Schlozman and Tierney 1986, 169). In fact, it is possible that the existence and activities of a particular interest group, or even a large coalition, may not have any impact on a policy outcome at all. Other influences on the policy making process, such as media coverage or the personal preferences of legislators, may have greater influence on policy decisions. It is especially difficult to judge the extent to which pressures have been brought to bear because policy communities, and the individual interests that they represent, are likely to posture and claim success as part of their organizational maintenance strategy, regardless of the degree of involvement they actually have had (Browne 1988, 192; Heinz et al. (1993, 384). After studying four different policy domains, John P. Heinz and his colleagues concluded that interest groups often affect policy decisions, but their role is rarely substantial enough to take credit or blame legitimately for those outcomes (58).

An additional way to look at the question of interest group influence is to examine to what extent public officials grant access to the group's representatives, listen to their concerns, and choose to devote their own time to advocacy on behalf of the group (Hansen 1991, 2). Rather than judging interest group influence on the basis of policy outcomes, therefore, one could judge it on the basis of a group's ability to call public officials' attention to its requests. Groups do that by bringing political intelligence and relevant information to the table (227–30). In so doing, they help to shape the agenda and to limit the range and direction of policy options under consideration (Heinz et al. 1993, 57–58). Policy makers are better-informed if they have information from interest groups, and groups rarely misrepresent the information they are providing because competitors could then expose their misinformation, which would lead to loss of access to policy makers (Wright 1996, 200–201). Though key congressional staff members maintain their own independent decision making capability (Whiteman 1995, 188–89), they often develop close alliances with policy analysts from the interest groups, to their mutual benefit (Malbin 1980). By providing the right information at the right time, the groups' spokespersons may be able to influence details in a policy decision, even though they are not determining the basic outcome (Schlozman and Tierney 1986, 310).

Probably the best indicator of a group's success is its ability to achieve its predetermined objectives, as it defines them. Those groups with narrow objectives, therefore, are more likely to be successful than those with broader objectives (Schlozman and Tierney 1986, 396). However, there may be no agreement on the meaning of success. People have differing expectations going into a policy decision, as well as different explanations of what transpired, and why, and who gets the credit or blame. In at least one-fifth of the policy making processes studied by Heinz and his colleagues, participants varied in their assessments of success (1993, 352). For example, when the authors asked specifically to what degree the participants achieved their objectives, a little more than one-third reported that all were achieved, while almost two-thirds disagreed and said that they had achieved most but not all of their objectives (214). But success is not just in the eye of the beholder. The fact that a policy battle is never really over, and that there are likely to be many rounds of activity in the future, means that success is also dependent on when the snapshot is taken (351).

PUBLIC OFFICIALS' PERCEPTIONS OF THE HIGHER EDUCATION COMMUNITY

There is no doubt that the higher education community achieved its policy objectives in the 104th Congress; the only doubt concerns the extent to which higher education leaders and associations deserve credit for the policy outcomes. Those who are in the best position to judge a group's lobbying effectiveness are those who work in that policy area, especially legislators, their aides, and other public officials (Hrebenar and Thomas 1987, 143, 149). While the major higher education associations historically had difficulty coordinating their efforts and often were regarded as only marginally effective (e.g., see Bailey 1975; Breneman and Finn 1978; Gladieux 1977; Hawkins 1992; King 1975; and Stewart 1975), the majority of public officials responded to interview and survey questions by saying that the Big Six are doing much better these days than they used to. They noted that this policy community always faces a big challenge because of the heterogeneity of the institutions it represents, but they commented on improvements in coordination among the associations, resulting in a better division of labor and a more focused approach to policy issues. They said the associations succeeded in activating more college and university presidents to engage in advocacy, not just the ones from the largest and most elite institutions. Public officials also noted that the associations are more likely to speak with one voice on policy issues now.

A number of public officials made positive comments about the quality of the people chosen to represent higher education. For example, the assistant secretary for postsecondary education said, "Higher ed is ethical and honest. . . . These are very solid folks" (Longanecker interview, 1995). Similarly, a congressional staffer, commented that the higher education lobbyists are "a rational group of people," and another Department of Education official said, "Higher ed is an independent thinking lot. It is less slick. It looks more real."

Public officials said they rely heavily on higher education lobbyists, especially association staff, for information. They said they call the associations for information, just as the association personnel call them. Most commented on the frequency of their communications. "Sometimes they have information about new policy proposals before I do, so they let me know what's coming down the pike, and tell me about emerging problems and also tell me about emerging issues in the higher ed community." Other public officials commented on the important role of association personnel in assessing the effects of proposed policies. For example, one official indicated that information provided by the associations was important because, as the official put it, "I need to know the impact of student aid changes on their institutions." Other officials indicated that their communication with association personnel allowed them to gauge more accurately where the associations stand on various policy issues. One official commented, "I ask them about the opinion of the higher ed community on legislative proposals."

This relationship between public officials and association personnel is a mutual and interdependent one, with officials also supplying association personnel with crucial information. One public official revealed, "I give them tip-offs and advance warning and information when they need it. The associations can challenge administration proposals. I can't because that's my boss." Often, officials supply information in an attempt to convince association personnel of the wisdom of a particular course of action. Said one public official, "Its a two-way street. They call us a bit more often than we call them, but the contact is constant. We try to work with them. We try to let them know what we're doing. We try to convince them to take a position that will let us work together, rather than being at odds." Another official commented, "[Secretary] Riley meets with the association presidents to tell them what the Department's positions are. He tries to get them on the same page." And an additional official similarly remarked, "We strategize. I ask for a letter of support for my bills and find out how they will affect local colleges."

An executive branch official went so far as to say she used the association staff just like her own and drew on their assistance in many areas. Some of the Republican congressional staffers noted that because they were new to majority status, they relied heavily on association staff to help them learn the ropes. The cutback in the number of congressional aides at the beginning of the 104th Congress had exacerbated their dependence on outside assistance. For example, a Republican staff member commented, "We have no idea how to be the majority. . . . Our staff was cut by one-third, and we don't know what we're doing. I don't know what I'd do without the higher ed lobbyists. I'm pretty content with them. We wouldn't survive if we couldn't ask them what they think. We call them for everything. We ask them to look at language and tell us whether it works. We try, as we craft legislation, to avoid causing people affected by the legislation to have to devote extra time and money unnecessarily. The higher ed lobbyists call us the right amount too, not constantly. And they call only when they have real problems. They've been here and they know what it's like."

Public officials' comments about higher education's effectiveness were often contextual. Many noted that public confidence has substantial impact on policy outcomes, and as described in chapter 3, there has been less public confidence in all established institutions in recent years, including colleges and universities. One official commented on the "slow decline in the influence of higher education since World War II," but the pace of the decline has seemed especially rapid in recent years. In the eyes of many officeholders, higher education has gone from being regarded as a public good, a national investment that leads to societal benefits, to being regarded as a special interest. The days when elected officials stood up as a university president entered the room, which was once literally true in the Illinois state legislature, are long gone. As one Clinton administration official put it, "People don't bow down before university presidents anymore." Therefore, the higher education community faces a greater challenge as it makes its policy appeals.

Public officials also raised a second issue of context. A period of retrenchment, such as the one that faced the 104th Congress as it worked to erase the federal deficit, presents a real challenge for all policy communities competing at the federal trough. In the 1960s and 1970s the public coffers were much fuller than they are now. It is harder for a community to seem effective when there is little federal discretionary money than it is during a growth era. Furthermore, the Republican majority's aggressive proposals for budget cuts made it difficult for many policy sectors, including higher education, to do more than react. Proactive initiatives are not likely in such a policy setting.

A third issue of context concerns a comparison of the higher education community to other interest groups. Most public officials said they regard higher education as a whole as "somewhere in the middle of the pack." One official specified that, in terms of sophistication and level of activity, there are three tiers of lobbyists: the bankers and financial people are among those in the top tier, and many grassroots public interest groups are among those in the bottom tier; higher education seems to fall into the large middle tier, as do many of the other major interests competing with each other for their share of the domestic discretionary budget. While higher education has become much more active, using more sophisticated and strategic tactics, so have other communities. The result has been that higher education has simply held its own in an increasingly competitive policy making environment.

While the majority of comments from public officials about the higher education community were fairly positive, there were of course a few detractors. A top official in the Department of Education said, "One Dupont Circle has not changed since 1979." Another Education official said, "The associations' lack of effectiveness and people's unawareness of that lack is typical of Washington, where often the emperor wears no clothes." There were comments about continuing turf battles among the associations and disputes over credit-claiming, and there were criticisms of the associations for refusing to take stands on tough issues. Some public officials felt that the associations had a responsibility to exercise leadership and speak up even in the absence of a consensus among members. For example, one expressed his frustration about the lack of association consensus on the direct loan issue: "Associations should take a position. . . . Trade associations are supposed to make decisions. They're supposed to push members to take reasonable stands, even when some members disagree." Another said, "ACE convenes the higher ed community but it does not take a principled stand, as it should. Usually it dishes out self-serving pablum."

Other public officials contended that although the higher education community fared well in the 104th Congress, its success was not due to having developed a political strategy in advance. Rather, said these observers, higher education simply took advantage of the fact that the Republican congressional majority overreached on its budget cutting plans and thereby stirred up student activism. Higher education also benefited from President Clinton's support and commitment to funding, but could not be given credit for that lucky break.

Stanley Ikenberry, now president of ACE, was still president of the University of Illinois when he was first interviewed for this book. At that time he said that many of the complaints about the effectiveness of the associations are really about policy outcomes based on issues over which the associations have little or no control. "Complaints about the effectiveness of One Dupont Circle organizations may derive not from an objective analysis of their work but from a dissatisfaction with the outcome of higher education policy making. That's not fair to the associations. They have no control over the purchase of a yacht at Stanford. . . . Or the problem may be the soaring costs of higher education, or the magnitude of the federal deficit, and the associations have no control over those things" (Ikenberry interview, 1995). There is a limit to what the Washington higher education community can accomplish.

ADVICE FOR THE HIGHER EDUCATION COMMUNITY

When public officials were asked, "Do you have any advice for higher education so that it can be more effective?" their responses were often reminiscent of the criticisms of the community made after the associations' debacle on the 1972 HEA (see chapter 2). While higher education lobbying clearly has improved over the years, certain weaknesses persist.

One suggestion from public officials concerned better policy analysis. As noted in chapter 8, the higher education community does not take full advantage of its resources, especially its constituents and supporters. There are policy specialists on every campus, and faculty members are adept at research and writing. However, administrators rarely call on them to use their expertise for policy advocacy, and faculty tend not to know how to deliver their research findings to policy makers. Because of the paucity of policy analysis, higher education lobbyists do not always have useful information ready for policy makers when they need it. The higher education community is fortunate to have a wealth of information and expertise, but using it effectively for public policy purposes is another story altogether.

Although a recent study concluded that members of Congress rely less on interest group policy analysis than they used to (Browne 1995, 159), presentation of specialized information continues to be an important way for groups to wield influence (Wright 1996, 75–96). Public officials commented on their need for good information from the higher education community. One executive branch official said that higher education is better at identifying issues than doing the policy analysis necessary to deal with them, and another said, "There is [only] one sophisticated policy analyst at One Dupont Circle who can supply the charts and graphs." A chief congressional aide on higher education said, "I've been disappointed with the quality of policy analysis. There is too little empirical data. . . ." A Department of Education official made a similar comment, "They need real data to lobby, not just anecdotal information." An underappreciated higher education policy analyst explained that while "technical knowledge puts you at the table during decision making . . . , higher ed folks think that policy analysts are just glorified clerks." Several interviewees echoed the comments of John Brademas, a former member of Congress who had worked effectively on behalf of federal aid to higher education during his years in office. In 1987 Brademas wrote about his "frustration at not having been able to obtain for our work thoughtful analyses from the higher education community" (57).

The ACE Board of Directors commissioned an independent review of ACE at the end of 1995, as a prelude to the search for a presidential successor to Robert Atwell. The review report's recommendations were accepted unanimously by the ACE Board. One of the recommendations was that ACE improve its policy analysis and research capacity (American Council on Education 1996, 13). A key congressional staffer agreed that policy analysis should have higher priority for ACE: "ACE should do better research. ACE is a sleeping giant and needs to be more aggressive. . . . I have tried for more help from the associations than I've gotten." From the associations' standpoint, having staff with good policy analysis capabilities would mean that they would be invited to the table to inform policy makers of the consequences of their proposals and could stay to express support for their favored alternatives. As one policy analyst put it, "Analytic expertise is the best way to work yourself into the policy process."

A second set of public officials' suggestions for higher education concerned the need to form better alliances with like-minded policy communities. As noted in chapter 8, there has been a shortage of standing coalitions. A Senate staffer said that higher education should reach out to mayors and city councils because a university's finances affect the whole community. It should reach out to senior citizens who benefit from the culture and activities it provides because they too could help lobby. A House staff member made similar comments, saying, "I don't hear from Mom and Dad or the taxpayers." A senator specifically recommended getting alumni/ae associations to do a better job of activating their members in support of higher education legislation. Another member of Congress repeated the same advice: "There has been a tendency for education people not to try to activate the parents, the students, the other constituents who will be affected by legislation, but it has to be done. Higher ed should tell the people in its communities about the policy issues it faces in Congress and in the state legislatures. Don't leave the debate in Washington."

A third word of advice concerned bipartisanship and the importance for the higher education community of working well with Republicans as well as Democrats. During the 104th Congress, bipartisanship was a real challenge. On one issue after another, the higher education leaders found themselves opposed to Republican congressional proposals and allied with the Clinton administration. Even so, many members of the community knew they should avoid overt partisanship. For example, a Democratic congressional aide described calls she got from lobbyists asking her to tone down the partisan rhetoric.

There may be many more Republican majorities in Congress, and it would behoove the higher education community to work effectively with both parties. In an era of political instability, like the one that characterized the 104th Congress, bipartisanship seemed to be a winning strategy. The higher education community thinks it takes a bipartisan approach. However, when congressional Republicans were asked in interviews if the higher education community had collaborated with them adequately during the 104th Congress, they all said that it had not. They said it simply benefited from the good fortunes of the Clinton administration to which it had hitched its star. Some eventual recognition of the importance of bipartisanship appeared in an analysis of 104th congressional policies written by ACE lobbyist Terry Hartle. Rather than continuing the military metaphors that had previously characterized much higher education rhetoric (such as referring to Republican opponents as the "enemy" and describing congressional outcomes as "victories"), Hartle noted that "members of the new Republican majority proved willing to listen to the arguments and revise their plans. Indeed, several Republicans proved to be strong supporters of the national investment in research and student aid" (Hartle, *Chronicle of Higher Education*, 28 June 1996).

Fourth, public officials counseled higher education to be more proactive and visionary. In the study done by Cosand et al. in 1979 national observers, including public officials, judged the higher education associations as "reactive to issues and problems." Little has changed since then.

When interviewees were also asked whether higher education was typically more "reactive" or "proactive," none said that the higher education community could be regarded as proactive. The *Report of the ACE Review Committee* (American Council on Education 1996) specifically mentioned that the community, especially ACE, tends to be overly reactive.

Many interviewees deplored the lack of "vision" of the higher education community, saying that all it wants to do is get more funding for current programs. For example, a Department of Education official characterized association voices as "oink, oink" and commented on their status quo orientation. Similarly, a member of Congress said that the community "retards innovation" with its reflexive lobbying for more funds and efforts to save every program, rather than thinking about how the existing programs might be restructured or supplanted. The assistant secretary for postsecondary education said, "Higher education associations tend to be too comfortable with the status quo. . . . Their institutional preservation comes first. Regardless of the issue, they want to preserve the same distribution of benefits by sector." (Longanecker interview, 1995.) One congressional staffer noted that the higher education policy outcomes of the 104th Congress could be defined as success for the community only if success means avoidance of change.

Two members of Congress specifically commented that those lobbying on behalf of higher education should have more vision. A representative said, "Higher ed and other Washington groups have no long-term vision or agenda for positive changes in the field. . . . I look at lifelong learning and new technologies, and I see that higher ed needs a new vision of what learning will be like in the future. Change is happening, and it would be better to have the people in higher ed lead the change." Similarly, a senator commented, "Higher ed should look to the future, establish priorities, and be more proactive. . . . We need to chart a course for the next decade and look at different approaches."

Interestingly, the 1996 *Report of the ACE Review Committee* reached a similar conclusion about the higher education community, saying, "Time and again we heard a call for ACE to look out over the horizon and lead in defining the primary questions affecting higher education and in resolving those questions." The *Report* suggested that higher education's Washington leaders embark on "innovative and even risky initiatives" (American Council on Education 1996, 7, 19). The *Report* also recognized higher education's need for a more visible spokesperson to articulate that vision. As noted earlier, in previous decades it was common to have college and university presidents serve as national spokespersons for higher education, and many of them had good public name recognition. However, in recent years the spokesperson role has been left primarily to Washington association leaders, especially the president of ACE. To enhance his ability to serve that function, the *Report* recommended that ACE hire an executive vice-president for internal management so that the new president could be more visible as spokesperson.

Fifth, some public officials said that higher education could be more effective in Washington if members of Congress and other officials were more often invited to campus. Members of Congress specified that such invitations are most valuable when they are home, in the district, and their schedules are less hectic. They said it is important to provide opportunities for these get-acquainted sessions at times when the university is not making a request and there is no sense of urgency.[1] Public officials commented on the pleasure of seeing the labs they have helped to fund, or hearing from faculty about exciting research, or meeting the students whose aid they have helped to arrange. They said it is vital to humanize lobbyists' entreaties by coming to campus, and seeing the projects, and meeting the people.

One Senate aide described going to a research university to attend a symposium. What really mattered to this aide, much more than what she learned at the symposium, was that the event gave her the chance to meet several faculty members—people she could call for advice and opinions and personal stories later on, when specific issues arose. She recommended that all staffers be invited to campuses for a few days, to get acquainted. Implementation of this suggestion, like the one regarding more policy analysis, could only happen if college and university administrators made more effort to share the lobbying tasks with other members of the higher education community.

One member of Congress said he thought campuses should do more to give candidates and public officeholders a platform, and he said, "Always invite the media to come and observe." Free media is better than purchased media, of course, and universities can help to provide it at groundbreaking ceremonies, and various academic events, especially with honorary degrees.

He said that higher education does not do enough to cultivate its congressional allies, and several others echoed the same refrain. One senator contended that without campaign finance reform, the leaders of the higher education community would have no choice but to form PACs eventually to bolster their congressional supporters (Simon interview, 1996). However, the majority of public officials contend that higher education should not develop PACs. Instead, they point out that colleges and universities should try to dole out more non-monetary rewards to their friends. A senator's comment was typical: "Unfortunately, the [higher education] community is wary of rewarding its friends and punishing its enemies to the extent I believe they should."

A final, and related, word of advice to higher education concerns simple gratitude. Several public officials advised higher education representatives to say "thank you" more often and spoke somewhat bitterly of having their work on behalf of colleges and universities taken for granted. A legislative aide for a key Senate supporter of student financial assistance said that in the six years she had worked for the senator, he had received only two letters from students thanking him for his efforts. Another congressional staffer said, "Universities constantly ask for more. You can never do enough for them. They never say thank you." A third staffer commented that many college and university presidents say, "Just put the money on the stump and leave us alone."

In the course of interviews for this book, it was not uncommon for public officials to use the verbs "whine" and "beg" in describing the higher education community's approach to advocacy. The allegorical story of the three dogs cited at the beginning of this book exemplifies the community's feeling of entitlement. The story's punch line says that college and university representatives have historically used whining and begging as their favored mode of lobbying. One observer made a comment that shows the resentment the community has engendered by using this approach: "The goddamn arrogance of higher education. Higher education tries to intimidate lawmakers at the same time it is begging. It knows that higher ed is the key to the American dream."

REMAINING QUESTIONS

While this book provides a new understanding of interest groups generally and the higher education community specifically, it raises a number of questions. The book has chronicled the spirited new federal relations of the higher education community during the 104th Congress, but an important question concerns the community's commitment to this new approach in the future. At the beginning of the 105th Congress in 1997, President Clinton gave special priority to enactment of the Hope Scholarships he had proposed during the 1996 election campaign. In spite of initial opposition from congressional Republicans and some Democrats, Congress eventually passed tax breaks worth $40 billion to defray the cost of tuition, as well as additional funding and expanded eligibility for Pell Grants.

During the 1997 debate on student aid, the higher education community did not sustain the consensus positions that characterized it throughout the 104th Congress. Nor did many higher education representatives take the lead in crafting the legislation or in resolving policy differences between the Clinton administration and Congress or among members of Congress (Lederman, *Chronicle of Higher Education*, 28 November 1997). Partly because of the behind-the-scenes maneuvers that typify changes in tax policy and partly because of its internal disagreements, the community made minimal use of ad hoc coalitions and campus-based resources to advocate its policy preferences. Nonetheless, the higher education community ultimately fared very well.

Some observers now liken the 1997 experience to the one during the reauthorization of the Higher Education Act in 1972. Then, too, Congress enacted a large amount of student aid even though most of the major associations were not on the bandwagon. The question, then, is the extent to which the lessons of the 104th Congress will apply in the future. Perhaps the higher education community can mobilize and lobby aggressively only when it faces a serious threat to current funding.

Another question is whether the major associations will continue to shape the community's lobbying strategies and messages, given the influx of new lobbying recruits from the campuses. Faculty, alumni/ae, board members, and of course students are gradually becoming players in the Washington policy making arena, so association leaders and college and university presidents will be sharing the stage with them. The major associations are likely to face more challenges to their leadership and adaptability than ever before.

Furthermore, with most of the Big Six having started, in 1997, to move out of the building which ACE manages at One Dupont Circle, it is likely to be more difficult for ACE to do consensus building and maintain its status as umbrella association. The Big Six meetings will continue, but it remains to be seen whether the association staff can supplement them as effectively with faxes, e-mail, and phone calls as they previously did with informal conversations in the hallways and elevators. Without their information-sharing network and semblance of unity, the Big Six may lose their dominant note in the higher education community.

For now, though, the higher education community has a distinctive organizational structure, and its associations and pattern of interactions have remained unchanged for many decades. While the community has experienced the same proliferation of Washington representatives and fragmentation of interests as other policy communities, it has usually maintained a high degree of consensus about process and policies. The Big Six may no longer be almost the only game in town, as they once were, but they are still the lead players. Questions remain about what it is that makes the community able to sustain an umbrella association and such a stable set of major associations, and whether other communities attach as much value to consensus building.

Other questions concern the extent to which the Big Six typify other institutional associations outside of higher education and whether the higher education community is unusual in its good citizen mentality and powerful peer pressure that prevents institutions from becoming free riders. The durability of institutional memberships merits continued examination because there are probably variations, depending on the policy community. It would be useful to learn how the views of college and university presidents about their institutional associations compare with those of chief executive officers in other policy communities—and how unique and domain-specific the behavior of the higher education community really is. Although there are several good studies of various domains (e.g., Browne 1988; Heinz et al. 1993; Laumann and Knoke 1987), it is time to give more thought to institutional association membership incentives, members' views of the effectiveness of federal relations, and the factors that influence decisions about membership renewal. Student groups may be an especially interesting topic for further study because their leadership is temporary and constantly shifting, which means they may have motivations and incentives that differ from those of more established groups. The effectiveness of the science/medicine lobby means that it too merits further discussion, especially in regard to organizational strategies and lobbying techniques.

In general, too little attention has been paid in the interest group literature to nonprofit occupational associations, such as those representing higher education, hospitals, and museums. Since these nonprofit enterprises contribute substantially to the general welfare, it is important to gain a better understanding of their federal relations. Like all policy communities, they feel the impact of federal policy changes and need to provide effective education of policy makers. However, their legal status precludes aggressive lobbying activities, as does their image as a public good. More research on the organization and lobbying strategies of nonprofit occupational associations would yield information about what is possible, and what is effective. It would be useful to find out whether the public officials' list of suggestions for higher education lobbying would apply to other nonprofit communities.

Finally, the election of the 104th Congress also reemphasized a theme of the Reagan presidency, namely, that the public has become increasingly disenchanted with the federal government and increasingly receptive to the transfer of policy making responsibilities to state governments. This book focuses solely on federal policy making, but in higher education as elsewhere, it is important to engage in study of state policy making and state level policy communities. As one college president put it, "More and more of my government relations concerns are shifting to the state level, so national associations don't help much." The state level is where policy action is more likely to take place in the future, and perhaps state higher education lobbyists will benefit from the lessons learned in Washington.

When the 104th Congress came to town, higher education faced substantial threats to the federal funding, programs, and agencies it had come to rely upon. Representatives of colleges and universities had always been concerned about the propriety of lobbying and had rarely pursued aggressive strategies in the past. However, they responded energetically to the challenges they faced in 1995–96 and achieved most of their legislative objectives. The reasons for their success are numerous and include President Clinton's decision to risk shutting down the federal government over spending cuts and then make education a key theme in the 1996 campaign. Though no one would argue that the higher education community is one of Washington's more sophisticated lobbies, it nonetheless deserves credit for taking the hand it was dealt and playing it wisely.

CONCLUSIONS

A review of the policy outcomes of the 104th Congress shows that the higher education community was remarkably successful in realizing its objectives. However, interest group *success* is difficult to define. One of the best means of measuring the effectiveness of an interest group's lobbying is to ask the public officials who are the targets of the lobbying.

On the whole, public officials gave a positive assessment of higher education lobbying in the 104th Congress and commented favorably about the major associations. Though some interviewees did not agree, the majority of those public officials who handle higher education issues talked about improvements in coordination among college and university representatives and the fact that they frequently succeeded in speaking with one voice in 1995–96. Many noted that associations had effectively mobilized campus-based constituents, especially college students and institutional presidents, by sounding a wake-up call that led to more concerted lobbying efforts and more varied techniques, including ad hoc coalitions. Public officials also gave the associations a vote of confidence by saying that they rely heavily on association staff to inform their own policy decisions.

Nonetheless, public officials had several words of advice for the higher education community. They suggest more and better policy analysis, more alliances with other policy communities, more bipartisanship, and more strategic, visionary thinking. Finally, they emphasize the significance to them of expressions of gratitude from constituents who benefit from their efforts. They especially appreciate campus invitations and other local rewards that colleges and universities can provide to policy makers.

Perhaps the most remarkable and salient feature of this list of suggestions is that none of them (with the exception perhaps of better policy analysis) would entail additional expenditures. Most public officials did not advise colleges and universities to establish PACs or engage in other expensive lobbying tactics. To implement the suggestions from public officials, higher education would not have to augment its funding for federal relations; it would simply have to be more strategic in its use of existing resources. Good lobbying may not depend as fully on financial resources as conventional wisdom proclaims.

When the 104th Congress came to town, higher education faced substantial threats to the federal funding, programs, and agencies it had come to rely upon. Representatives of colleges and universities had always been concerned about the propriety of lobbying and had rarely pursued aggressive strategies in the past. However, they responded energetically to the challenges they faced in 1995–96 and achieved most of their legislative objectives. The reasons for their success are numerous and include President

Clinton's decisions to risk shutting down the federal government over spending cuts and then make education a key theme in the 1996 campaign.

Though no one would argue that the higher education community is one of Washington's more sophisticated lobbies, it nonetheless deserves credit for taking the hand it was dealt in the 104th Congress and playing it wisely. Not every policy community's leaders respond to policy challenges as effectively, and the response bodes well for the future of higher education. Although colleges and universities are among the oldest institutions in the Western world and are steeped in tradition that they are often reluctant to change, in Washington in 1995–96 their representatives proved able to adapt when necessary. That is fortunate because, given the erosion of public confidence in higher education, along with budget constraints, the higher education community is likely to be grappling with federal relations challenges for many years to come.

Chapter Eleven

AN OVERVIEW FOR COLLEGE AND UNIVERSITY PRESIDENTS

Most presidents of institutions of higher learning are likely to find this book pertinent to the federal relations decisions they face. Since they responded generously to the survey and interviews for this book, it is appropriate to reciprocate by providing a convenient executive summary that highlights the findings and recommendations that are most relevant to them. This overview may be of use and interest to others as well.

BENEFITS OF THE MAJOR ASSOCIATIONS

One of this book's topics is an examination of the Big Six associations in Washington, namely, the American Association of Community Colleges (AACC), the Association of American Universities (AAU), the American Association of State Colleges and Universities (AASCU), the National Association of Independent Colleges and Universities (NAICU), the National Association of State Universities and Land-Grant Colleges (NASULGC), and their umbrella association, the American Council on Education (ACE). Collectively known as "the Big Six," they provide a myriad of services and programs unrelated to federal relations, but presidents expressed particular interest in having an evaluation of the associations' federal relations work.

Presidents often ask whether the Big Six membership dues are worth paying. The short answer is yes, for a variety of reasons. First, their peers regard affiliation with these major associations as the professional equivalent of civic duty—"the price of good citizenship," as Derek Bok reportedly put it. Because the whole higher education community benefits from association lobbying, regardless of affiliation, there is considerable peer pressure to share the cost of association support. Presidential peers are critical, especially in the smaller associations, of those institutions and chief executives who do not belong. Furthermore, given that most institutions withdraw only because of financial pressures, peers may view lack of affiliation as a public sign of institutional fragility.

A second and more important reason for affiliation is that federal policy making has become increasingly consequential for colleges and universities, and their need for a higher education voice in Washington is greater than ever. Given the current absence of well-known college or university spokespersons, the major associations, especially ACE, usually fill that role for public officials and the media. Additionally, survey results show that nearly every president thinks the major associations are effective in regard to federal relations, and presidents say they depend on the associations' information and early warning systems. Most public officials use association staff to inform their own policy decisions.

LIMITATIONS OF THE MAJOR ASSOCIATIONS

When college and university presidents criticize the Big Six, they often mention the associations' tendency to take generic, lowest-common-denominator policy positions, which may not reflect the views of their type of institution. Nearly a third of the presidents think the associations represent some institutions more than others, and many contend it is the larger institutions they represent best. Presidents also note that the major associations rarely handle institution-specific issues, i.e., the ones that concern their own institution individually.

To supplement or supplant the major associations, nearly half of the presidents turn to the more than two hundred specialized associations in Washington, to their own campus federal relations staff, or to hired guns (i.e., for-profit law, consulting, or lobbying firms). Larger institutions with research and doctoral emphases are the ones that tend to use the widest array of Washington representatives, while smaller institutions and those with fewer resources are more likely to rely exclusively on one or more of the Big Six for federal relations assistance. The number of Washington higher education representatives has mushroomed over the last fifteen years, but most public officials say the added numbers do not provide added clout for the community as a whole, only for institutions with their own representatives. Public officials especially bemoan the use of hired guns to lobby for academic earmarks, i.e., special appropriations for a specific institution or group of them. Officials say that this kind of lobbying makes higher education look like any other special interest. Though most association leaders agree, they have been unable to curtail this practice among their member institutions.

Those presidents who especially want a voice in Big Six association decisions can aspire to board membership. Association leaders listen to their boards and use them for everything from agenda-setting on policy issues to testifying before Congress. Presidents can also pick up the phone and complain to association leaders when they disagree, and many do so.

Association leaders are usually responsive to squeaky wheels but, conversely, most of the major associations do not get a full view of member preferences because they rarely conduct systematic surveys.

LOBBYING ADVICE

At the end of the 104th (Gingrich) Congress in 1996, one higher education lobbyist said, "We won everything we ever dreamed of." There were a number of reasons for the favorable outcomes in 1995–96, not least of which was the priority President Clinton put on higher education appropriations. However, this book contends that the higher education community also deserves credit, especially because of its move to more spirited advocacy. While the major associations were not solely responsible for the change in lobbying techniques, they initially sounded the alarm and then led some of the efforts to devise new strategies.

Members of Congress are increasingly sympathetic to entreaties from constituents rather than from association staff, so campus-based lobbying was especially useful during the 104th Congress. Presidents were better-informed and more active in Washington, and students demonstrated how effective their participation could be. In the future, presidents may want to improve the flow of information about institutional concerns to all campus colleagues, including faculty, students, trustees, and alumni/ae, so they too can contact public officials in an informed manner. During the 104th Congress, ad hoc coalitions, which focus on specific policy concerns, were another key to success because they could respond quickly and lobby aggressively, using many techniques that were unusual for the higher education community. These coalitions, along with campus-based lobbying, represent the new paradigm for higher education lobbying.

Nonetheless, ad hoc coalitions cannot take the place of major associations because they are not able to do the same consensus building. The higher education community is carefully structured, with different associations representing different kinds of institutions, and with the American Council on Education (ACE) serving as the umbrella association. There is some messiness to overlapping association memberships, and there are more major associations and specialized ones than cost-conscious institutional presidents would prefer to support. Nonetheless, structural overlap facilitates collaboration, as does physical proximity. As this book goes to press, three of the Big Six are moving out of the National Center for Higher Education at One Dupont Circle, which leaves only two of the organizations still housed there. The relocations will make it more difficult for ACE to continue to serve as the umbrella association and for the Big Six to maintain their previous level of cooperation. This is unfortunate since consensus helped the community make a stronger case on Capitol Hill during the

104th Congress. Institutional presidents should encourage their associations to reach consensus positions whenever possible.

Another way for presidents to advance the cause of higher education is to invite public officials to campus. Officials said they appreciate contact with faculty members and students who put a human face on dry policy issues, and they welcome media coverage of their campus visits to underline their interest in and support for higher education. Officials commented on their desire for more expressions of gratitude. The gratitude they have in mind is not necessarily monetary since many of them agree, along with the overwhelming majority of presidents, that PAC contributions would be inappropriate for colleges and universities.

It is noteworthy that when asked to provide advice to the higher education community, public officials did not suggest changes that entail much expense. Rather than advising an increase in funding for federal relations activities, public officials simply advised a change in attitude and more strategic use of existing resources.

CONCLUSION

There once was a time when the higher education community could stay above the Washington fray and fare well nonetheless. Those days are gone now. The decline of public confidence in higher education, coupled with budget constraints, means that there will be federal relations challenges for the foreseeable future. Given the growing impact of federal policies on colleges and universities, it has become even more important for presidents to participate in the process of making friends and educating federal officials. Prior to the 1994 election, one college president asserted, "I do not wish to politicize our work." Another commented, "Education already has adequate priority in the government arena." Thanks to the wake-up call from the 104th Congress, most higher education leaders understand now that their work is already politicized and that the future of colleges and universities is on the line.

APPENDICES

NOTES

BIBLIOGRAPHY

INTERVIEWEES

INDEX

Appendix A

SURVEY SENT TO COLLEGE AND UNIVERSITY PRESIDENTS

CENTER FOR THE STUDY OF HIGHER
AND POSTSECONDARY EDUCATION

THE UNIVERSITY OF MICHIGAN

*Presidential Views of the Federal Relations Activities
of the Washington Higher Education Associations*

It will take you only 5 minutes to fill out this questionnaire, and if you want a report of the survey results, please return the reply card. This survey is completely confidential; your name and institution will never be connected with your answers. Please fill in the circles completely, using either a pencil or pen.

This questionnaire asks about your views of the federal relations activities of the six major presidentially based higher education associations located in Washington, D.C. Please share your opinions about the federal relations work of the association(s) you know best. The associations are:

American Council on Education (ACE)
American Association of Community Colleges (AACC)
American Association of State Colleges and Universities (AASCU)
Association of American Universities (AAU)
National Association of Independent Colleges and Universities (NAICU)
National Association of State Universities and Land-Grant Colleges (NASULGC)

1. Please indicate which of the six associations your institution currently belongs to:
   AACC ❏   AASCU ❏   AAU ❏   ACE ❏   NAICU ❏   NASULGC ❏
   None of the six ❏
   (If you are not a member of any of the six, please skip to Question 7.)

2. Have you joined any of the six associations in the past 10–15 years? Yes ❏   No ❏

3. If yes, which one(s)?
   AACC ❏   AASCU ❏   AAU ❏   ACE ❏   NAICU ❏   NASULGC ❏

4. Have you discontinued membership in any of the six associations in the past 10-15 years?   Yes ❏   No ❏

5. If yes, which one(s)?
   AACC ❏   AASCU ❏   AAU ❏   ACE ❏   NAICU ❏   NASULGC ❏

6. Why did you withdraw? (Indicate the one most important reason. If the reason varies for different associations, please explain.)
   ❑ Budgetary reduction by my institution.
   ❑ Association programs or services did not justify fees.
   ❑ Our needs are served adequately by other associations.
   ❑ Concerns of institutions like mine are not met by the programs and services of this association.
   Comments: _____

7. The six major higher education associations do not have political action committees (PACs) to make campaign contributions to Congressional candidates and incumbent members of Congress. Do you think they should have PACs?
   Yes ❑   No ❑

8. If your answer to question 7 was "no," please explain why, indicating all the answers that apply:
   ❑ Forming a PAC would diminish higher education's special status, moving it from a public interest to a "special interest."
   ❑ The difficulties of forming and maintaining effective PACs outweigh the possible benefits that might be derived.
   ❑ Other _____

Besides PACs, associations may use a variety of other tactics, both direct and indirect, to influence what goes on in government. Please indicate your views about the tactics of the six major associations. Here is a list of possible educational and lobbying tactics:

(A) Associations do now and do well
(B) Associations do now, but do not do well
(C) Associations don't do now, but should do
(D) Associations don't do now, and should not do

		(A)	(B)	(C)	(D)
9.	Monitor changes in rules, regulations, or laws	❑	❑	❑	❑
10.	Alert colleges and universities about policy issues	❑	❑	❑	❑
11.	Develop policy positions or strategies	❑	❑	❑	❑
12.	Resolve policy conflicts among member institutions	❑	❑	❑	❑
13.	Coordinate policy positions or strategies with other associations	❑	❑	❑	❑
14.	Publish policy papers	❑	❑	❑	❑
15.	Purchase advertising in newspapers and other media to express association opinions on policy issues	❑	❑	❑	❑
16.	Arrange meetings between members of Congress (and/or staff) and college presidents (and/or staff)	❑	❑	❑	❑
17.	Arrange personal contacts between association staff and members of Congress and/or staff	❑	❑	❑	❑
18.	Organize letter-writing campaigns to Congress by college and university presidents	❑	❑	❑	❑
19.	Organize telephone campaigns for calls to Congressional district offices or Washington offices	❑	❑	❑	❑
20.	Testify at hearings	❑	❑	❑	❑
21.	Assist in developing legislation, or rules and regulations	❑	❑	❑	❑

22. Which of the six major associations is most often your *primary association* for the federal issues of greatest importance to your institution?
    AACC ❑   AASCU ❑   AAU ❑   ACE ❑   NAICU ❑   NASULGC ❑

None of the six ❑
*Questions 23-28 refer to your **primary association**. If you answered "none of the six," please skip to Question 29 (top of next page).*

23. How effective is your *primary association* in regard to federal relations?
Very effective ❑   Somewhat effective ❑   Somewhat ineffective ❑
Very ineffective ❑

24. Indicate the extent to which your primary association should give a higher or lower priority to federal relations:
Much higher than now ❑   Somewhat higher than now ❑   Same as now ❑
Somewhat lower than now ❑   Much lower than now ❑

25. In regard to federal relations, do you feel your primary association represents the needs of all its member institutions equally, or do you feel it represents some institutions more than others (e.g., rural or urban, large or small, public or private, etc.)?
Represents all equally ❑   Represents some more than others ❑   No opinion ❑

26. If you think it represents some more than others, what type of institutions does your primary association mostly represent?

_____

27. Are the institutional benefits of membership in your primary association worth the present costs?
Definitely yes ❑   Probably yes ❑   Uncertain ❑   Probably not ❑   Definitely not ❑

28. Are you committed to continuing your membership in your primary association?
Definitely yes ❑   Probably yes ❑   Uncertain ❑   Probably not ❑   Definitely not ❑

Questions 29-35 concern only ACE because ACE is the "umbrella association" for higher education in that its membership includes the other five major associations.

29. Do you consider ACE to be the major voice for higher education in Washington?
Yes ❑   No ❑

30. How effective do you consider ACE to be in regard to federal relations?
Very effective ❑   Somewhat effective ❑   Somewhat ineffective ❑
Very ineffective ❑

31. Indicate the extent to which you think that ACE should give a higher or lower priority to federal relations:
Much higher than now ❑   Somewhat higher than now ❑   Same as now ❑
Somewhat lower than now ❑   Much lower than now ❑

32. In regard to federal relations, do you feel ACE represents the needs of all its member institutions equally, or do you feel it represents some types of institutions more than others?
Represents all equally ❑   Represents some more than others ❑   No opinion ❑

33. If you think ACE represents some more than others, what type of institution does ACE mostly represent?

34. If you are an ACE member, do you think the institutional benefits are worth the present costs?
Definitely yes ❏   Probably yes ❏   Uncertain ❏   Probably not ❏   Definitely not ❏

35. If you are an ACE member, are you committed to continuing your membership?
Definitely yes ❏   Probably yes ❏   Uncertain ❏   Probably not ❏   Definitely not ❏

36. How many full-time equivalent persons (FTEs), or portions of FTEs, does your campus employ in *federal relations*? _____

37. Does your institution have a *full-time* staff member in Washington? Yes ❏ No ❏

38. If yes, approximately how long have you had a full-time staff member in Washington?
Less than 5 years ❏   Between 5 and 10 years ❏   Between 10 and 15 years ❏
Over 15 years ❏

39. Does your institution have a *part-time* staff member in Washington? Yes ❏ No ❏

40. If yes, approximately how long have you had a part-time staff member in Washington?
Less than 5 years ❏   Between 5 and 10 years ❏   Between 10 and 15 years ❏
Over 15 years ❏

41. If your institution has a Washington representative, is that because of insufficient federal relations help from the major presidentially-based associations?
Yes ❏ No ❏

42. In general, when different associations have different positions on an issue, do you think they *now* are most likely to: (*Choose one.*)
❏ Arrive at a compromise and present a unified higher education position to the federal government.
❏ Recognize the conflicting interests and present the different positions to the federal government.

43. When different associations have different positions on an issue, you think they most often *should*: (*Choose one.*)
❏ Arrive at a compromise and present a unified higher education position to the federal government.
❏ Recognize the conflicting interests and present the different positions to the federal government.

44. In addition to the six major presidentially-based associations, there are many campus offices and specialized groups and firms that represent higher education in Washington. To represent the interests of your institution in Washington, do you usually rely: on one or more of the six major associations: on other offices, groups, and firms; or on both?
one or more of the six associations ❏ other offices, groups, and firms ❏ both ❏

45. Has your institution employed a for-profit Washington law firm, consulting firm, or lobbying firm to deal with a special federal relations problem?
Yes, often ❑   Yes, occasionally ❑   No, never ❑

46. Does your institution have a PAC (political action committee) for federal relations?
Yes ❑   No ❑

47. In general, how effective do you consider all of higher education to be in regard to federal relations? (This question is asking not just about the major associations; it is asking about the effectiveness of the Washington higher education community as a whole.)
Very effective ❑   Somewhat effective ❑   Somewhat ineffective ❑
Very ineffective ❑

48. Is your institution public or private?   Public ❑   Private ❑

49. How does the Carnegie Foundation classify your institution?
❑ Research
❑ Doctoral
❑ Comprehensive (Master's)
❑ Liberal Arts (Baccalaureate)
❑ Associate of Arts

50. Do you run the central office of a multi-campus institution?   Yes ❑   No ❑

51. Size of your institution (FTE students):
Less than 1,000 FTEs ❑   1,001-5,000 FTEs ❑   more than 5,001 FTEs ❑

52. How long have you served as president or chancellor of your institution?
Less than one year ❑   2-3 years ❑   4-5 years ❑   More than 5 years ❑

53. On what did you base the views you expressed in this survey?
Intimate knowledge ❑   Informed opinion ❑   General impression ❑

54. Do you have any additional comments about the associations or higher education representation in Washington?

Thank you for your time. Please return your completed questionnaire in the enclosed reply envelope, or mail it to:

Dr. Constance E. Cook
The University of Michigan
Center for the Study of Higher and Postsecondary Education
3300 School of Education Building
Ann Arbor, Michigan 48109-1259

If you would like a copy of the results of this survey, just return the enclosed reply card.

Funding for this survey comes from a grant from the Office of Research at the University of Michigan.

Appendix B

COMPARISON OF SURVEY RESPONDENTS AND OVERALL POPULATION OF COLLEGES AND UNIVERSITIES IN THE UNITED STATES

	Survey	Population	X^2
Control			143.71*
Public	60.2	44.9	
Private	39.8	55.1	
Carnegie classification			133.57*
Associate of Arts	37.8	51.4	
Baccalaureate	24.8	22.0	
Master's	24.3	18.5	
Doctoral	6.5	3.9	
Research	6.6	4.3	
Size, in full-time equivalent students [FTEs]			243.94*
Small (<1,000 FTEs)	17.4	36.6	
Medium (1,000 to 5,000 FTEs)	52.7	39.2	
Large (>5,000 FTEs)	29.9	24.2	

Source: Population data based on the *Chronicle of Higher Education Almanac* (2 September 1996) and Fact Files (6 April 1994), http://www.chronicle.com.
* $p < .001$

This sample is not statistically representative of the entire population of institutions in the United States in that private, associate of arts, and small colleges are underrepresented.

NOTES

PREFACE (pages xi–xxi)

1. Appendix B has a statistical comparison of survey respondents and the overall population of colleges and universities in the United States.

2. Although the survey was addressed to the presidents, there is no way to tell whether the president was the person who actually filled it out. In some cases, it was probably a government relations officer or presidential assistant who actually answered the questionnaire.

CHAPTER 1 (pages 3–18)

1. The Lobbying Disclosure Act defines *lobbying* as oral or written communications to high level executive or legislative branch officials regarding the selection of federal officials or the formulation, modification, or adoption of federal legislation, regulations, and programs.

2. An explanation of the implications of 501(c)(3) tax status appears in chapter 8.

3. These figures do not include proprietary (for-profit) institutions.

4. While *FY1998* is commonly used in federal documents when referring to the 1998 fiscal year, this book is using instead the terms *fiscal year 1998* or *the 1998 fiscal year* to be sure that the meaning is clear to readers less familiar with federal parlance.

5. The *Big Six* are also known as *The Six*.

6. There are a small handful of institutions that can belong to four of the Big Six, such as MIT, Tuskegee, and Cornell University, which are land-grant universities and, therefore, can be NASULGC members in spite of their private status. (Cornell in fact has both public and private components.)

7. The 1995 dues of the Big Six were the following: AAU: $38,000 for all U.S. members; AACC: $700–4,890, based on enrollment; NASULGC: $7,700–38,200, based on enrollment and general fund expenditures; NAICU: $600–9,000, based on enrollment and general expenditures; AASCU: $1,550–10,450, based on enrollment; ACE: $804–12,292, based on enrollment and general expenditures.

8. The Carnegie system is even more complex than indicated here because, in fact, there are both Research Universities I and II, Doctoral Universities I and II, Master's Universities and Colleges I and II, and Baccalaureate Colleges I and II.

9. While these specialized institutions are considered part of the higher education community, they were not included in the survey of presidents that is described in this book.

10. Although the judiciary is the not the subject of this book, it is worth noting that interest groups try to influence judicial policy making, just as they try to influence policy in the executive and legislative branches of government (see, for example, Cook 1980).

CHAPTER 2 (pages 19–33)

1. *Banding Together: The Rise of National Associations in American Higher Education, 1887–1950* by Hugh Hawkins (1992) provides an authoritative history of the Big Six associations before 1950. The following information is distilled from it except where noted.

2. As this book goes to press, three of the Big Six—AASCU, NASULGC, and AAU—are moving out of One Dupont Circle. Since NAICU is already located elsewhere, ACE will continue to serve as landlord only for AACC.

3. Moynihan made his remark after learning that university presidents had used the short meeting he had arranged for them with President Nixon not to present their case for a major infusion of federal aid to institutions, as he had anticipated, but rather to lobby for a relatively small program concerning foreign language instruction (Berdahl interview, 1996).

4. *Iron triangle* (or occasionally *cozy triangle*) is a term used by political scientists to describe the interactions between interest groups and policy makers. The three parts of the triangle are the relevant interest groups, the relevant legislators and their staff (usually a single congressional committee or subcommittee), and the relevant personnel from a specific agency in the executive branch. Their interactions consist of exchanges of information for their mutual benefit. The chief characteristics of an iron triangle are the relatively small number of its participants, the lack of permeability of its *iron* boundaries so that those outside cannot intercede in the relationships within the triangle, and the collusion of the three sets of participants on policy preferences. The term *iron triangle* has sometimes been used synonymously with *subgovernment,* which also denotes an autonomous, fixed set of players who are interdependent. As the number of participants in policy decisions has grown and the boundaries of the policy communities have become porous, the term *issue network* has come to replace the terms *iron triangle* and *subgovernment* (Heclo 1978, 87–124). *Issue network* does a better job of describing what Salisbury characterizes as "the shifting, almost kaleidoscopic configurations of groups involved in trying to shape policy" (Salisbury 1992, 347).

CHAPTER 3 (pages 34–52)

1. The U.S. Navy (and its Office of Naval Research, which was the cognizant agency for Stanford University research) eventually said it did not "'have a claim' that Stanford engaged in 'fraud, misrepresentation, or other wrongdoing'" (Cordes, *Chronicle of Higher Education*, 26 October 1994).

2. Accreditation of postsecondary institutions is a complex topic. There are three categories of accrediting associations: the six regionals (North Central Accrediting Association, for example); the nationals, such as the Rabbinical and Talmudic Schools and the Bible Colleges, the Accrediting Council for Independent Colleges and Schools (mostly proprietary business schools), the Accrediting Commission of the Distance Education and Training Council, Council on Occupational Education, Accrediting Commission for Career Schools and Colleges of Technology (proprietary trade schools); and the specialized accreditors, such as those in dentistry, journalism, law, medicine, nursing, etc. There are two groups which recognize accreditors: the new Council on Higher Education Accreditation (CHEA) and the U.S. Department of Education, through its National Advisory

Committee on Institutional Quality and Integrity, which provides recognition for purposes of participation in federal programs. CHEA recognizes fewer accreditors than does the Department since it limits itself to higher education, rather than including postsecondary education more generally (Fuller letter, 2 December 1996).

CHAPTER 4 (pages 53–63)

1. Historically, faculty have supported Democratic candidates and policies over Republican ones. It is well-known that academics are an exception to the generalization that individuals with higher income and education levels are more likely to support Republicans.

2. It was the fact that Gingrich channeled tax-exempt contributions for these courses to his political action committee, GOPAC, that led to his reprimand by the House of Representatives in January 1997. Federal law prohibits use of tax-exempt contributions for partisan political activities.

3. Steven Waldman's *The Bill* (1995) provides an excellent description of the development and passage of this legislation.

CHAPTER 5 (pages 64–87)

1. Mark Nemec of the University of Michigan co-authored an early version of this chapter.

2. According to Heinz et al. (1993) there used to be two peak associations in agriculture, the American Farm Bureau Federation (AFBF) and, later, the National Farmers Union (NFU), but by the 1960s there were internal divisions, and they had lost their dominant positions. In the energy field there are several major associations, such as the American Petroleum Institute, the American Gas Association, and the National Coal Association, but in the 1970s these fuel interests began playing a more modest role because they lost their capacity to speak authoritatively for the individual corporations that were their members. In labor, there is an adversarial relationship between two polarized camps, with the AFL-CIO dominating one side and the Chamber of Commerce, National Association of Manufacturers, and Business Roundtable dominating the other. In the health sector the American Medical Association was the hegemonic interest group on health policy from the 1940s until the 1960s, but since then there has been a fragmentation of interests, with no dominant groups or coalitions.

3. The major associations paid annual dues of about $2,000 for membership in ACE in 1996. Fuller information about institutional dues can be found in chapter 1.

4. See the fuller explanation of the implications of this tax status in chapter 8.

5. The Monday Group includes the Association of Community College Trustees (ACCT), Association of Catholic Colleges and Universities (ACCU), Association of Governing Boards (AGB), Association of Jesuit Colleges and Universities (AJCU), Council of Independent Colleges (CIC), Hispanic Association of Colleges and Universities (HACU), National Association of College and University Business Officers (NACUBO), National Association for Equal Opportunity in Higher Education (NAFEO), National Association of Student Financial Aid Administrators (NASFAA), and United Negro College Fund (UNCF).

6. ACE typically coordinates amicus curiae briefs for the higher education community.

7. Some observers say that ACE was less often an autonomous player during the two decades when Hartle's predecessor, Charlie Saunders, served as Vice President for Government Relations.

8. The University of Notre Dame, for example, has been hoping to be admitted for some time.

9. In recent years the rivalry has been minimal at the presidential level but more intense among the government relations personnel.

10. For example, the American Association for Higher Education (AAHE) and the Association of American Colleges and Universities (AAC&U) both play an important role in improving the quality of higher education, but neither is very active in federal relations; AAHE's promotion of assessment of student learning has sometimes involved it in federal relations, and AAC&U, the association that promotes the liberal arts and deals with curricular issues, was once a major Washington player but was succeeded in that role by NAICU in 1976.

11. Although NASFAA's president, Dallas Martin, was once called "Washington's most effective lobbyist for higher education" (Roark 1980), observers view NASFAA as somewhat less influential now than it used to be. Interviewees said the decline in influence is due to the increasingly technical nature of student financial aid, coupled with problems caused by a divided board. Furthermore, the Big Six have developed their own student aid expertise, making them less dependent on NASFAA.

12. NCEOA comprises ten regional associations. Its principal concern is sustaining and improving educational opportunity program services, specifically the federally funded TRIO projects that operate in over a thousand postsecondary institutions and more than ninety community agencies. (TRIO projects are under Title IV of the HEA and are operated by the U.S. Department of Education.) NCEOA's savvy president, Arnold Mitchem, has successfully championed the educational opportunity programs.

13. For the last few years UNCF's visibility has increased because it has been led by the former Democratic Whip in the House of Representatives, William Gray, who is a well-known figure in Washington.

14. USSA is a forty-year-old association that suffers both from the transient nature of its membership and also from its periodic involvement in issues not directly related to higher education policy. The USSA board is made up of current students, and the staff of eight is mostly composed of recent graduates or those taking a leave from their studies; each has a fixed term of office of one or two years. USSA was a very active and effective player in the 1995 student aid debates.

15. AAUP has a Washington office and is a member of the Higher Education Secretariat. Although it joined the Action Committee for Higher Education in the early 1980s and the Alliance to Save Student Aid in 1995, it usually does not lobby with the rest of the higher education establishment. AAUP's counterparts, the National Education Association (NEA) and the American Federation of Teachers (AFT), both represent some unionized campuses. Although they play a strong role in elementary and secondary education, these two organizations do not have as much visibility or effect on higher education policy issues.

16. There are other effective lobbying groups that deal with student aid issues

but are not considered part of the higher education community, e.g., the National Council of Higher Education Loan Programs (which represents guarantee agencies) and the Consumer Bankers Association (which represents banks that provide student loans).

17. For example, AAMC works with the Association of Schools of Nursing, and it also works with a variety of associations outside of higher education, such as the American Hospital Association, the American Medical Association, and the American College of Surgeons.

18. CASE is the association for institutional advancement, i.e., communications, fund-raising, and alumni/ae relations. Its membership of about three thousand includes not only institutions of higher learning but also independent elementary and secondary schools.

19. Proprietary schools offer certificate and degree programs in such fields as accounting, auto mechanics, beautician work, computer programming, business administration, paralegal work, medical technician roles, graphic design, truck driving, and aviation maintenance.

20. Both AACC and ACE include members from some of the accredited proprietary schools; AACC includes fewer of them because it requires members to have regional accreditation.

21. Interviews with public officials fifteen or twenty years ago, contrasted to current interview data, would of course have made possible a more authoritative conclusion about the effect of additional interest groups. With no pre/post data available, the next-best approach is to rely on the memories of those who have experienced the changing numbers themselves.

CHAPTER 6 (pages 88–114)

1. Pearson's $r = .475$, $p < .01$.

2. According to the president of AASCU (Appleberry interview, 1995), that association's recent membership survey showed that government relations is the number one priority for its member institutions, and he said that a similar survey showed the same thing three years ago. Nonetheless, phone interviews with presidents on the AASCU board yielded the same information as those with the board members of the other associations, namely, that federal relations is important, but neither the sole reason for the organization nor its number one priority.

3. Pearson's $r = .364$, $p < .01$.

4. Pearson's $r = .740$, $p < .01$.

5. Pearson's $r = -.358$, $p < .01$.

6. Pearson's $r = -.121$, $p < .01$.

7. Affiliation with AAU, which is an elite club of research universities with an eager waiting list, confers prestige on its member institutions. No matter how dissatisfied the members may be with AAU's federal relations or other programs and services, institution presidents said they would not seriously consider withdrawing.

8. There are some well-endowed institutions that are not members of major associations but whose nonparticipation would not be interpreted as a sign of institutional fragility; for example, Northwestern University is not a member of NAICU.

9. Both of AAU's annual membership meetings are presidents-only events.

CHAPTER 7 (pages 115–137)

1. The consensus ethos extends to the internal workings of the associations, as noted in the *Report of the ACE Review Committee* (ACE 1996). It said that ACE is run much like a college, with a decentralized administration and elaborate consultation by all players, on all topics. The *Report* discussed the "profound commitment throughout the organization to a consultative and consensus-based decision process" (11).

2. ANOVA, $df = 6$, $F = 10.938$, $p < .001$.

3. Pearson $X^2 = 145.037$, $df = 4$, $p < .001$.

4. ANOVA, $df = 4$, $F = 9.929$, $p < .001$.

5. $t = 4.042$, $p < .001$.

6. ANOVA, $df = 5$, $F = 8.264$, $p < .001$.

7. Pearson $X^2 = 19.072$, $df = 2$, $p < .001$.

8. ANOVA, $df = 5$, $F = 12.114$, $p < .001$.

CHAPTER 8 (pages 138–172)

1. Berry surveyed 83 public interest groups, or citizens' groups. Walker's survey included 892 voluntary associations, i.e., ones that are open to members, as opposed to trade unions, for example. Knoke studied 459 national associations, especially professional societies, recreational organizations, and women's associations.

2. Schlozman and Tierney used a random sample that was weighted to include more of the large, active, and affluent groups with Washington offices. They conducted interviews with 175 Washington representatives.

3. In Schlozman and Tierney's classification of lobbying tactics, it is evident that trade associations lobby much the same way as the corporations they represent, so the distinction between trade associations and corporations in their analysis is of little utility (1986, 431). Trade associations for nonprofit industries make up only a small percentage of those surveyed by Schlozman and Tierney.

4. Grassroots mobilization used to be the sole province of labor and citizen groups, but that is no longer the case. That technique is now used by both insiders and outsiders. Corporations have learned to mobilize grassroots activism from the top down, out of their public affairs offices, using employees, suppliers, customers, and stockholders (Walker 1991, 51).

5. Though higher education clearly benefits society at large, it has come to be regarded as a personal benefit because the payback of a college education to the individual student is considerable. Studies show that those with a bachelor's degree have lifetime earnings of $600,000 more than those with a high school degree, plus an additional $800,000 for a master's degree and $1.3 million for a professional school degree (Hartle, *Chronicle of Higher Education*, 28 June 1996). Some believe that the implication of this payback is that tuition funding should come from the ultimate beneficiary, the student, rather than from taxpayers.

6. NAICU used to be the only member of the Big Six with both 501(c)(3) and also 501(c)(6) components. However, in 1995 NAICU became entirely a 501(c)(3) organization. According to its president, David Warren, the reason for the change was to give all employees the benefit of TIAA-CREF, the retirement plan available to those in organizations with 501(c)(3) status.

216

7. In a 1994 report on the level of public confidence in social institutions, higher education fared better than twenty other institutions, including health, environmental, human services, arts and cultural organizations; organized labor; the media; major corporations; and federal, state, and local government (National Center for Education Statistics 1995, 33).

8. In the course of over one hundred interviews, only once was there mention of any difficulty in scheduling appointments for university officials with members of Congress, and that comment came from the Washington representative of a large state system that has personnel from many institutions competing for the attention of the congressional delegation. Most interviewees said that legislators were always available to college and university presidents, especially those from their own district.

9. Representative Dick Chrysler, a Democrat from Michigan, said that he and Representative Sonny Bono, a Republican from California, were the only two members of Congress in 1995–96 who had never attended college (Chrysler interview, 1996).

10. *First Session* refers to the first year of a two-year Congress, and *Second Session* refers to the second year.

11. Association leaders and college and university presidents have often written letters to the editors of newspapers to express their views, rather than taking out ads.

12. According to C. Brown, the collaboration between public relations and government relations staff was unprecedented (1985, 12).

13. Secretary of Education Riley is reported to have told President Clinton that without NAICU's efforts, student financial aid would have been lost in 1995 (Fuller interview, 1996a).

14. James Rowe, Harvard University's Vice President for Government, Community and Public Affairs, and John Crowley, Special Assistant to the President and Director of the Washington Office of the Massachusetts Institute of Technology, played leadership roles in the creation of the Science Coalition.

15. A January 1996 letter to university colleagues from then-President James J. Duderstadt of the University of Michigan and President Charles M. Vest of MIT urged their support for the Science Coalition and detailed its strategy and founding principles.

16. Student groups often demonstrate in support of or in opposition to various public policy initiatives that are largely unrelated to higher education policy.

17. The bill concerned the tax on loan volume.

18. The bill, an amendment to the 1997 fiscal year Labor, HHS (Health and Human Services), and Education Appropriations Bill, was introduced by Representative Ernest Jim Istook (R-Oklahoma) in July 1996.

19. In "America's professoriate: Politicized, yet apolitical," Jacoby hypothesizes that faculty have so politicized their approach to teaching their own disciplines that they already believe they "'give' at the office" and, therefore, do not have to devote their energies to practical politics. (*Chronicle of Higher Education*, 12 April 1996).

20. While trustees can be influential lobbyists, they are less likely than presidents to have a full understanding of institutional policy issues, and the political savvy that got them elected or appointed in the first place may work to their disad-

vantage when lobbying members of Congress, especially if they represent the wrong party (Helms 1993, 122–30).

21. The fact that many of the Christian colleges' boards of trustees include major Republican Party donors made that prospect especially attractive.

22. Since almost all of the interviews were conducted after the 1994 election, it is not surprising that interviewees emphasized the importance of avoiding close identification with the Democratic Party.

23. She surveyed 230 presidents of private coeducational colleges and universities in 1991 and had a 73 percent response rate.

24. Bornstein (1995) reports that a survey of private institution presidents revealed that 19 percent say they endorse candidates publicly.

25. AAU signed on late to the creation of the Science Coalition, and its staff admitted to concern about it. They said they hoped it would disband when its objectives are achieved.

26. A conference at Columbia University in the fall of 1996 drew many well-known academics. They discussed ways that academe might shore up the declining strength of the labor movement.

27. There are about two dozen higher education political action committees operating in at least six states, especially Texas and Michigan. The PAC contributors range from university administrators and faculty to alumni/ae and other local supporters. Only one of the PACs, at Ferris State University, contributes to candidates for national office (Lederman, *Chronicle of Higher Education*, 18 April 1997).

28. A group of Washington lobbyists also attempted to form a PAC in 1981 after Reagan was elected (Wilson, *Chronicle of Higher Education*, 11 November 1987).

29. The Bornstein (1995) survey of private institution presidents found that 10 percent report hosting fundraising events for candidates, and 37 percent attend them. While 55 percent contribute to political campaigns, several said they do so in amounts small enough so their contributions do not have to be reported to the public. They worry that their own political leanings would commit their institutions inappropriately.

30. For example, when Representative John Brademas, one of higher education's best allies, lost his seat in the House in 1980, many observers noted that the community's weak financial support for his re-election may have contributed to his loss (O'Keefe 1985, 12; Wilson, *Chronicle of Higher Education*, 11 November 1987).

CHAPTER 9 (pages 173–182)

1. Congressman George Brown's (D-California) fight against earmarks (described in chapter 3) was assisted by other congressional earmark opponents, such as House Appropriations Committee Chair Robert Livingston (R-Louisiana), as well as by the pressure to reduce discretionary spending and balance the federal budget.

2. Two-thirds of the 350 Javits Fellows waged an aggressive e-mail campaign to save the Javits program from elimination in 1996, but they did so without prompting by higher education institutions or associations (Burd, *Chronicle of Higher Education*, 1 March 1996).

3. In September 1996, organized labor joined the fray with a series of paid political advertisements aimed at unseating Republican members of Congress who voted against student aid.

CHAPTER 10 (pages 183–197)

1. Helms's (1993) interviews with members of Congress found the same emphasis on the importance of "friend-raising" to ensure the effectiveness of community college lobbying efforts.

★ ★ ★ ★ ★ ★

BIBLIOGRAPHY

Abrahams, Edward. 1996. The Washington connection: Brown and the federal government. *Faculty Bulletin* 8 (3).

Ainsworth, Scott, and Itai Sened. 1993. The role of lobbyists. Entrepreneurs with two audiences. *American Journal of Political Science* 37: 834–66.

American Association of State Colleges and Universities (AASCU). 1994. Membership. Washington, D.C.: AASCU.

———. 1995. 1995 public policy agenda. Washington, D.C.: AASCU.

American Council on Education (ACE). 1996. *Report of the ACE Review Committee.* Washington, D.C.: ACE.

Anderson, Jack, and Michael Binstein. 1993. The soaring cost of 'earmarks'. *Washington Post,* 30 August.

Anderson, Martin. 1992. *Impostors in the temple.* New York: Simon & Schuster.

Ann Arbor News. 1995. Gingrich takes swing at 'elitists'. 27 April.

Ashworth, Kenneth H. 1972. *Scholars and statesmen: Higher education and government policy.* San Francisco: Jossey-Bass.

Association of American Colleges (AAC). 1985. *Integrity in the college curriculum: A report to the academic community.* Washington, D.C.: AAC.

Atwell, Robert H. 1992. Globalism or localism: Must we choose? Speech given at 74th Annual Meeting of the American Council on Education, 23 January, Washington, D.C.

———. 1994. Republicans likely to seek domestic program cuts. *Higher Education and National Affairs,* 21 November.

Austen-Smith, David, and John Wright. 1994. Counteractive lobbying. *American Journal of Political Science* 38: 25–44.

Babbidge, Homer D., Jr., and Robert M. Rosenzweig. 1962. *The federal interest in higher education.* New York: McGraw-Hill.

Bailey, Anne Lowrey. 1988. Higher-education groups in Washington charged with weak leadership. *Chronicle of Higher Education,* 20 April.

Bailey, Stephen K. 1975. *Education interest groups in the nation's capital.* Washington, D.C.: American Council on Education.

Baker, Donald P., and Bart Barnes. 1980. College lobbyists flocking here in quest for funds. *Washington Post,* 28 January.

Bauer, Raymond A., Ithiel de Sola Pool, and Lewis A. Dexter. 1963. *American business and public policy.* New York: Atherton Press.

Bell, Terrel H. 1988. The federal imprint. In *New Directions for Community Colleges,* edited by David B. Wolf and Mary Lou Zoglin. San Francisco: Jossey-Bass (64): 9–14.

Bendor, Jonathon and Dilip Mookherjee. 1987. Institutional structure and the logic of ongoing collective action. *American Political Science Review* 81 (1): 129–54.

Bennett, W. J. 1984. *To reclaim a legacy: A report on the humanities in higher education.* Washington, D.C.: National Endowment for the Humanities.

220

BIBLIOGRAPHY

Berry, Jeffrey M. 1977. *Lobbying for the people*. Princeton, N.J.: Princeton University Press.

———. 1997. *The interest group society*. 3rd ed. Glenview, Ill.: Scott, Foresman/Little, Brown.

Blank, Jared. 1996. Science Coalition works for university research funding. *The University Record*, 17 September.

Blocker, Clyde E., Louis W. Bender, and V. Martorana. 1975. *The political terrain of American postsecondary education*. Fort Lauderdale, Fla.: Nova University Press.

Bloland, Harland G. 1969. *Higher education associations in a decentralized education system*. Berkeley, Calif.: Center of Research and Development in Higher Education, University of California.

———. 1985. *Associations in action: The Washington, D.C., higher education community*. ASHE-ERIC Higher Education Report No. 2. Washington, D.C.: Association for the Study of Higher Education.

———. 1992. *Higher education in the Washington lobby system: Old and new politics*. Paper presented at Annual Meeting of the Association for the Study of Higher Education.

Bloom, Allan. 1987. *The closing of the American mind: How higher education has failed democracy and impoverished the souls of today's students*. New York: Simon and Schuster.

Bok, Derek C. 1980. The federal government and the university. *The Public Interest* 58: 80–101.

———. 1992. Reclaiming the public trust. *Change*, July/August, 13–19.

Bornstein, Rita. 1995. Back in the spotlight: The college president as public intellectual. *Educational Record* 76 (4): 57–62.

Brademas, John. 1987. *The politics of education: Conflict and consensus on Capitol Hill*. Norman: University of Oklahoma Press.

Breneman, David W., and Chester E. Finn, Jr., eds. 1978. *Public policy and private higher education*. Washington, D.C.: Brookings Institution.

Brick, Michael. 1963. The American Association of Junior Colleges: Forum and focus for the junior college movement. Ph.D. diss., Columbia University.

Brown, Carol L. 1985. The role of the government relations representative in the efforts of some national higher education associations to influence federal education policy: A case study analysis of the Action Committee for Higher Education. Ph.D. diss., University of Maryland, College Park.

Brown, George E. 1993. *Academic earmarks: An interim report by the Chairman of the Committee on Science, Space and Technology*. 103rd Con., 2d sess.

Brown, Patricia E. 1985. The organization and management of state-level lobbying efforts of different types of institutions of higher education. Ph.D. diss., University of Virginia.

Browne, William P. 1976. Benefits and membership: A reappraisal of interest group activity. *Western Politics Quarterly* 29: 258–73.

———. 1977. Organizational maintenance: The internal operation of interest groups. *Public Administration Review* 37: 48–57.

———. 1985. Variations in the behavior and style of state lobbyists and interest groups. *Journal of Politics* 47: 450–68.

———. 1988. *Private interests, public policy, and American agriculture*. Lawrence: University Press of Kansas.

———. 1990. Organized interests and their issue niches: A search for pluralism in a policy domain. *Journal of Politics* 52: 477–509.

———. 1995. *Cultivating Congress: Constituents, issues, and agricultural policymaking.* Lawrence: University Press of Kansas.

Browne, William P., and Won K. Paik. 1993. Beyond the domain: Recasting network politics in the postreform Congress. *American Journal of Political Science* 37: 1054–78.

Browne, William P., and Robert H. Salisbury. 1972. Organized spokesmen for cities: Urban interest groups. In *People and politics in urban society,* edited by Harlan Hahn. Beverly Hills: Sage.

Burd, Stephen. 1996. Student-run campaign may save Javits program from elimination. *Chronicle of Higher Education,* 1 March.

———. 1996. At the last minute, Clinton and Congress agree on big increases for student aid. *Chronicle of Higher Education,* 11 October.

———. 1996. Many owners of proprietary schools gave generously to members of congress. *Chronicle of Higher Education,* 8 November.

Burd, Stephen, et al. 1997. One day on Capitol Hill for higher education. *Chronicle of Higher Education,* 25 April.

Cameron, Kim S., and David A. Whetten. 1983. Models of the organizational life cycle: Applications to higher education. *The Review of Higher Education* 6: 269–99.

Chong, Dennis. 1991. *Collective action and the civil rights movement.* Chicago: University of Chicago Press.

Chronicle of Higher Education. 1980. Many presidents feel American Council fails to represent all members equally. 25 August.

———. 1992. In box. 15 April.

———. 1992. Advertisement. 28 October.

———. 1995. Almanac issue. 1 September.

———. 1996. Almanac issue. 2 September.

———. 1996. Tuition costs outpace incomes. 6 September.

———. 1996. Getting the next generation of voters to go to the polls. 27 September.

———. 1996. Many academic leaders back Clinton's bid for re-election. 1 November.

———. 1996. Clinton won the college vote. 15 November.

Clark, Peter B., and James Q. Wilson. 1961. Incentive systems: A theory of organization. *Administrative Science Quarterly* 6 (2): 129–66.

Clifford, F. 1968. Washington outpost: More schools find use for a man in the capitol, *Science* 159 (3821), 22 March, 1334, 1339–40.

Cook, Constance E. 1980. *Nuclear power and legal advocacy: The environmentalists and the courts.* Lexington, Mass.: Lexington Books (D.C. Heath).

———. 1983. *Membership involvement in public interest groups.* Paper presented at Annual Meeting of the American Political Science Association, Chicago.

———. 1984. Participation in public interest groups. *American Politics Quarterly* 12 (4): 409–30.

Cordes, Colleen. 1991. Washington lobbyists continue to sign up university clients, capitalizing on academe's demand for political expertise. *Chronicle of Higher Education,* 9 October.

———. 1993. Curbing earmarks. *Chronicle of Higher Education,* 3 November.

BIBLIOGRAPHY

————. 1994. The power of pique. *Chronicle of Higher Education*, 29 June.

————. 1994. Settlement for Stanford. *Chronicle of Higher Education*, 26 October.

————. 1994. King of the earmarks. *Chronicle of Higher Education*, 2 November.

Cordes, Colleen, and Charles Ornstein. 1994. Academe's pork barrel. *Chronicle of Higher Education*, 3 August.

Cordes, Colleen, and Dylan Rivera. 1995. Trimming academic pork. *Chronicle of Higher Education*, 8 September.

Cosand, Joseph P., Gerald Gurin, Marvin W. Peterson, and Frank R. Brister. 1979. Presidential views of higher education's national institutional membership associations. Unpublished summary report. University of Michigan Center for the Study of Higher Education, Ann Arbor, Mich.

Costain, W. Douglas, and Anne N. Costain. 1981. Interest groups as policy aggregators in the legislative process. *Polity* 14: 249–72.

Council for the Advancement and Support of Education (CASE). 1990. Attitudes about American colleges 1990. Washington, D.C.: National Higher Education Week.

Crawford, E. M. 1981. The role of presidents and trustees in government relations. *New Directions for Institutional Advancement* 12: 25–34.

Curtis, Mark H. 1989. Crisis and opportunity: The founding of AAC. *Liberal Education* 75 (1): 6–15.

Davis, Bob. 1990. Federal budget pinch may cut amount of 'pork' to colleges living off of the fat of the land. *Wall Street Journal*, 2 May.

Delco, Wilhelmina, Mel Elfin, Louis Harris, Clifford Smith, and Frank Newman. 1992. Seeing ourselves as others see us. *AAHE Bulletin* 44 (10): 3–7.

DeLoughry, Thomas J. 1991. In Washington, outlook for colleges worsens as bad publicity abounds. *Chronicle of Higher Education*, 8 May.

DiBiaggio, John. 1990. Ten tips for higher education leaders. *Educational Record* 71: 17–20.

D'Souza, Dinesh. 1991. *Illiberal education: The politics of race and sex on campus.* New York: Free Press.

Eaton, Judith S. 1991. *The unfinished agenda: Higher education and the 1980s.* New York: American Council on Education and Macmillan Publishing Co.

Encyclopedia of American Associations. 1956. Detroit, Mich.: Gale Research Co.

Encyclopedia of Associations. 1968. Detroit, Mich.: Gale Research Co.

————. 1976. Detroit, Mich.: Gale Research Co.

————. 1986. Detroit, Mich.: Gale Research Co.

————. 1996. Detroit, Mich.: Gale Research Co.

Evans, Diana. 1990. Lobbying the committee: Interest groups and the House Public Works and Transportation Committee. In *Interest group politics*, 3rd ed., edited by Allan J. Cigler and Burdett A. Loomis. Washington, D.C.: Congressional Quarterly Press.

Fenno, Richard F., Jr. 1978. *Home style.* Boston: Little, Brown.

Fields, C. 1979. Higher education's Washington lobbyists. *Chronicle of Higher Education*, 19 March.

Finn, Chester E., Jr. 1978. *Scholars, dollars and bureaucrats.* Washington, D.C.: Brookings Institute.

Fiorina, Morris P. 1974. *Representatives, roll calls, and constituencies.* Lexington, Mass.: Lexington Books.

Fisher, James L. 1982. Battle of the budget. *Case Currents* (July, August): 9–11.

Flawn, Peter T. 1990. *A primer for university presidents: Managing the modern university*. Austin: University of Texas Press.

Freeman, Jo. 1975. *The politics of women's liberation*. New York: McKay.

Fretwell, E. K., Jr. 1981. Association report. *Educational Record* 62 (1): 78–80.

Gais, Thomas L., and Jack L. Walker. 1991. Pathways to influence in American politics. In *Mobilizing interest groups in America: Patrons, professions, and social movements*, edited by Jack L. Walker. Ann Arbor: University of Michigan Press.

Gardner, John W., Robert H. Atwell, and Robert O. Berdahl. 1985. *Cooperation and conflict: The public and private sectors in higher education*. Washington, D.C.: Association of Governing Boards.

Gerdes, Wylie. 1993. Grants to state colleges criticized as pork barrel. *Detroit Free Press*, 15 February.

Gingrich, Newt. 1995. *To renew America*. New York: Harper Collins.

Gladieux, Lawrence E. 1977. Education lobbies come into their own. *Change 9* (3): 42–43.

————. 1978. Appraising the influence of the educational lobbies: The case of higher education. In *The changing politics of education: Prospects for the 1980s*, edited by Edith K. Mosher and Jennings L. Wagoner, Jr. Berkeley, Calif.: Phi Delta Kappa/McCutcheon Publishing.

Gladieux, Lawrence E., Arthur M. Hauptman, and Laura Greene Knapp. 1994. The federal government and higher education. In *Higher education in American society*, 3rd ed., edited by Philip G. Altbach, Robert O. Berdahl, and Patricia J. Gumport. Amherst, N. Y.: Prometheus Books.

Gladieux, Lawrence E. and Thomas R. Wolanin. 1976. *Congress and the colleges: The national politics of higher education*. Lexington, Mass.: Lexington Books.

Gleazer, Edmund J. 1985. Governance and the shifting role of the board of trustees. In *New Directions for Community Colleges*, edited by William L. Deegan and James F. Gollattscheck. San Francisco: Jossey-Bass (49) 41–52.

Gollattscheck, James F. 1988. The AACJC and curriculum reform. In *New Directions for Community Colleges*, edited by David B. Wolf and Mary Lou Zoglin. San Francisco: Jossey-Bass (64): 15–22.

Gray, Virginia, and David Lowery. 1996a. A niche theory of interest representation. *Journal of Politics* 58 (1): 91–111.

————. 1996b. *The population ecology of interest representation*. Ann Arbor: University of Michigan Press.

Grenzke, Janet M. 1989. PACs and the congressional supermarket: The currency is complex. *American Journal of Political Science* 33: 1–24.

Greve, Frank. 1994. Bringing it home. *Detroit News and Free Press*, 7 August.

Grossman, Ron, Carol Jouzaitis, and Charles Leroux. 1992. The bottom line rules on campus. *Chicago Tribune*, 21 June.

Haider, Donald. 1974. *When governments come to Washington: Governors, mayors, and intergovernmental lobbying*. New York: Free Press.

Hall, Richard L, and Wayman, Frank W. 1990. Buying time: Moneyed interests and the mobilization of bias in congressional committees. *American Political Science Review* 84: 797–820.

Hamilton, Bette E. 1977. Federal policy networks for postsecondary education. Ph.D. diss., University of Michigan.

BIBLIOGRAPHY

Hansen, John Mark. 1985. The political economy of group membership. *American Political Science Review* 79: 79–96.

———. 1991. *Gaining access: Congress and the farm lobby, 1919–1981.* Chicago: University of Chicago Press.

Hardin, Russell. 1982. *Collective action.* Baltimore: Johns Hopkins University Press.

Hartle, Terry. 1993. Direct lending proposal expected to save billions, improve loan system. *Higher Education and National Affairs,* 17 May.

———. 1996. The specter of budget uncertainty. *Chronicle of Higher Education,* 28 June.

Hartle, Terry W., and Fred J. Galloway. 1997. Federal guidance for a changing national agenda. In *Planning and management for a changing environment: A handbook on redesigning postsecondary institutions,* edited by Marvin W. Peterson, David D. Dill, Lisa A. Mets, and Associates. San Francisco: Jossey-Bass.

Hawkins, Hugh. 1992. *Banding together: The rise of national associations in American higher education, 1887–1950.* Baltimore: Johns Hopkins University Press.

Hayes, Michael T. 1978. The semi-sovereign pressure groups: A critique of current theory and an alternative typology. *Journal of Politics* 40 (1): 134–61.

———. 1981. *Lobbyists and legislators: A theory of political markets.* New Brunswick, N.J.: Rutgers University Press.

———. 1983. Interest groups: Pluralism or mass society? In *Interest group politics,* edited by Allan J. Cigler and Burdett A. Loomis. Washington, D.C.: Congressional Quarterly Press.

———. 1986. The new group universe. In *Interest group politics,* 2nd ed., edited by Allan J. Cigler and Burdett A. Loomis. Washington D.C.: Congressional Quarterly Press.

Heclo, Hugh. 1978. Issue networks and the executive establishment. In *The new American political system,* edited by Anthony King. Washington, D.C.: American Enterprise Institute.

Heinz, John P., Edward O. Laumann, Robert H. Salisbury, and Robert L. Nelson. 1990. Inner circles or hollow cores? Elite networks in national policy systems. *Journal of Politics* 52: 356–90.

———. 1993. *The hollow core: Private interests in national policy making.* Cambridge, Mass.: Harvard University Press.

Helms, Phyllis E. 1993. The identification of effective strategies used by community college leaders to lobby members of Congress involved in higher education legislation affecting community colleges. Ph.D. diss., North Carolina State University.

HEP 1994 Higher Education Directory. 1994. Falls Church, Va.: Higher Education Publications.

Heyns, Roger. 1973. The national educational establishment. *Educational Record* 54 (2): 93–99.

Higher Education and National Affairs. 1993a. Major changes in aid program likely. 19 April.

———. 1993b. Group proposes service, direct loan provisions. 19 April.

———. 1993. Clinton unveils national service, student loan reform proposals. 3 May.

———. 1993. Lawmakers scale back service proposal. 16 August.

———. 1994. Associations release analysis of proposed SPRE, accrediting regs. 7 March.

———. 1994. Budget plan would cut aid, cap Pell recipients. 27 June.

———. 1994. Educators seek funding increase in spending bill. 15 August.

———. 1995. Riley urges Republicans to maintain ed funding. 23 January.

———. 1995. House budget resolution would eliminate aid programs, interest exemption on student loans. 22 May.

———. 1995. Presidents oppose direct loan program cap. 13 November.

Hinsdale, Burke A. 1906. *The history of the University of Michigan*. Edited by Isaac N. Demmon. Ann Arbor: University of Michigan.

Hirsch, E. D., Jr. 1988. *Cultural literacy: What every American needs to know*. New York: Vintage Books.

Hirschman, Albert. 1970. *Exit, voice, and loyalty*. Cambridge, Mass.: Harvard University Press.

Hobbs, Walter C., ed. 1978. *Government regulation in higher education*. Cambridge, Mass.: Ballinger.

Hojnacki, Marie. 1997. Interest groups' decisions to join alliances or work alone. *American Journal of Political Science* 41: 61–87.

Honan, William H. 1994. At the top of the ivory tower the watchword is silence. *New York Times*, 24 July.

———. 1996. Spared budget cutting, colleges remain fearful. *New York Times*, 19 June.

Horton, Nancy, and Charles Andersen. 1994. Linking the economy to the academy. *American Council on Education Research Briefs*, 5 (4).

Hrebenar, Ronald J., and Clive Thomas. 1987. *Interest group politics in the American west*. Salt Lake City: University of Utah Press.

Hunt, Susan. 1977. NAICU's growing pains. *Change* 9 (2): 50–51.

Jacoby, Russell. 1996. America's professoriate: Politicized, yet apolitical. *Chronicle of Higher Education*, 12 April.

Jaschick, Scott. 1992. President of black-college lobbying group stirs furor with claim ACE is racist. *Chronicle of Higher Education,* 8 January.

———. 1992. Black-college presidents plan a 'summit' amid displeasure with lobbying group. *Chronicle of Higher Education,* 15 January.

———. 1994. A modest retreat on accrediting. *Chronicle of Higher Education,* 4 May.

Johnson, Marvin D. 1981. The rationale for government relations. In *New Directions for Institutional Advancement,* edited by Marvin D. Johnson. San Francisco: Jossey-Bass (12): 1–8.

Jordan, Mary. 1993. Funds from friends in high places. *Washington Post,* 10 October.

———. 1993. Congressional 'earmarking' on the wane, review finds. *Washington Post,* 3 November.

Kerr, Clark. 1994. *Troubled times for American higher education: The 1990s and beyond.* Albany: State University of New York Press.

King, David C., and Jack L. Walker. 1992. The provision of benefits by interest groups in the United States. *Journal of Politics* 54: 394–426.

King, Lauriston R. 1975. *The Washington lobbyists for higher education*. Lexington, Mass.: Lexington Books (D.C. Heath).

BIBLIOGRAPHY

Kingdon, John W. 1981. *Congressmen's voting decisions.* New York: Harper and Row.

———. 1984. *Agendas, alternatives, and public policies.* Boston: Little, Brown and Company.

Knoke, David. 1990. *Organizing for collective action: The political economies of associations.* Hawthorne, N.Y.: A. deGroyter.

Lane, Neal. 1996. We must explain why science matters to society. *Chronicle of Higher Education,* 6 December.

Langbein, Laura I. 1986. Money and access: Some empirical evidence. *Journal of Politics* 48: 1052–62.

Laumann, Edward O., and David Knoke. 1987. *The Organizational state: Social choices and national policy domains.* Madison: University of Wisconsin Press.

Lederman, Douglas. 1996. Who is a lobbyist? *Chronicle of Higher Education,* 8 March.

———. 1997. Political action committees help lawmakers who help universities. *Chronicle of Higher Education,* 18 April.

———. 1997. The politicking and policymaking behind a $40-billion windfall. *Chronicle of Higher Education,* 28 November.

Loomis, Burdett. 1993. The politics of interests: Interest groups transformed. *American Political Science Review* 87: 221–22.

Lowi, Theodore J. 1979. *The end of liberalism.* 2nd ed. New York: W. W. Norton & Company.

Luttbeg, Norman R., and Harmon Zeigler. 1966. Attitude consensus and conflict in an interest group: an assessment of cohesion. *American Political Science Review* 60: 655–66.

Malbin, Michael. 1980. *Unelected representatives: Congressional staff and the future of representative government.* New York: Basic Books.

Manegold, Catherine S. 1994. In campaign to curb bad student loans, U. S. warns of audits, and colleges protest. *New York Times,* 10 August.

Mann, Lawrence R. 1979. The National Association of State Universities and Land-Grant Colleges: A political interest group and its congressional relations, 1887–1958. Ph.D. diss., University of Illinois at Urbana-Champaign.

Mansbridge, Jane J. 1986. *Why we lost the ERA.* Chicago: University of Chicago Press.

Mayhew, David R. 1974. *Congress: The electoral connection.* New Haven, Conn.: Yale University Press.

McMillan, Jeff. 1996. Clinton won the college vote, polls indicate. *Chronicle of Higher Education,* 15 November.

McMillen, Liz. 1991. Higher education is said to face the toughest PR challenge ever. *Chronicle of Higher Education,* 24 July.

Michels, Robert. 1915. *Political parties.* New York: Dover.

Milbrath, Lester. 1963. *The Washington lobbyists.* Chicago: Rand McNally.

Miller, Warren E., and Donald E. Stokes. 1966. Constituency influence in Congress. In *Elections and the political order,* edited by Angus Campbell, et al. New York: John Wiley.

Moe, Terry M. 1980a. A calculus of group membership. *American Journal of Political Science* 24: 593–632.

———. 1980b. *The organization of interests: Incentives and the internal dynamics of political interest groups.* Chicago: University of Chicago Press.

————. 1981. Toward a broader view of interest groups. *Journal of Politics* 43: 531–43.

Mosher, Edith K., and Jennings L. Wagoner, Jr. 1978. *The changing politics of education: Prospects for the 1980s.* Berkeley, Calif.: Phi Delta Kappa/McCutcheon Publishing.

Moynihan, Daniel P. 1975. The politics of the higher education lobby. *Daedalus* 104 (1): 128–47.

Murray, Michael A. 1976. Defining the higher education lobby. *Journal of Higher Education* 47 (1): 79–92.

National Center for Education Statistics. 1995. *Digest of education statistics 1995.* U. S. Department of Education Office of Educational Research and Improvement. Washington, D.C.: GPO.

National Institute of Education (NIE). 1984. *Involvement in learning: Realizing the potential of American higher education.* Washington, D.C.: NIE

Ness, Frederic W. 1989. Cooperation and competition: A look at higher education associations. *Liberal Education* 75 (1): 16–21.

O'Keefe, Michael. 1985. Self-inflicted laryngitis. *Change* 17 (2): 11–13.

Olson, Mancur. 1965. *The logic of collective action.* Cambridge, Mass.: Harvard University Press.

Park, Robert L. 1996. Fall from grace. *The Sciences,* May/June, 18–21.

Parsons, Michael D. 1997. *Power and politics: Federal higher education policymaking in the 1990s.* Albany: State University of New York Press.

Petracca, Mark, ed. 1992. *The politics of interests: Interest groups transformed.* Boulder, Colo.: Westview Press.

Pedersen, Robert. 1995. The St. Louis conference: The junior college movement reborn. *Community College Journal* 65 (5): 26–30.

Pianin, Eric. 1992. 'Academic pork' fills favored school larders. *Washington Post,* 23 September.

Powell, Lynda W. 1982. Issue representation in Congress. *Journal of Politics:* 658–78.

Pratt, Henry J. 1976. *The gray lobby.* Chicago: University of Chicago Press.

————. 1993. *Gray agendas: Interest groups and public pensions in Canada, Britain, and the United States.* Ann Arbor: University of Michigan Press.

Rauch, Jonathan. 1994. *Demosclerosis: the silent killer of American government.* New York: Random House.

Ripley, Randall B., and Grace A. Franklin. 1982. *Bureaucracy and policy implementation.* Homewood, Ill.: Dorsey Press.

Roark, Anne C. 1980. Washington's 'most effective' lobbyist for higher education. *Chronicle of Higher Education,* 6 October.

Rosenzweig, Robert. 1965. Education lobbies and federal legislation. In *Challenge and change in American education,* edited by Seymour Harris. Berkeley, Calif.: McCutcheon.

Rothenberg, Lawrence S. 1983. Organizational maintenance and the retention decision in groups. *American Political Science Review* 82 (4): 1129–52.

————. 1992. *Linking citizens to government: Interest group politics at Common Cause.* Cambridge: Cambridge University Press.

Sabatier, Paul. A., and Susan McLaughlin. 1990. Belief congruence between interest group leaders and members: An empirical analysis of three theories and a suggested synthesis. *Journal of Politics* 52 (3): 914–35.

Salisbury, Robert H. 1969. An exchange theory of interest groups. *Midwest Journal of Political Science* 13 (1): 1–32.

———. 1984. Interest representation: The dominance of institutions. *American Political Science Review* 78 (1): 64–76.

———. 1990. The paradox of interest groups in Washington — More groups, less clout. In *The new American political system*, 2nd ed., edited by Anthony King. Washington, D.C.: American Enterprise Institute.

———. 1992. *Interests and institutions: Substance and structure in American politics.* Pittsburgh: University of Pittsburgh Press.

Salisbury, Robert H., John P. Heinz, Edward O. Laumann, and Robert L. Nelson. 1987. Who works with whom?: Interest group alliances and opposition. *American Political Science Review* 81 (4): 1217–34.

Samors, Bob. 1996. Washington update. *DRDA Reporter*, 11 November, 2–3.

Saunders, Charles B., Jr. 1981. The role of the national associations. In *New Directions for Institutional Advancement*, edited by Marvin D. Johnson. San Francisco: Jossey-Bass (12): 49–58.

Schlozman, Kay Lehman, and John T. Tierney. 1986. *Organizational interests and American democracy.* New York: Harper and Row.

Schuster, Jack H. 1982. Out of the frying pan: The politics of education in a new era. *Phi Delta Kappan* 63 (9): 583–91.

Scully, M. G. 1979. Michigan center, 'Gang of Six' to study performance of 8 education associations. *Chronicle of Higher Education*, 10 December.

Semas, Philip W. 1972. Few changes thus far in higher education's Washington 'umbrella'. *Chronicle of Higher Education,* 30 October.

Smith, Richard A. 1984. Advocacy, interpretation, and influence in the U. S. Congress. *American Political Science Review* 78: 44–63.

Stanfield, Rochelle L. 1983. The education lobby reborn. *National Journal,* 1452–56.

Stewart, Donald M. 1975. Politics of higher education: A study of the American Council on Education. Ph.D. diss., Harvard University.

Sykes, Charles J. 1988. *Profscam: Professors and the demise of higher education.* Washington, D.C.: Regnery Gateway.

Terenzini, Patrick T. 1996. Rediscovering roots: Public policy and higher education research. *The Review of Higher Education* 20 (1): 5–13.

Tierney, John T. 1992. Organized interests and the nation's capital. In *The politics of interests: Interest groups transformed,* edited by Mark Petracca. Boulder, Colo.: Westview Press.

Thurber, James A. 1991. Dynamics of policy subsystems in American politics. In *Interest group politics*, edited by Allan J. Cigler and Burdett Loomis. 3rd ed. Washington, D.C.: Congressional Quarterly Press.

Truman, David B. 1951. *The governmental process.* New York: Knopf.

Vaughan, George B. 1995. *The community college story: A tale of American innovation.* Washington, D.C.: American Association of Community Colleges.

Vobejda, Barbara. 1987. The humbling of higher education. *Washington Post National Weekly Edition*, 9 March.

Wahlke, John C., Heinz Eulau, William Buchanan, and L. C. Ferguson. 1962. *The legislative system: Explorations in legislative behavior.* New York: Wiley.

Waldman, Steven. 1995. *The bill.* New York: Viking.

Waldo, Robert G. 1981. New trends in lobbying and higher education. In *New Directions for Institutional Advancement,* edited by Marvin D. Johnson. San Francisco: Jossey-Bass (12): 9–14.

Walker, Jack L. 1983. The origins and maintenance of interest groups in America. *American Political Science Review* 77 (2): 390–405.

————. 1991. *Mobilizing interest groups in America: Patrons, professions, and social movements.* Ann Arbor: University of Michigan Press.

Washington, D.C., Higher Education Associations. 1994. U. S. Department of Education notice of proposed rulemaking on recognition standard for accrediting agencies and the establishment of state postsecondary review entities. Duplicated.

Washington Post. 1992. House panel criticizes surge in college costs. 15 September.

Watkins, Beverly. 1978. American Council to reorganize. *Chronicle of Higher Education,* 10 July 16, 5.

Wells, Nan S. 1990. Congress, campuses, and an education lobbyist's life in Washington. *Educational Record* 71: 24–28.

White, Robert M. 1996. The Science advocacy dilemma. *Technology Review,* May/June, 66.

Whiteman, David. 1995. *Communication in Congress: Members, staff, and the search for information.* Lawrence: University Press of Kansas.

Williams, Roger L. 1991. Colleges need some 19th century savvy in dealing with Washington. *Chronicle of Higher Education,* 4 December.

Wilson, James Q. 1973. *Political organizations.* New York: Basic Books.

Wilson, John T. 1982. *Higher education and the Washington scene.* Chicago: University of Chicago Press.

Wilson, Robin. 1987. Lobbyists and college presidents debate need for political action committee. *Chronicle of Higher Education,* 11 November.

————. 1988. Outspoken critic of colleges' lobbying strategy takes a Capitol Hill job where he'll see a lot of it. *Chronicle of Higher Education,* 6 July.

Wolanin, Thomas. 1976. The national higher education associations: Political resources and style. *Phi Delta Kappan* 58 (2): 181–84.

Wooton, Graham. 1985. *Interest groups: Policy and politics in America.* Englewood Cliffs, N. J.: Prentice-Hall.

Wright, John R. 1989. PAC contributions, lobbying, and representation. *Journal of Politics*: 51: 713–29.

————. 1990. Contributions, lobbying, and committee voting in the U. S. House of Representatives. *American Political Science Review* 84 (2): 417–38.

————. 1996. *Interest groups and Congress: Lobbying, contributions, and influence.* Needham Heights, Mass.: Allyn & Bacon.

Wyatt, Joe B. 1993. Pork barrel science. *New York Times,* 12 October.

Zook, Jim. 1994. Storm over accreditation: College lobbyists say proposed regulations are still too burdensome. *Chronicle of Higher Education,* 2 February.

————. 1994. Proposed rules on accreditation draw unusual outpouring of critical comments. *Chronicle of Higher Education,* 6 April.

————. 1994. Despite changes, accrediting rules still trouble some colleges. *Chronicle of Higher Education,* 25 May.

INTERVIEWEES

Interviewees and Their Positions at Time of Interview
All interviews were by the author.

Abrahams, Edward. 1995. Director of Government and Community Relations, Brown University. Washington, D.C., 2 May.

Adams, Michael. 1995. President, Centre College; Chair, National Association of Independent Colleges and Universities Board of Directors. Telephone interview, 18 April.

Adelsheimer, Erica. 1996. Legislative Director, United States Student Association. Telephone interview, 3 December.

Alfred, Richard. 1994. Professor of Higher Education, University of Michigan. Ann Arbor, Mich., 7 February.

Appleberry, James B. 1995. President, American Association of State Colleges and Universities. Washington, D.C., 15 June.

Atwell, Robert. 1995. President, American Council on Education. Washington, D.C., 15 June.

Baime, David. 1995. Director of Government Relations, American Association of Community Colleges. Washington, D.C., 11 April.

———. 1996a. Director of Government Relations, American Association of Community Colleges. Washington, D.C., 5 June.

———. 1996b. Director of Government Relations, American Association of Community Colleges. Telephone interview, 25 November.

Beering, Steven. 1995. President, Purdue University; Vice Chair, Association of American Universities Executive Committee. Telephone interview, 3 April.

Belcher, Jacqueline. 1995. President, Minneapolis Community College; Chair, American Association of Community Colleges Board of Directors; member, American Council on Education Board of Directors. Telephone interview, 6 April.

Benjamin, Ernest. 1996. Associate General Secretary and Director of Research of the American Association of University Professors. Atlanta, Ga., 19 January.

Berdahl, Robert. 1993. Professor, University of Maryland. Washington, D.C., 11 October.

———. 1996. Professor, University of Maryland. Memphis, Tenn., 1 November.

Blair, Stephen J. 1995. President, Career College Association. Washington, D.C., 17 May.

Bloland, Harland. 1993. Professor, University of Miami. Orlando, Fla., 14 November.

———. 1994. Professor, University of Miami. Orlando, Fla., 14 April.

Boyer, Kevin. 1995. Executive Director, National Association of Graduate and Professional Students. Washington, D.C., 28 June.

Boyer, Violet. 1996. President, Committee for Education Funding. Washington, D.C., 5 June.

231

Brown, George. 1996. Congressman (D-California), Ranking Minority Member, Science Committee, U. S. House of Representatives. Telephone interview, 1 February.

Butts, Thomas. 1993. Associate Vice President for Government Relations, University of Michigan. Telephone interview, 30 August.

———. 1996. Associate Vice President for Government Relations, University of Michigan. Ann Arbor, Mich., 31 May.

———. 1996. Associate Vice President for Government Relations, University of Michigan. Telephone interview, 20 December.

Cardenas, Raul. 1995. President, Paradise Valley Community College; member, American Council on Education Board of Directors. Telephone interview, 20 April.

Cartwright, Carol. 1995. President, Kent State University; member, American Council on Education Board of Directors; member, National Association of State Universities and Land-Grant Colleges Board of Directors. Telephone interview, 3 July.

Chrysler, Dick. 1996. Congressman (R-Michigan), Government Reform and Oversight Committee, U. S. House of Representatives. Telephone interview, 15 January.

Clarkson, Shirley. 1992. Assistant to President, University of Michigan, Ann Arbor, Mich.

Cole, Elsa. 1995. General Counsel, University of Michigan. Ann Arbor, Mich., 4 April.

Combs, Michael. 1996a. Coordinator of Grassroots Development, National Association of Independent Colleges and Universities. Washington, D.C., 5 June.

———. 1996b. Coordinator of Grassroots Development, National Association of Independent Colleges and Universities. Washington, D.C., 14 November.

DeFleur, Lois. 1995. President, State University of New York at Binghamton; Chair-elect, National Association of State Universities and Land-Grant Colleges Board of Directors; member, American Council on Education Board of Directors. Telephone interview, 6 April.

Douthat, James. 1994. President, Lycoming College. Telephone interview, 8 April.

Duderstadt, James. 1991. President, University of Michigan; former member, Association of American Universities Executive Committee. Ann Arbor, Mich., 19 May.

———. 1993. President, University of Michigan; former member, Association of American Universities Executive Committee. Ann Arbor, Mich., 13 September.

———. 1996. President, University of Michigan; former member, Association of American Universities Executive Committee. Ann Arbor, Mich., 5 May.

Dunlop, Susan. 1996. Special Assistant to the President, AFL-CIO. Telephone interview, 13 November.

Duvall, Betty. 1995. Liaison for Community Colleges, U. S. Department of Education. Washington, D.C., 3 May.

Ehlers, Vernon. 1996. Congressman (R-Michigan), Vice Chair, Science Committee, U. S. House of Representatives. Telephone interview, 4 January.

El-Khawas, Elaine. 1993. Vice President, American Council on Education. Ann Arbor, Mich., 3 March.

Elliott, Peggy. 1995. President, University of Akron; Secretary/Treasurer, American Association of State Colleges and Universities Board of Directors; member, Government Relations Committee, American Council on Education Board of Directors. Telephone interview, 20 April.

Elmendorf, Edward. 1994. Vice President, Government Relations, American Association of State Colleges and Universities. Washington, D.C., 17 February.

————. 1995. Vice President, Government Relations, American Association of State Colleges and Universities. Washington, D.C., 10 April.

Evans, David. 1995. Staff Director, Subcommittee on Education, Arts, and Humanities, Labor and Human Resources Committee, U. S. Senate. Washington, D.C., 2 June.

Flanagan, Sarah. 1995. Vice President for Government Relations, National Association of Independent Colleges and Universities. Washington, D.C., 11 April.

Ford, William. 1996. Former Congressman (D-Michigan), Chair, Subcommittee on Postsecondary Education, Education and Labor Committee, U. S. House of Representatives. Telephone interview, 29 March.

Fuller, Jon. 1994. Senior Fellow, National Association of Independent Colleges and Universities. Washington, D.C., 20 January.

————. 1995a. Senior Fellow, National Association of Independent Colleges and Universities. Washington, D.C., 11 April.

————. 1995b. Senior Fellow, National Association of Independent Colleges and Universities. Washington, D.C., 10 September.

————. 1996a. Senior Fellow, National Association of Independent Colleges and Universities. Washington, D.C., 29 January.

————. 1996b. Senior Fellow, National Association of Independent Colleges and Universities. Letter to author, 2 December.

Fuller, Jon, and Carol Fuller. 1996a. Senior Fellow, National Association of Independent Colleges and Universities, and Assistant Vice President for Research and Policy Analysis, National Association of Independent Colleges and Universities. Washington, D.C., 1 June.

————. 1996b. Senior Fellow, National Association of Independent Colleges and Universities, and Assistant Vice President for Research and Policy Analysis, National Association of Independent Colleges and Universities. Washington, D.C., 14 November.

Galloway, Fred. 1996. Director of Federal Policy Analysis, American Council on Education. Ann Arbor, Mich., 2 April.

Gobstein, Howard. 1994. Vice President, Association of American Universities. Washington, D.C., 19 January.

Grafton, Steven. 1996. Director, Alumni Association, University of Michigan. Ann Arbor, Mich., 5 April.

Harrison, Walter. 1996. Vice President for University Relations, University of Michigan. Ann Arbor, Mich., 10 April.

Hartle, Terry. 1995. Vice President and Director, Division of Government Relations, American Council on Education. Washington, D.C., 16 June.

———. 1996. Vice President and Director, Division of Government Relations, American Council on Education. Washington, D.C., 29 January.

Hasselmo, Nils. 1995. President, University of Minnesota; 1996 Chair, National Association of State Universities and Land-Grant Colleges Board of Directors. Telephone interview, 4 May.

Hattan, Susan. 1996. Staff Director, Committee on Labor and Human Resources, U. S. Senate. Washington, D.C., 14 November.

Hayford, Elizabeth. 1994. President, Associated Colleges of the Midwest. Telephone interview, 17 March.

Hill, Barbara. 1995. President, Sweet Briar College; member, Government Relations Committee, National Association of Independent Colleges and Universities Board of Directors. Telephone interview, 12 April.

Hoekstra, Peter. 1996. Congressman (R-Michigan), Budget Committee and Economic and Educational Opportunities Committee, U. S. House of Representatives. Telephone interview, 25 February.

Holland, Barbara. 1996. Associate Vice Provost, Portland State University. Memphis, Tenn., 1 November.

———. 1996. Associate Vice Provost, Portland State University. Letter to author, 12 November.

Ikenberry, Stanley. 1995. President, University of Illinois; member, Association of American Universities Executive Committee. Telephone interview, 7 April.

———. 1996. President, American Council on Education. Memphis, Tenn., 1 November.

Ingram, Richard T. 1995. President, Association of Governing Boards of Universities and Colleges. Washington, D.C., 16 May.

Kassebaum, Nancy. 1996. Senator (R-Kansas), Chair, Labor and Human Resources Committee, U. S. Senate. Telephone interview, 25 January.

Kealy, Edward R. 1995. Executive Director, Committee for Education Funding. Telephone interview, 29 June.

Kelly, Eamon. 1995. President, Tulane University; Chair, Association of American Universities Executive Committee. Telephone interview, 19 April.

Knapp, Richard. 1995. Executive Vice President for Government Relations, American Association of Medical Colleges. Washington, D.C., 15 June.

Kornfeld, Leo. 1995. Senior Advisor to the Secretary, U. S. Department of Education. Washington, D.C., 3 May.

Lane, Neal. 1995. Director, National Science Foundation. Washington, D.C., 23 June.

Long, Edward. 1995. Former Staff Director, Subcommittee on Labor, Health and Human Services, and Education, Appropriations Committee, U. S. Senate. Telephone interview, 31 May.

Longanecker, David A. 1995. Assistant Secretary, Office of Postsecondary Education, U. S. Department of Education. Washington, D.C., 3 May.

Lovett, Clara. 1993. President-elect, Northern Arizona University. Washington, D.C., 2 October.

Magrath, Peter. 1995. President, National Association of State Universities and Land-Grant Colleges. Washington, D.C., 15 June.

Malloy, Edward. 1995. President, University of Notre Dame; Immediate Past Chair, American Council on Education Board of Directors. Telephone interview, 24 April.

Marchese, Theodore. 1991. Vice President, American Association for Higher Education. Washington, D.C., 3 October.

———. 1992. Vice President, American Association for Higher Education. Washington, D.C.

———. 1995. Vice President, American Association for Higher Education. Washington, D.C., 10 April.

Martin, Dallas. 1995. President, National Association of Student Financial Aid Administrators. Washington, D.C., 16 May.

McClintock, Laura. 1995. Legislative Director, United States Student Association. Telephone interview, 28 June.

McKenna, Margaret. 1995. President, Lesley College; member, Government Relations Committee, National Association of Independent Colleges and Universities Board of Directors. Telephone interview, 13 April.

Merkowitz, David. 1995. Director, Office of Public Affairs, American Council on Education. Washington, D.C., 11 April.

Mertz, Francis. 1995. President, Fairleigh Dickinson University; member, Government Relations Committee, National Association of Independent Colleges and Universities Board of Directors. Telephone interview, 13 April.

Mingle, James. 1994. Executive Director, State Higher Education Executive Officers. Ann Arbor, Mich., 2 May.

Mitchem, Arnold. 1995. Executive Director, National Council of Educational Opportunity Associations. Washington, D.C., 16 May.

Myers, Michael. 1995a. Staff Assistant for the House Subcommittee on Labor, Health and Human Services, and Education, Appropriations Committee, U. S. House of Representatives. Washington, D.C., 2 June.

———. 1995b. Staff Assistant for the House Subcommittee on Labor, Health and Human Services, and Education, Appropriations Committee, U. S. House of Representatives. Washington, D.C., 14 November.

Narum, Jeanne. 1993. President, Independent Colleges Office. Washington, D.C., 10 October.

———. 1995a. President, Independent Colleges Office. Washington, D.C., 9 April.

———. 1995b. President, Independent Colleges Office. Washington, D.C., 2 May.

Nassirian, Barmak. 1996. Director, Federal Policy Analysis, American Association of State Colleges and Universities. Washington, D.C., 14 November.

Needham, Ray. 1995. President, Tacoma Community College; member, American Association of Community Colleges Board of Directors. Telephone interview, 26 April.

Novack, Richard. 1995. Association of Governing Boards of Universities and Colleges. Washington, D.C., 16 May.

Nowack, Judith. 1995. Office of the Vice President for Research, University of Michigan. Ann Arbor, Mich., 8 May.

Obear, Frederick. 1995. President, University of Tennessee at Chattanooga; Chair, American Association of State Colleges and Universities Board of Directors. Telephone interview, 6 April.

Odems, Constance. 1994. Senior Vice President, American Association of Community Colleges. Washington, D.C., 18 February.

Palmer, Roberta. 1994a. Vice President for Governmental Affairs, Wayne State University. Ann Arbor, Mich., 1 February.

———. 1994b. Vice President for Governmental Affairs, Wayne State University. Ann Arbor, Mich., 4 April.

Pell, Claiborne. 1996. Senator (D-Rhode Island), Ranking Minority Member, Subcommittee on Education, Arts, and Humanities, Labor and Human Resources Committee, U. S. Senate. Letter to author, 25 January.

Perry, Barbara. 1995. Director, Federal Governmental Relations, University of California. Washington, D.C., 16 May.

Petri, Thomas E. 1996. Congressman (R-Wisconsin), Economic and Educational Opportunities Committee, U. S. House of Representatives. Telephone interview, 18 November.

Pierce, David. 1995. President, American Association of Community Colleges. Washington, D.C., 16 June.

Pings, Cornelius. 1995. President, Association of American Universities. Telephone interview, 21 June.

Rivers, Lynn. 1996. Congresswoman (D-Michigan), Budget Committee and Science Committee, U. S. House of Representatives. Ann Arbor, Mich., 8 January.

Roschwalb, Jerold. 1994. Director, Federal Relations and Higher Education, National Association of State Universities and Land-Grant Colleges. Telephone interview, 8 April.

———. 1995. Director, Federal Relations and Higher Education, National Association of State Universities and Land-Grant Colleges. Washington, D.C., 10 April.

Samors, Robert. 1996a. Government Relations Officer, University of Michigan. Ann Arbor, Mich., 28 March.

———. 1996b. Government Relations Officer, University of Michigan. Telephone interview, 31 May.

———. 1996c. Government Relations Officer, University of Michigan. Telephone interview, 17 December.

Segal, Eli. 1996. Founding Chief Executive Officer, Corporation for National Service. Ann Arbor, Mich., 15 November.

Shay, John. 1995. President, Marygrove College; member, Government Relations Committee, National Association of Independent Colleges and Universities Board of Directors. Telephone interview, 17 April.

Shireman, Robert. 1995. Legislative Director to Senator Paul Simon, Labor and Human Resources Committee, U. S. Senate. Washington, D.C., 1 June.

Simon, Paul. 1996. Senator (D-Illinois), Labor and Human Resources Committee, U. S. Senate. Telephone interview, 12 December.

Smith, Hoke. 1994. President, Towson State University; former Chair, American Association of State Colleges and Universities Board of Directors; former Chair, American Council on Education Board of Directors. Atlanta, Ga., 29 January.

Smith, Michael. 1995. Undersecretary, U. S. Department of Education. Washington, D.C., 2 May.

Speert, Arnold. 1995. President, William Patterson College of New Jersey; member, American Association of State Colleges and Universities Board of Directors. Telephone interview, 3 April.

Spencer, Clayton. 1995. Chief Education Counsel, Labor and Human Resources Committee, U. S. Senate. Washington, D.C., 1 June.

Stephens, Michael. 1995. Staff Assistant, Labor, Health and Human Services, and Education Subcommittee, Appropriations Committee, U. S. House of Representatives. Washington, D.C., 1 June.

Stewart, Donald M. 1994. President, The College Board. Ann Arbor, Mich., 17 January.

Stroup, Sally. 1995. Staff Member, Economic and Educational Opportunities Committee, U. S. House of Representatives. Washington, D.C., 2 June.

Sullivan, Leila. 1995. President, Middlesex Community College; member, American Association of Community Colleges Board of Directors. Telephone interview, 27 April.

Taylor, Ray. 1995. President, Association of Community College Trustees. Telephone interview, 29 June.

Timmons, Rebecca. 1994. Director of Congressional Relations, Division of Governmental Relations, American Council on Education. Washington, D.C., 17 February.

————. 1995. Director of Congressional Relations, Division of Governmental Relations, American Council on Education. Washington, D.C., 11 April.

Tolo, Kenneth. 1995. Assistant to Undersecretary, U. S. Department of Education. Washington, D.C., 2 May.

VanEyck, Laila. 1995. Government Relations Program Coordinator, Council for Advancement and Support of Education. Washington, D.C., 17 May.

Vaughn, John. 1995a. Executive Officer & Director of Education Policy, Association of American Universities. Telephone interview, 22 March.

————. 1995b. Executive Officer & Director of Education Policy, Association of American Universities. Washington, D.C., 11 April.

————. 1995c. Executive Officer & Director of Education Policy, Association of American Universities. Telephone interview, 28 April.

————. 1996. Executive Officer & Director of Education Policy, Association of American Universities. Washington, D.C., 27 March.

Warren, David. 1995. President, National Association of Independent Colleges and Universities. Washington, D.C., 15 June.

Wentworth, Eric. 1995. Director of Federal Government Relations, Council for Advancement and Support of Education. Washington, D.C., 17 May.

Wheelan, Belle S. 1995. President, Central Virginia Community College; member, American Association of Community Colleges Board of Directors. Telephone interview, 6 April.

White, Barry. 1995. Education Bureau Chief, Human Resources Division, Office of Management and Budget. Washington, D.C., 3 May.

Widder, Joel. 1995. Director, Legislative Affairs Division, National Science Foundation. Washington, D.C., 2 May.

Wilson, James. 1995. Professional Staff Member, Science Committee, U. S. House of Representatives. Washington, D.C., 2 June.

Wolanin, Thomas R. 1995. Deputy Assistant Secretary for Legislation, U. S. Department of Education. Washington, D.C., 3 May.

INDEX

academic research (funding of), 33, 43, 75, 123–124, 128; and hired guns, 75, 82; lobbying for, 155, 162; and Republicans, 54; and two-year colleges, 124

accreditation, 20–21, 44–46, 212 n.2b. *See also* State Postsecondary Review Entities (SPREs)

Accrediting Commission for Career Schools and Colleges of Technology, 212 n.2b

Accrediting Commission of the Distance Education and Training Council, 212 n.2b

Accrediting Council for Independent Colleges and Schools, 212 n.2b

Action Committee for Higher Education (ACHE), 148, 214 n.15

Ad Hoc Group for Medical Research Funding, 157, 163

Ad Hoc Tax Group, 157

ad hoc groups. *See* coalitions

advertising. *See* lobbying: technique of: — advertising as

affirmative action, 7, 61–62, 70, 176, 179; critics of, 56; and student admission and retention, 7; and student aid, 7–8

AFL-CIO, 213 n.2b

Adelsheimer, Erica: interview, 152

Alliance to Save Student Aid, 65, 148–150, 151–152, 156, 170, 214 n.15; CCA, 84; effectiveness of, 78, 156, 181; and publication of: *Stop the Raid on Student Aid,* 149; public support for, 173;

American Association for the Advancement of Science (AAAS), 40

American Association of Community and Junior Colleges (AACJC), 24. *See also* American Association of Community Colleges

American Association of Community College Trustees (AACCT), 73, 156, 213 n.5

American Association of Community Colleges (AACC), 11–13, 24, 29, 69, 83, 153, 156, 198; dues of, 211 n.7; and legal immigrants aid, 124, 178; as lobbyist, 143; location of, 212 n.2a; and membership participation, 90, 109; membership profile of, 73, 215 n.20; and Pell Grants, 124; and political action committees (PACs), 131, 167

American Association of Governing Boards (AGB), 156, 213 n.5

American Association of Higher Education (AAHE), 214 n.10

American Association of Junior Colleges (AAJC), 24. *See also* American Association of Community Colleges

American Association of State Colleges and Universities (AASCU), 11–13, 24–25, 43, 55, 106, 111, 198; and ACE; 68, 69, 70; and campus representatives, 81; and direct lending, 123; dues of, 211 n.7; and federal relations, 215 n.2; as lobbyist, 143; location of, 212 n.2a; and member communication, 100; membership profile of, 74; and NASULGC, 74; and proprietary schools, 84

American Association of University Professors (AAUP), 78, 214 n.15

American Chemical Society, 78, 89

American College of Surgeons, 215 n.17

American Council on Education (ACE), xix, xxi, 10–13, 14, 22–24, 54; and ad hoc groups, 164–165; and amicus curiae briefs, 214 n.6; as bipartisan, 158–159; Board of Directors of, 189; conflicting roles of, 70; and consensus building role, 76, 86–87, 121, 127, 194; and cooperation, 26 86; critics of, 68, 188; and direct lending, 59; dues of, 211 n.7; 213 n.3; and earmarked fund-

238

CONSTANCE EWING COOK is associate professor of higher education at the Center
for the Study of Higher and Postsecondary Education at the University of Michigan.
She is a political scientist who first became familiar with the Washington higher education associations when she worked for the U.S. Department of Education. Later, as executive assistant to the president of the university of Michigan, she learned about higher
education lobbying from a campus perspective.